MEMOS TO A NEW MILLENNIUM
THE FINAL RADIO PLAYS OF
NORMAN CORWIN

EDITED BY MICHAEL JAMES KACEY
FOREWORD BY WILLIAM SHATNER

Memos to a New Millennium: The Final Radio Plays of Norman Corwin
© 2011 Norman Corwin. All Rights Reserved.

Excerpts from poems #38 and #87 in THE PEOPLE, YES by Carl Sandburg, copyright 1936 by Harcourt, Inc. and renewed 1964 by Carl Sandburg, reproduced by permission of Houghton Mifflin Harcourt Publishing Company. All rights reserved.

Excerpt from "Times Gettin' Hard, Boys" THE AMERICAN SONGBAG, copyright 1927 by Harcourt, Inc. and renewed 1955 by Carl Sandburg, reproduced by permission of Houghton Mifflin Harcourt Publishing Company. All rights reserved.

No part of this book may be reproduced in any form or by any means, electronic, mechanical, digital, photocopying or recording, except for the inclusion in a review, without permission in writing from the publisher.

The plays in this volume are fully protected by copyright. No performances of them, public or private, whether for gain or charity, may be made without the written permission of the author's estate. All inquiries should be made via the official Norman Corwin website: *www.NormanCorwin.com*.

Published in the USA by:
BearManor Media
PO Box 1129
Duncan, Oklahoma 73534-1129
www.bearmanormedia.com

ISBN 978-1-59393-692-1

Printed in the United States of America.
Book design by Brian Pearce | Red Jacket Press.

TABLE OF CONTENTS

FOREWORD BY WILLIAM SHATNER 5

INTRODUCTION 9

CITIZEN OF THE WORLD 12

DOCUMENT A/777 42

THE STRANGE AFFLICTION 72

NATIONAL HOLIDAYS SERIES 94

FIFTY YEARS AFTER 14 AUGUST 112

NO LOVE LOST 124

THE WRITER WITH THE LAME LEFT HAND 150

THE CURSE OF 589 180

**OUR LADY OF THE FREEDOMS
AND SOME OF HER FRIENDS** 210

THE SECRETARIAT 240

MEMOS TO A NEW MILLENNIUM 266

GLOSSARY OF TERMS USED IN THIS BOOK 281

ABOUT THE AUTHOR 285

ABOUT THE EDITOR 287

INDEX 289

FOREWORD BY WILLIAM SHATNER

His voice had a bit of a quiver in it or is that a quaver as in quavering voice? Nonetheless, it did not have the resonance and the vitality that marked my appreciation of Norman. He delicately and quietly asked me to come to his 100th birthday. It was going to be celebrated at Norman Lear's house and would I come? Would I come? My dear friend, Norman Corwin had reached this benchmark of 100 years and would I come to celebrate? I would have climbed Mount Everest, I would have forged the Amazon, I would have climbed the slate grey mountains of Yosemite to come to his birthday. Fortunately, all I had to do was to find Norman Lear's house buried in the Bel Air region of Los Angeles. And finally through the mists and the gates and the unpaved roads, the pine trees and the sagebrush, I located Mr. Lear's home and as fate would have it, both the birthday boy and I arrived at the same time. Now he was being wheeled in a chair. The vigor gone not only from his voice, but from his body. Yet unmistakably, that humor and precision of words was there, untarnished, untouched by the years.

There was a small group of his friends at the lunch. Each telling their anecdote regarding their relationship with Norman each one more amusing than the other. I remember laughing and enjoying the camaraderie of men, most unusually, older than me. There was a sense of joy tinged with sadness because at 100 years of age, the future is not entirely open. One could expect calamity at any moment. But there were no surprises and the afternoon was memorable. Not only for the stories, but for the love that filled the room. All of us murmuring and touching and cooing over this gentle, old man. 100 years! My God, what is the man's diet?

There was another Norman in my life. Nearly fifty years earlier, I had just come in from New York where I had just arrived a couple of years earlier from Montreal, where I had gone to McGill University a couple of years before that and had studied Norman Corwin delivered by stuffy and arid professors who knew very little of the delight of the words and rhythm and dramaturgy of a Corwin script. Oh the poetic joy of studying Norman Corwin! The lyricism, the art of the chosen word, the mechanics that were hidden beneath scenes of great emotion. I knew his name, I knew his reputation. He was a legend to me at McGill. And now I am standing outside a gymnasium on Sepulveda Boulevard on a hot summer evening and Norman Corwin had called me. Was this a joke? He wanted to speak with me about a script he had. So, I met Norman Corwin for the first time, this dark haired, vital, nasal-voiced, lanky, tweedy guy who seemed so ordinary. Actually he seemed like one of the professorial types, like one of the guys I had left a few years prior at McGill. He had written a play and would I do it? Would I do it? Would I do it? "Yes, I would," I said, trying not to be obvious about how deeply I felt. There was an unreality about the whole situation and that sense of unreality didn't leave me for the longest time.

Ultimately we opened that play at the University of Utah to extravagant notices. There were parts of the play that I thought rivaled Shakespeare. Indeed I collared a Shakespeare professor at the university and told him how I felt. The prof came back stage after one performance and in somewhat hushed and awed tones, told Norman that he agreed that pieces of Norman's poetry were as profound as some of Shakespeare's. I never forgot that moment. We were Broadway bound except I received a phone call from Desilu Studios telling me that the pilot that I had made the previous year had sold and would now go on the air. That pilot was named *Star Trek* and it meant that I couldn't go to Broadway with the play that Norman had written for me.

Over the subsequent years, I did a lot of Norman Corwin's radio dramas. In one form or another I was an Orson Welles substitute and he and I became fast friends. He listed among his friends many of his old radio cohorts. So there came a time some years later that PBS wanted to do a retrospect of Corwin's work and what it would have been like to be in a studio doing one of those massive Corwin radio dramas with Bernard Herrmann conducting the CBS Symphony Orchestra, with numerous special effects people and several interns rushing around doing everyone's bidding. There would have been hundreds of people in a studio, with the tension of a gathering storm, as broadcast time loomed. And then the orgiastic moment of truth as an hour of great drama would take place on American radio to which millions tuned their sets. We didn't have those minions of course. In a forlorn empty studio, disconnected from the rest of the world, with a few old microphones with cables that led nowhere, we reproduced for the four cameras that were filming us what it might have been like at a Norman Corwin broadcast in 1945. This of course was 1970 and Norman's work had been forgotten in many places. But not by us. And we were his cohorts, we were his sycophants, we were the old radio actors who did a lot of listening to their voice, mimicked by Gary Owens of *Laugh In* who showed the American television audience what a radio actor's covered voice was like (that was what it was called). An actor who was so tuned in to his own voice that he was listening to it as though it was disembodied. There was a mechanical feel to it and several of the cohorts were of that mentality.

The PBS film group stayed about an hour yelling cut about every 10 minutes to reload their cameras. By the second time they yelled cut, the cohorts, Corwin, and other assorted actors like myself paid no mind to the film director's desire to stop. Somewhere buried in our subconscious, the idea that we were going to broadcast in several hours came into being. Of course it was pure fantasy. There was nobody outside of this room who knew what we were doing. There was dust on the microphones and when Norman got behind the glass walls of the control room and threw a finger toward the non-existent Bernard Herrmann, only we of the drama group heard the CBS Symphony. Only us radio cohorts heard the special effects of the non-existent sound engineers. By the end of an hour, PBS had all of the film that they needed, they packed up their film cameras, their executive notes, and beat a somewhat mystified retreat as they saw Corwin and Company in a frenzy of creativity. We put on the last great radio show that was only heard by the covered voices. We finished with a flourish and we finished right on the minute as Norman spread his hands in the final moment and as the clock ticked the empty hour that didn't exist anywhere but in our imagination. Exultant, we slapped each other on the back and the highest compliment that we could receive was a pat on the shoulder and a gentle smile from the king of radio himself. We all went home in ecstasy.

That's the Norman I remember, triumphant, vital, Herrmann at his beck and call, and all he had to do was point a finger and people jumped, then another finger, this time at me, and I would speak beautiful words that only he could write. What a memory.

William Shatner

INTRODUCTION

"The Word had authority. Ideas had authority."

Voice resolute, eyes intense, Norman Corwin commanded the room. He was describing the power of radio during his tenure at CBS as I interviewed him for a documentary film. It was the very first time I met him. Those words have never left me.

Corwin began his career as a newspaperman and it showed. His style was singular: he wrote with the eye of a journalist and the soul of a poet. He knew how to harness the power of words. Some were soft as a lover's whisper or fragile as a falling snowflake; but others were crafted into tightly packed phrases that hit with the force of a Joe Louis uppercut. Corwin wanted his audience to both think and feel. The result was intoxicating. Through his use of language, important ideas found cohesion and form.

Norman Corwin personally selected the plays included in this book. At his behest, I retrieved his original scripts from the American Radio Archives at the Thousand Oaks Library, and as I retyped them into book format, he jotted down his thoughts about each play. At age 101, his energy was waning, but his passion for this project remained strong. He had just finished the notes when I met with him in late September 2011. We spoke for a while. His voice was only a whisper at the end, his eyes soft, but as I took my leave, we shook hands and I marveled aloud at the firmness of his grip. For a moment, it seemed he wouldn't let go. It was the last time I saw him.

I would like to personally thank Cristian Borjas, Peggy Webber, Mary Beth Kirchner, Jeanette Berard, Kathleen Hays, and Robin Kacey for their kind assistance with this project. Special recognition and appreciation goes to Richard Fish, who originated the idea of this collection.

The format of this book mirrors that of Corwin's three previous collections of radio plays: *Thirteen by Corwin* (1942), *More by Corwin* (1944), and *Untitled and other Radio Dramas by Norman Corwin* (1947). Each play is preceded by a title page consisting of basic broadcast information: date, time, network, cast, and so forth. This is followed by the text of the radio play itself. Music and sound cues are indented and italicized; dialogue and acting directions are likewise formatted as in the previous books. Following each play are the notes penned by Norman Corwin. Additional notes from myself, as editor, follow. The book concludes with a glossary of terms. Footnotes have been added with the goal of enhancing the reader's experience.

Norman Corwin sometimes feared that he had "written on water," that all he had committed to paper and guided through the airwaves would inevitably vanish into the echoes of time. He didn't want to be reduced to a footnote in a chapter on radio history buried in some college course textbook. He wanted his words to live. After reading this book, I hope you will as well.

Michael James Kacey

CITIZEN OF THE WORLD

The show was produced by the CBS Documentary Unit and was broadcast on Sunday July 10, 1949, 10–11 p.m. It was Corwin's first show in two years. Starring Lee J. Cobb with Paul Bouchon, Joseph de Santos, Robert Dryden, Steven Hill, Charles Irving, Gerald Kean, Paul Mann, Bryna Rayburn, Ann Shepherd, Karl Swenson, and Hans van Stuwe.

Produced by Werner Michel with music composed and conducted by Alexander Semmler. The author directed.

Music: Excitement of departure, under.

Plane in full flight, under.

NARRATOR. One of them took a fast plane to Kashmir to stop a war…

Music: Swallows the sound, and goes into:

Train in flight: hold under.

NARRATOR. One of them took a night train to Poland to fight beetles and Bang's disease…

Music: Up and into:

A boat whistle.

NARRATOR. One of them took a slow boat to China, trailing a dope smuggler.

Music: Moderate toward resolution, and dip behind:

NARRATOR. And one fed a million children, and one got shot in an ambush, and one stopped an epidemic, and one was a poet, and one was an emperor, and one was a prophet, and one was a businessman, and at first there were only a few, scattered around the world, but now there are many, and growing, and they're around you, and for all you know, you may be one yourself!

Music: Up to resolution; then an opening statement, which backs for a short way and then drops under:

NARRATOR. Friends, Romans, Countryman, Men of Athens, People of Mexico, Fellow Americans: We are gathered around a hot microphone tonight to consider what kind of a bird is the citizen of the world — who he is, where he comes from, why he does what he does, and what he has to do with you.

Ever see one? Would you know him if you saw him? If not, be advised you can't tell him from the cut of his clothes or the blend of his tobacco. Not one ever swam the English Channel or flew solo across the Atlantic, hence there have been no confetti parades in his honor.

Few were ever considered distinguished by a whiskey company. And their words and deeds have been as varied as Sanskrit and Pidgin English, as wide apart as the Golden Horn and the Golden Gate.

Sometimes their work is unglamorous, like the announcement by one of them in a routine report out of Geneva, Switzerland, not long ago:

EPIDEMIOLOGIST. One plague infected rat found in Bombay.

NARRATOR. And sometimes they have spoken centuries ago, and solemnly sitting on cushy upholstery, as did an Emperor-type named Aurelius in Rome:

AURELIUS. Mankind are under one common law; and if so, they must be fellow citizens…from whence it will follow that the whole world is but one commonwealth.

NARRATOR. Sometimes their work is hard and rough, and the hours are long, as Dr. Leo Eloesser of San Francisco found out in China not too long ago. He went there with a medical team to set up health services and train people to help themselves:

DR. ELOESSER. They had one doctor for every eighty-six thousand people, which is better than in some other parts of China. Many hospital wards had two patients in a bed, but the two at least had the same kind of disease. In the town of Shin-chia-chuang one night, we had a lone visitor drop in after visiting hours…

Bomb drop and crash.

DR. ELOESSER. Took us forty hours of surgery, without a break, to take care of the casualties.

Music: Brief punctuation.

NARRATOR. Sometimes they meet in committee to act on complaints and petitions, like this one from an ex-chief in Tanganyika:

KUDILILWA. To the United Nations: I, Wamba Kudililwa, at present residing at Buchosa, Uzinza, in the district of Mwanza, have unreasonably and suddenly been dethroned from my chiefdom, which I inherited from my parents. I humbly beg your lordships that I may be throned again.

NARRATOR. Sometimes they are pitching for time off with pay as in the case of Mildred Fairchild of Chicago, who's been after countries to improve conditions for working women:

DR. FAIRCHILD. We've already got seventeen countries to agree to give expectant mothers twelve weeks off with pay — from public funds. And the mother is guaranteed her job back at the end of the twelve weeks.

Music: A little color behind.

NARRATOR. Surgery in China, working hours, dead rats, rivers, libraries — the world citizen is interested in all those things and in all other things if, and as, they relate to the well-being of his fellow man. He's not a goody-goody about it; you can't spot him by a self-made halo around his homburg, if he wears a homburg. He thinks of himself as practical. And as a rule he's right. Only he's practical on a bigger scale than most of us. When he goes in for farming...
SEED. See that seed? Something new. Little thing like this may mean the difference between life and death to people in famine areas. It's a strain of hybrid corn that's tough, fights off diseases and gives a terrific yield.
NARRATOR. When he vaccinates a million cattle, or paddles up the Amazon to explore jungles, or searches for kids that were lost or stolen during the war, he means to benefit more than his bank account or his hometown. Whether he's a poet or an engineer, his slant on things is the kind that curves over the horizon and keeps going — take a poet named Carl Sandberg, sitting in his living room in Flat Rock, North Carolina, and telling the world about other citizens of the world — saying it in lines he wrote fifteen years ago, before the United Nations came along.
SANDBURG. This free man is a rare bird and when you meet
    him take a good look at him and try
    to figure him out because
Some day when the United States of the Earth
    gets going and runs smooth and pretty there
    will be more of him than we have now.[1]
NARRATOR. They're not so hard to figure out, these birds, and neither are they as rare as they used to be; in fact, their habitat is very often among those alphabetical international agencies whose careers we somehow follow much less closely than that of local baseball clubs... You've heard of some of them:
WHO. WHO.

---

1. Excerpt from Poem #87 of Carl Sandburg's *The People, Yes.* (1936)

NARRATOR. By which is meant not the pronoun or the song of the same name, but the World Health Organization.
UNESCO. UNESCO.
NARRATOR. Isn't the trade name of a biscuit. Stands for United Nations Educational, Scientific and Cultural Organization.
ICAO. ICAO.
NARRATOR. Could be the name of a town in the Philippines, but it isn't. Stands for International Civil Aviation Organization.
AGENCIES. FAO, UNICEF, UNSCCUR, ITU, UPU, EC&SOC, Commission on Human Rights *(Fading down behind Narrator:)* Commission on the Status of Women, International Refugee Organization, International Trade Organization, Inter-governmental Maritime Consultative Organization, Narcotics Commission, United Nations Appeal for Children, International Labor Organization, International Telecommunications Organization, Universal Postal Union...
NARRATOR. Clerk in Geneva, poet in North Carolina, surgeon in North China, engineer in Brazil. If you were to ask one of them — a citizen of the world — how he got that way, he'd give you a long answer, with illustrations, and before you know it, the whole world would be in your lap. He'd ask you questions too — questions like:
CITIZEN. Think the world has little to do with you, your friends, your deals, and what's hanging in the closet of your room?
NARRATOR. He'd argue that you're all so mixed up with the world right this minute, inside and out, past and present, that you can't tell where you begin and the world leaves off. And no matter what country you're a citizen of, he'd point to your foreign relations...
CITIZEN. You really think you're an American, one hundred percent self-sufficient, owing nothing to any foreign parts or people?
NARRATOR. And he'd advance his argument with a case in point.
CITIZEN. Take at random a typical American, hundred percent self-sufficient, relaxing at home after his dinner. He lives, let's say, in Memphis, Tennessee...
NARRATOR. (Named after the capital of ancient Egypt.)
CITIZEN. ...and he's just finished drinking coffee.
NARRATOR. (From Venezuela.)
CITIZEN. He sits back and strikes a match...
NARRATOR. (Invented in France.)
CITIZEN. ...lights up a cigar...
NARRATOR. (Invented in Cuba.)
CITIZEN. ...and picks up the evening paper...
NARRATOR. (Invented in China.)

CITIZEN. ...to read in bold print...
NARRATOR. (Invented in Germany.)
CITIZEN. ...that the state of Florida...
NARRATOR. (Named by Spaniards.)
CITIZEN. ...will be spared a new hurricane.
NARRATOR. (So called by the Carib Indians.)
CITIZEN. Relieved, he glances at a clock...
NARRATOR. (Invented in Holland.)
CITIZEN. Notes that the time is now 10:05...
NARRATOR. (Numerals invented in Arabia.)
CITIZEN. ...realizes that he missed a program on the radio...
NARRATOR. (Discovered in Italy.)
CITIZEN. ...goes over and turns on his television set...
NARRATOR. (Invented in Scotland.)
CITIZEN. ...and he watches a telecast. However, as his eyes are bad and he needs glasses...
NARRATOR. (Invented in England.)
CITIZEN. ...he gets a headache, and takes an aspirin.
NARRATOR. (Invented in Germany.)
CITIZEN. Feeling better, he decided to go out for a walk in the rain; so he puts on his felt hat...
NARRATOR. (Felt invented in Asia.)
CITIZEN. ...slips rubbers on his feet...
NARRATOR. (The rubbers, not the feet, invented in Mexico.)
CITIZEN. ...takes his umbrella...
NARRATOR. (Invented in Assyria.)
CITIZEN. ...and goes out through the door.
NARRATOR. (First slammed by the Romans.)

Door slam.

Music: Exclamation mark.

NARRATOR. But the world citizen wouldn't let you off there. He'd argue that even if you don't drink coffee, smoke cigars, get headaches, go through doors, or live in Memphis — and all that's possible — you could still, no matter what the situation, be part of the world's pattern; he'd tell you that the very *currents* of the world flow right through you...
CITIZEN. Take this same fellow — back from his walk. He thinks he's alone in his little room, and out of touch with things. But actually the whole of America is crowded into that room, and right behind

America, presses the world. Right this minute there is passing through his room and his body a hundred vibrations of light, sound and speech — a chowchow of amateurs, aircraft, short-wave, TV, AM, FM flowing right through him; not only ordinary broadcasts, but also things like Facsimile, by which newspapers are send through space...

Facsimile beam.

CITIZEN. And the conversation of ships at sea...

Montage of codes, building.

CITIZEN. And scrambled speech, by which private radio conversations are hashed up to confound eavesdroppers...

A strand of scrambled speech.

CITIZEN. And Pidgin English to the backwoods of New Guinea, over Station 9PA, Port Moresby...
STATION 9PA. Good day all aboy. This fella he wireless belong Port Moresby. Now you harim talk talk...Me like askum you along helphim all pikininy about all place, all he no got something, no got clothes, no got kai kai, no got medicine.
CITIZEN. And short-waves...oh, short-waves from everywhere...

A quick montage of short-wave programs, accelerating and culminating until it dips momentarily behind:

CITIZEN. All crowded into a little room that was just minding its own business in Memphis.

Effect up to peak, at which:

Music sweeps away the effect, then moderates and fades under:

NARRATOR. The same citizen of the world, if he were patient, would put down all this as Step Number One — getting you to agree that the world outside us is all mixed up with what's inside us and behind us and around us. He'd most likely say:
CITIZEN. Not only are you not isolated in the world, but the world you're not isolated in, is getting smaller and smaller. In fact, if you have

scientific toys to play with, the earth can be just a big balloon, and you can do tricks with time and distance.

NARRATOR. And to show how easy it is to bring people together, our man of the world might take a couple of kids living twelve thousand miles apart, and get them to sing a duet without their ever meeting or speaking to each other, like this twelve-year-old in Sweden.

EVA. I am a Swedish schoolgirl and I am twelve years old. My name is Eva Rossngard and I live in Westervegen, twenty-seven, in Stockholm, Sweden.

NARRATOR. And an eleven-year-old down and across the globe…

JENNIFER. I am Jennifer Tyler of Corona Avenue, Roseville, Sydney, Australia.

NARRATOR. And though neither Jennifer nor Eva ever stirred outside her country, or met each other, or talked to each other, or sung to each other — by radio or telephone — they nevertheless can sing a duet across a shrunken world.

Both singing a duet on "Old MacDonald Had a Farm."

NARRATOR (*over it*). It's authentic; we'll let you guess at how it was done.

Duet up briefly.

NARRATOR (*over fading duet*). The young citizen of today, who sings blind duets across the globe, sees his country shrink and his world shrink, and notes, if he's old enough to understand, that the electronic tube and the airplane have brought the far places together, and with them — their problems, interlocked in a network of cause and effect, a chain reaction of trouble.

Take that dollar shortage in Europe…itself the result of a chain reaction that included two world wars. Further along in that reaction, was a familiar link:

EUROPEAN. We are obliged to limit the importation of American automobiles.

NARRATOR. And in Detroit, men are laid off. And *that* set off further troubles. But chain reaction can also be put in reverse gear. Take that situation in Italy when they thought they'd have to shut down the steel mills because they had no furnace brick. There was a meeting of industrial experts — men who were not hiring out their services to a company, but just doing jobs as world citizens. Said the man from Italy:

ITALIAN. The bricks we need can be made in Germany if the quartzite for them can be got from the mines in the French zone.
NARRATOR. Said the Frenchman:
FRENCHMAN. But there's no manpower for the quartzite mines in our zone.
NARRATOR. Said the Italian:
ITALIAN. We'll send the manpower.
NARRATOR. Said the Frenchman:
FRENCHMAN. But even if we have the manpower, we need digging equipment.
NARRATOR. Said the Englishman:
BRITON. Look, we'll help you get it.
NARRATOR. Said the Frenchman:
FRENCHMAN. Even so, winter is coming; the ground may be too hard to work for months.
NARRATOR. Said the American:
AMERICAN. Tell you what I'll do, I'll cable Washington for information on how we mine quartzite in Alaska.
NARRATOR. Said the Frenchman:
FRENCHMAN. That'll do it.
NARRATOR. Said the Italian:
ITALIAN. Thank you very much.

Music: Hit neatly, then into a variation of "Old MacDonald Had a Farm," that is punctuational rather than transitional.

NARRATOR. A citizen of the world, when he becomes one, (and there are no formalities about it — it happens gradually, like growing up) lets himself in for a fairly sobering experience. He finds that an awful lot of the facts of life in this vale of troubles range from sad to horrible: there are cold wars, hot wars, prophecies of gloom, supersonic rockets, atomic bombs, bacteriological weapons, tensions, crises, moves, counter-moves.

And apart from political matter, apart from protests, rejections-of-protests, and live shooting, he finds that ordinary, everyday life turns up enough grim facts to make an imaginative man shiver in a Turkish bath. He doesn't know whether to call in a poet or a statistician to interpret the figures:
STATISTICIAN. Two-thirds of the people of the world are undernourished.[2]
NARRATOR. That's so massive a number it means nothing to anybody. Try it again.

---

2. By way of comparison, according the FAO in 2011, one in seven people are undernourished. (1.02 billion)

STATISTICIAN. Upwards of one billion, six hundred million people live from day to day not getting enough to eat.

NARRATOR. Still doesn't do it. Too enormous to latch onto, let alone be moved by. But if you compress these hundreds of millions into a single family, the tragedy of statistics begin to take on some meaning. Pinpoint a starving child or study the face of its mother, and you catch the barest glimpse of the infinite anguish of world hunger…It could be anywhere…a beggar pulling your sleeve in Egypt….

ARAB (*weakly*). Hasanaa lellah…hasanaa lellah…

NARRATOR. Or in the town of Jacmel, in tropical Haiti, the woman who walked seventeen miles across a mountain to trade five wild mangoes for a cupful of rice to feed her family of five, and who told a UNESCO man:

HAITIAN (*wearily*). Depuis une semaine on n'a rien a se mettre sous la dent que quelques mangues. On an tombe tres malade. Les champs sont sec.

INTERPRETER. "All we have had to eat for a week is a few wild mangoes. They have made us very sick. The fields are parched."

NARRATOR. Of the many things that make up a citizen of the world, awareness of the suffering of others is one of the greatest. He has a talent for translating statistics into humanity; and sometimes he sees for himself how low are the lowest depths.

Five years ago, a world citizen named John Muehl, of Michigan, witnessed a famine in India:

MUEHL. For them there was only the bare sidewalk where they begged for food till they were too weary and sick. All over the province rice was dear and life was cheap. The streets were glutted with the dead and dying, sprawled together on the pavement and in the gutter.

The human mind can adjust to almost anything…but I never realized how quickly until the day in Calcutta when I found myself eating a candy bar, disinterestedly watching a woman die…

Music: Hit angry with hunger theme, then retard and diminish mournfully behind:

NARRATOR. Sometimes it's slow hunger, wasting a people year after year; sometimes it's famine that sweeps like flame. And all lands have known the scourge of it. Rome…when thousands drowned themselves in the Tiber rather than slowly starve; a seven-year famine in Egypt; cannibalism, in one of the Indian famines; ten million dead in Bengal in one year; famine in Ireland, China, Russia…

Music: A surge, then down, and moderate to a brighter mood behind:

NARRATOR. The world citizen attacks famine as he would an enemy, and in a group like FAO — Food and Agriculture Organization — he organizes action against it. One of the first things he goes after is:

FAO MAN. Rats. We've got to figure ways of trapping the rats and killing the vermin that destroy thirty-three million tons of food every year...a full tenth of the world's supply.

NARRATOR. And he approaches the problems of supply from all angles...

2ND FAO. There's got to be more production from farms (we're helping in that); there's got to be better transportation of foods, less spoilage, bigger hauls, faster freights...

NARRATOR. And sometimes actually shows up with the victuals, as did Dr. Manuel Seigel of U.N.'s Children Emergency Fund in the little town of Radomir, Bulgaria, recently. The children of the village hadn't drunk milk in any form for years, and they had never *heard* of milk in powdered form; and they were so suspicious of it that the mayor of Radomir, Simeon Dinev, had to bring them together in the public square and work on them. Now Mr. Dinev can't speak any English, so I'll make like the mayor of Radomir, and we'll act out what actually happened that morning in the square...picture the children standing all around, sullen-like and scared...I'm the mayor...(*Clears throat.*)

(*Projecting.*) My dear children...now just look at this milk here. Cool. Wet. Tastes delicious. It was sent to us by all the nice friends of Bulgaria, because it's what you *need*. Who'll step up and drink some? (*No answer.*) Now you *know* our friends wouldn't send anything harmful. Don't you know that? I'm *surprised*! You older children — wouldn't you take a chance to show that the United Nations would never send us bad milk? (*Pause.*) Not one of you?

BOY (*off*). I will drink it!

NARRATOR. Just one? (*Pause.*) All right, Georgi. Come on up here.

Crowd murmur; ad lib.

NARRATOR. Now you taste this and see if I'm wrong. Here.

Effect of milk being poured into a glass.

NARRATOR. All right. Stand back — let him drink it...Like the taste, Georgi?

BOY. It's good, but not as good as raw milk.
NARRATOR. You feel sick from poison?
BOY. No. I feel all right.
NARRATOR. You still able to walk?
BOY (*giggling*). Sure. I feel fine.
NARRATOR. You like some more?
BOY. Yes. Plenty.
NARRATOR (*up*). There, children. You see?

Crowd effect; over which:

NARRATOR. Georgi drank it, liked the taste, didn't keel over, and they day was won.

Music: Blackout.

NARRATOR. But hunger has partners in crime. Nature is one of them — droughts and floods, notably — frosts, blights, locusts — but Man contributes his share of damage. Good old man. He alone is almost entirely responsible for erosion, one of the five biggest problems on earth. You ask a world citizen.
CITIZEN. Erosion? It's a staggering world problem. There's not a country on earth, from the poorest to the richest that doesn't suffer from it.
NARRATOR. The abused topsoil of continents washing out to sea on the flood crests of rivers, or being blown away by winds — once fertile land which man turned into dust bowl by axe, plow, fire and gun — the destruction of forests, the tearing up of farmlands…the handiwork of man…

Sneak wind effect under:

NARRATOR. And the good earth, that has taken centuries to build, sickens, dies, decays, and blows off in the wind; the face of Australia drifts out over the Tasman Sea; the soil of Oklahoma darkens the sky over New York; dust rises from the dongas of South Africa; rain cuts deeper into the barrancos of Guatemala; man's larder and his garden crumble into powder, and are whisked away like puffs of smoke…farmers lose their crops, their land, their homes; times grow hard; they look around for places to go…they sing mournful songs about it…
SINGER (*hums under foregoing: "Times Gettin' Hard, Boys, Money Gettin' Scarce"*).

(*Up with text.*) If times don't get better, boys, I'm gonna leave this place...
Every wind that blows, boys, every wind that blows...
Is carrying my old farm away, heaven only knows...
Times gettin' hard, boys, money gettin' scarce,
If times don't get better, boys, I'm gonna leave this place...[3]

NARRATOR (*over effect*). But times won't get better, boys, unless something is done about it on a world scale...and the boys that are hoping to do it are world citizens. In fact, they're already at it, hacking away at problems that underlie erosion and hunger. Countries in trouble can, and do, ask for specialists to examine 'em where it hurts, and prescribe treatment. Specialists like G. F. Danhof, of Apeldoorn, Holland, who goes to Siam[4] with five other experts from China, India, Africa and the United States. As a team, they examine the country; and Mr. Danhof reports:

DANHOF. We advise the Siamese government to look after its forests better or there won't be any left. Why, timber is being *stolen*. My colleagues and I have 127 other specific recommendations to offer.

NARRATOR. Across the world, in South America, the republic of Venezuela finds itself dangerously low on edible fats and oils, so it asks for a similar team of experts. K.S. Markley of New Orleans, chief of the team, recommends, among other things:

MARKLEY. Well, er — plant African and American oil palms; develop a good nut-cracking machine to get the oil from the palm-nuts; and get going on large-scale mechanized farming.

NARRATOR. And in a potato field on the outskirts of Wroclaw, Poland, Dr. W. A. Rawlins of Cornell, tells a group of Silesian farmers how to get rid of an international nuisance known as the Colorado potato beetle:

RAWLINS. All right, turn on the spray please, and walk with it.

Spray, alone, for a moment.

RAWLINS. Interpreter, tell him to walk slower so that he covers the foliage on all sides. Tell him to hold the nozzle of the sprayer closer to the plants. Got that?

INTERPRETER. Yes. (*Up.*) Prosze isc wolniej, tak aby spryskiwać liscie po obu stronach. Rozumie Pan? Prosze trzymac koniec rozplyacza blizej do roslin. Prosze trzymac...

---

3. Excerpt from Carl Sandburg's *The American Songbag*. (1927)
4. Now Thailand.

NARRATOR (*as both the spraying and the Polish fade simultaneously*). And while Rawlins of Cornell is in Poland spraying bugs, Gray of Australia is in Ethiopia inoculating animals; Kalbfleisch of Canada is in Hungary demonstrating farm machinery; Van der Ord of Holland is in China advising on flood control; and all over the world specialists like them are sweating it out in the sun, or shivering in the cold, or swallowing dust on washboard roads.

The battle is just beginning…just the first set of skirmishes in what could develop into a grand-scale attack against hunger and erosion, if only the world citizen and his fellow citizens can work in peace.

Music: Up briefly in the clear.

NARRATOR. You'd think hunger and erosion would be grief enough for a single earth in any one millennium…but they're only a couple of clumps in the heavy sack the world is toting; millstones that no nation, however strong, can pack up in an old kit bag and smile away. Plenty of other troubles vex and worry the citizen of everywhere — some of them too famous and nasty to need much description…killers like disease —

Music: Upsurge.

NARRATOR. — and poverty

Music: Upsurge.

NARRATOR. — and war.

Music: A stern punctuation, modulating and diminishing behind:

NARRATOR. A child in California gets trapped in a well in an accident, and the sympathy of the world hangs on the desperate attempt of a whole community to rescue her. The child dies, and there is public grief.[5] But every day of the year, tens of thousands of children are trapped by preventable diseases, and every day thousands of them die. The roll call is an unending death march…

DISEASE. Malaria…three hundred million cases every year.[6]

---

5. Three-year-old Kathy Fiscus died April 8, 1949 after she fell into a well in San Marino, California. The rescue attempt was covered by live television on KTLA, Los Angeles.
6. According to the WHO in 2010, there were 216 million cases and 655,000 deaths.

NARRATOR. (Eight thousand die of it every day.)
DISEASE. Tuberculosis...fifty million cases every year.[7]
NARRATOR. (Fourteen thousand die of it every day.)
DISEASE. Venereal diseases...parasitic diseases...virus diseases...polio[8], trachoma, cholera, (*fading*) plague, typhus, smallpox, yellow fever, influenza...
NARRATOR. And never quite enough medicine or doctors to go around. The report from Ethiopia, telling us:
ETHIOPIA. This country has a hundred and fifty doctors of medicine for a population of over fifteen million.
NARRATOR. The report from India:
INDIA. In India it's somewhat better...one doctor for every eight thousand people.
NARRATOR. And in the wealthiest country in the world:
AMERICA. There's one doctor for every 915 people in the United States[9], and *that's* not enough.
NARRATOR. Germs have no politics and no frontiers, and down the centuries they have killed a thousand times more than all the wars of history. And in spite of available vaccines and sulfa drugs and attabrine and penicillin, disease — preventable disease — is still doing its dirty work. The death knell tolls for too many before their time...

Music: A funeral bell.

MADAGASCAN. Dead: Flavien Antand Roy, aged eight, of Tananarive[10], Madagascar; of smallpox.

Music: Another bell.

SAMOAN. Dead: Tamasi, twenty-one, of Ofa, Samoa; of Schistosomiasis.

Music: Another bell.

POLE. Dead: Stanislaw Karycki, sixteen, of Kraków, Poland; of tuberculosis.

---

7. 5.7 million in 2010 according to WHO.
8. Since Dr. Jonas Salk's polio vaccine was announced in 1955, most countries have eradicated the disease. According to WHO only 1,349 cases were reported worldwide in 2010.
9. As of 2009, the ratio is one doctor for every 392 people in the United States, according to the Association of American Medical Colleges.
10. Now called Antananarivo.

NARRATOR (*as bell fades*). The citizen of the north has enough on his mind without worrying about the yaws or leprosy of the tropics; the citizen of the tropics can't worry about influenza in the north; but the citizen of the world is concerned with both; and he writes his concern into the constitution of one of those alphabetical international agencies — the World Health Organization:

Music: Institutional muted strings behind:

CONSTITUTION (*on echo*). "Enjoyment of the highest attainable standard of health is one of the fundamental rights of every human being… and is fundamental to the attainment of peace and security."

Music out.

NARRATOR. But it isn't just solemn words and high-sounding resolutions. Why, only *one* of its dozens of activities throughout the world, this band of world citizens called the WHO operates a network of fourteen radio stations to keep shipping of all countries alert to health conditions in all ports.

A stream of code to ships at sea.

SINGAPORE (*over effect*). One plague infected rat found in Bombay town — quarantine restrictions against Canton on account of smallpox…217 cases of typhus in Columbia…nine dead…Foochow[11] free from plague…(*Fading.*) Tenanarive, plague, one imported; Damietta, smallpox, one; Baghdad, typhus, one; Saigon, smallpox deaths, six; Allahabad, plague, one imported.

NARRATOR. The work of world health wouldn't get far if it merely *reported* disease — although that's a big first step. It also gets there in a hurry with the medicines, as in the case of that fierce cholera epidemic in Egypt last year.[12]

Music: In.

NARRATOR. Three thousand Egyptians a week were dying from cholera, when Cairo appealed for help, and in no time, six thousand miles away…

---

11. Now spelled Fuzhou.
12. The cholera epidemic lasted from September 1947 to February 1948 and claimed over 20,000 lives.

A siren, coming up under:

NARRATOR. ....a truck bearing vaccine and medical supplies was rushed, with police escort, from drug manufacturing plants in Philadelphia, up the pike, through the Holland Tunnel, and out to LaGuardia airfield in New York.

Cross-fade sirens to airplane motors.

NARRATOR. The medicines were loaded on a waiting plane, and the shipment went on its way to Egypt. Meanwhile, WHO rounded up its member nations.

No one country in the world had enough anti-cholera vaccine on hand to stop that epidemic. So several pitched in.

Music: Effect.

AFGHANISTAN. From Afghanistan, seventy-five thousand cc's of vaccine...

Music: Effect.

CHINA. From China, a million cc's...

Music: Effect.

IRAQ. From Iraq, two hundred thousand cc's...

Music: Effect.

USSR. From the Soviet Union, six hundred thousand cc's...

Music: Effect.

BRITAIN. From the United Kingdom, twelve ambulances...

Music: Effect.

USA. From the United States, a million tablets of sulfa drugs...

Music: Effect.

NYC. From New York City's Health Department, three thousand syringes…

Music: Effect.

ITALY. From Italy, one and a half million cc's…

Music: The turning point…Music out.

NARRATOR. When the goods arrived, deaths from cholera were passing three thousand per week…Then overnight…

Music: A surge; then a diminishing effect in which the orchestration is thinned out at each interval until extinguished at the end of the following:

NARRATOR. Eighth week of epidemic, three hundred thirty deaths; (*Effect.*); ninth week, seventy-nine; (*Effect.*); tenth week, thirty-nine; (*Effect.*); eleventh week, nine; (*Effect.*); twelfth week, two; (*Effect.*); thirteen week, one; (*Effect.*); fourteenth week, none.

Music: A moment of one faint fermata on a flute; Silence. Then a triumphant passage.

NARRATOR. The results aren't always as dramatic as in that cholera epidemic; the figures don't always shoot up and down that fast… but fantastic figures are involved at all times…such as one hundred million, count them — one hundred million — children being inoculated against TB by workers of the U.N.'s Children Emergency Fund.

Music: An upsurge, but still tragic in mood; then a return to the institutional motif under:

CONSTITUTION (*on echo*). "Highest attainable standard of health is one of the rights of every human being…and is fundamental to attainment of peace and security."

Music: Up to resolution.

NARRATOR (*repeating*). "Attainment of peace and *security*?" Did someone mention security? That old pot of porridge at the end of the rainbow?

That mirage slippery as a greased eel? That meal ticket that entitles you to live across the tracks from a rifled garbage pail?

You mean to say social security, like health and hunger and erosion, is a world problem? Well, ask the fellow whose name is Per Capita — the brother of Anon — ask the average American, the richest member of the Per Capita family, what his per-capita income is:

AMERICAN. Fourteen hundred bucks a year.[13]
NARRATOR. Canadian?
CANADIAN. A thousand dollars a year.
NARRATOR. Norwegian?
NORWEGIAN. Eleven hundred krone — about 555 dollars a year.
NARRATOR. Argentine?
ARGENTINE. Three hundred a year.
NARRATOR. Yugoslav?
YUGOSLAV. Hundred and thirty dollars a year.
NARRATOR. Brazilian?
BRAZILIAN. Fourteen hundred cruzeiros. About seventy dollars a year.
NARRATOR. Indian?
INDIAN. Forty-two dollars a year average income.
NARRATOR. Chinese?
CHINESE. Twenty-five American dollars a year.[14]
NARRATOR. Hunger, erosion, disease, poverty…and on top of all this, war! (*Laughs wryly.*) Well, what can you say about war? That it's hell? It is. That it's a world problem? Of course. That it's uncivilized? Yeah. That it's expensive? Rather. Open the till.

Cash register opening.

NARRATOR. Reach into the till for the cost of killing a man.

Do you know how much it cost to kill each enemy soldier in World War II?
STATISTICIAN. Two hundred and forty-five thousand dollars per man.
NARRATOR. Now reach in for the price of saving a life. Do you know how much it costs to inoculate a child against tuberculosis?
STATISTICIAN. Ten cents.

---

13. $44,872 according to United Nations statistics for 2009.
14. According to United Nations statistics for 2009, the numbers are now $39,795 for Canada, $78,674 for Norway, $7,666 for Argentina, $8,114 for Brazil, $1,075 for India and $3,769 for China. Yugoslavia no longer exists as a single nation.

Music: A sharp commentary, followed by dark muttering in the horns and strings under the following:

NARRATOR. War…the fiercest face in the rogue's gallery of world problems — king of the beasts — and trailing behind it, Disease, Famine, Poverty, Erosion, Overpopulation…but every one of these problems has been around a long time. Even back in the dimmest days of antiquity, there lived world citizens who took on the tough ones. They usually were martyred for their pains.

In Greece, golden Greece in the time of its glory, a stubborn old man who well loved his country and his city could say:

SOCRATES. I am neither an Athenian nor a Greek, but a citizen of the world.

NARRATOR. His name was Socrates. The early world citizen had only himself, or, if persuasive, a few disciples to go with him…but always he was a man of courage, wherever he turned up…as in Israel, seven hundred years before Christ, the stern prophet Isaiah, saying:

ISAIAH. Let all the nations be gathered together, and let the people be assembled…they shall beat their swords into ploughshares and their spears into pruning hooks; nation shall not lift up sword against nation, neither shall they learn war any more…

NARRATOR. And in China in a time of famine, the sage Confucius took his brush one day and put down four words:

CONFUCIUS. Under heaven, one family.

NARRATOR. Two thousand years further along, in the New World, Ben Franklin of Philadelphia, goose-quilling into his notebook:

FRANKLIN. God grant that not only the love of liberty but a thorough knowledge of the rights of man may pervade all the nations of the earth, so that a philosopher may set his foot anywhere on its surface and say, "This is my country."

Music: Up punctuationally, and out.

NARRATOR. In the near and far yesterdays, in times as old as the Old Testament there were world citizens who stood against the enemies of mankind.

Against Poverty, how many famous, fated attempts by brave, lonely men, to help the poor? But the work of their lives was as a candle to the icecap of Greenland.

Against Erosion, there were ancient warnings too, but nevertheless the hanging gardens fell, the terraced walls crumbled, the pastures blew away, the sands of the desert covered Nineveh and Troy, and Babylon was a bucket of ashes.

Against Disease, sacrifices to the gods, incantations, blood-letting, mumbo-jumbo.

Against War — every formula from women denying love to their husbands, as suggested by a Greek named Aristophanes[15], to launching a peace ship, as done by an American named Ford[16]. And all the time, weaving like a shuttle between the nations, the diplomats.

The treaties and pacts and covenants added up to a hundred small wars and two global wars; and out of it all, only the unvanquished Big Five remaining as menacing as ever…the Big Five of Hunger, Poverty, Disease, Erosion and War.

Music: A curdling cue, sneak.

NARRATOR. And the Big Five have their satellites: ignorance, suspicion, hysteria, thought control, persecution, crime. And off in the uneasy neutral corner, grimmest of all: the atom bomb.

Music: Up stinging, then moderates to brighter spirit under.

NARRATOR. And all this could be gloom, despondency and despair, except there is a difference now…the World Citizen has multiplied his numbers. Where once he was a solitary prophet, a poet, a monk, an emperor, far separated across time and geography, he is now organized as never before, into a dozen or more great alphabetical international organizations, and into x-teen smaller, non-governmental societies and associations…some going in the same general direction as the United Nations, others in different directions — some in a hurry, others patient — one headed by a housewife, one by a count, another by a bridge expert, others by an ex-prime minister named Churchill, a twenty-seven-year-old war vet named Whitehouse, a Supreme Court justice named Roberts. And still others have sprung up all over the map:

ARGENTINE. Association Pacifista Argentina, Gal Paz, Córdoba, Argentina.

DUTCHMAN. Wereldfederalisten Beweging, Amsterdam, Netherlands.

INDIAN. Indian Movement for World Government, Dalmia Jain Nivas, New Delhi.

ITALIAN. Associazione Pax Per Gli Stati Uniti del Monde, Roma, Italia.

---

15. His play *Lysistrata*.
16. Henry Ford led a private peace delegation to Europe in 1915 to try to end World War I.

NORWEGIAN. Rosla For Verdens Forente Stater, Oslo, Norway.
FRENCHMAN. Front Humain des Citoyens du Monde, Boulevard Victor Hugo, Neuilly, France.
BRITON. United Nations Association, 11 Maiden Lane, London WC2, England.
AMERICAN. Unitarian Service Committee, Boston; American Friends' Service Committee, Philadelphia; Rotary International, Chicago...
NARRATOR (*over*). These outfits have more different approaches than a putting green, but they are all aiming at the same objective — service, security, peace.

    But the U.N. itself, and the agencies connected with it, are by all odds the favorite locations of the full-time citizen of the world. They attract him because they're best equipped to get things done, and they go after the biggest game — Hunger, Poverty, Disease, Erosion, War. But more than attacking great Evil — they're on the alert to support great Good. Certain things can't wait until all the hungry are fed and the sick are healed, but have to go forward at the same time — massive things like Education, Culture, the freedoms, human rights — even the matter of flying through the air with the greatest safety, is something the world citizen worries about. Take for example, that romantic but little-known Atlantic patrol...

Four-motor plane in flight; interior perspective. It holds under:

NARRATOR. You're a passenger in a plane over the North Atlantic at night, flying through an overcast at eighteen thousand feet; there's no land below for a million square miles. Nevertheless, cutting through on the radio is a voice from down in the stormy darkness. It's the voice of Weather Ship Charlie, passing along to you, as to all North Atlantic planes, the latest dope around fifty-one degrees North and thirty-five West:
CHARLIE (*on filter, through static*). Clipper Six Zero, Clipper Six Zero, Weather Ship Charlie, Weather Ship Charlie...Visibility one-two miles, one-two miles; Temperature two-nine, two-nine; Wind, one-nine, one-nine...Barometer two-nine point three-zero, falling, Barometer two-nine point three-zero, falling...

Effect continues behind:

NARRATOR. Pilots on the eastward run often give Charlie in exchange the latest intelligence from the mainland:

PILOT. Clipper Six Zero to Weather Ship Charlie, Yanks are playing a night game, but I can tell you the score of some of the others: Brooklyn 6, Brooklyn 6, Giants 2, Giants 2; Red Sox 11, Red Sox 11, Detroit 5, Detroit 5...

Continues and fades under:

NARRATOR. Charlie is one of thirteen weather ships stationed in the Atlantic by another international outfit — ICAO — to promote safety of overseas plane traffic.
 The frontiers in the fight for a safer, saner, healthier world are everywhere — in the cabin of an airplane flying at eighteen thousand feet, and at the bottom of a Pennsylvania coal mine being inspected by world labor experts. And far more than airplanes and equipment are surveyed for the general good. The mind of man is inspected, too.
 Archibald MacLeish, former Librarian of Congress and one of the world's top-flight poets, helped to draft into the constitution of UNESCO a sentence that may well become one of the great slogans of our century. Here is the sentence, spoken by its author:

MACLEISH. Since wars begin in the minds of men, it is in the minds of men that the defenses of peace must be constructed.

NARRATOR. In the council room, and radiating outward to all compass points, the work goes on, the work of raising the battered head of humanity. Sometimes it takes the form of an epic Declaration on Human Rights, sponsored by forty-eight countries; sometimes it's as little as four words long:

MEXICAN. Cada uno enseña uno.

NARRATOR. The Mexican slogan — "Each one teach one," the battle cry of a drive to wipe out illiteracy. (*Pause.*) They used the same slogan in China...

CHINESE. E gha run chow E gha run...

NARRATOR. The credo of the world citizen is to help people to help themselves in every way. George Townsend of Australia, U.N. Trusteeship specialist on the Southwest Pacific, explained the philosophy for this program:

TOWNSEND. The aim is not to force backward people to become what we might think they ought to be, but to help them improve and develop the way of life which they have chosen, and in which they can be happy.

NARRATOR. A good example of this was a program in Haiti officially called "Pilot Project in Fundamental Education," and it took in not only teaching, but a drive against hunger, poverty, erosion and disease.

Music: Sneak in authentic recorded Haitian music.

NARRATOR. It was a warm and human experience, staking out in a single rugged valley among thirty thousand poor, hungry, illiterate people, a model for self-improvement that the rest of Haiti and the world could look to. To hear one of the UNESCO mission tell it:

UNESCO WOMAN. When we first got there, hoping to teach the people how to be self-sufficient, it was heartbreaking. Our students were dying of starvation and disease. There had been a drought, the land was eroded to begin with, there was no food, the water supply was polluted. The people were sick, superstitious and desperately poor. They expressed their misery in song...song that at least cost them nothing to sing...

Music: Plaintive Haitian song up briefly in the clear for a moment.

NARRATOR. And then one day:

Music: A sledge-hammer punctuation from the orchestra, obliterating the folk tune.

The sharp, clean crack of a hammer on a nail, followed by a fading series of construction noises under:

NARRATOR. They built a training center. It consisted of a clinic...
DR. REX. Malaria injections, on the left. Injections for yaws, on the right.
NARRATOR. ...and a library...
UNESCO. For those who can read, here are books about the history of Haiti. For those who can't, classes tomorrow at eight...
NARRATOR. ...and a classroom...
CHILD (*haltingly: in French*). a, b, c, d, e, f, g, h, i, j, k, l, m...
NARRATOR. ...and a demonstration farm...
TEACHER. ...and only by planting trees on hills where the ground has eroded, will you be able to hold the water. Now about planting vegetable seeds...
NARRATOR. And word got around the countryside that a new thing called UNSECO had come to help the people, and they pitched in, regardless of wages. They learned first of all...

TEACHER. Bad water means sickness. If the water is sick, and you drink it, you will get sick too.
HAITIAN. Pretre du voodoo dit; maladie c'est mauvais esprits qui punissent...
TEACHER. I know the voodoo man says sickness is punishment from evil spirits. But let me explain something to you...
NARRATOR. And they even got the voodoo man to cooperate. The Valley Folk got together and dug a deep well, singing at their work...

Music: Working song in, and under:

NARRATOR. They built a seventeen-mile road without being commissioned to...They went at it on no more than a suggestion. And the word spread around, until Haitians showed up who had walked thirty and forty miles across mountains to get a single injection, or to learn more about the exciting new thing called reading. After a while, the people began to look and feel better. They held their heads high in a way they had never done before. And in due time, there were actually two christenings, and an honorary dubbing which came as a bouquet from the people of Marbial Valley to the project of UNESCO. In the Etienne family:
PRIEST. This boy is named Unesco Febrius Etienne.
NARRATOR. And over at the Beauvoirs:
HAITIAN WOMAN. I have named my little girl Unesca Beauvoir.
NARRATOR. The honorary dubbing fell to a small white terrier:
BOY (*calling*). Here, Unesco! Here, Unesco!

Music: Travel motif, happy this time.

NARRATOR. In some ways, the world citizen is like a country doctor, on a world scale. If an ailing country calls him, he's there in a jiffy with machines or vaccines or new types of seed.
But none of these activities can amount to much if the world can't get rid of Public Enemy Number One — War...And don't think our citizen hasn't tackled War itself. And brought it down. He stopped no less than three wars in the past year...three out of three tries.
It was no ordinary day for the cause of peace when, a few weeks ago, an American Negro, grandson of a slave, sat before a short-wave microphone in a studio on the Isle of Rhodes, and announced the result of his mediation of the Palestinian War. Here is that announcement — the voice of Dr. Ralph Bunche, U.N. mediator, speaking from Rhodes, as he told the world of the armistice:

DR. BUNCHE. In the interest of peace and in the interest of the peoples of the Near East who have suffered from a tragic and unnecessary war, I am highly gratified that these negotiations have succeeded, and that for the first time in the long history of the Palestine dispute, Arab, and Jewish representatives have met, negotiated and signed a formal agreement.

Music: A triumphant cue; when it ends, there is already Hindu music established, under it, which backs:

NARRATOR. Thousands of miles from Palestine, the new nations of India and Pakistan were at war — an undeclared war which killed thousands of Muslims and Hindus. Armies were ready to decide whether the Princely States of Kashmir and Jammu went to Pakistan or India. Then suddenly...

Music: Snare drum roll, then lightly backing.

TRUCE. Truce! Cease-Fire.
NARRATOR. Cease-Fire brought about by a team of mediators doing in India what Dr. Bunche did in Palestine. And both sides calmed down and agreed to settle it with ballots.

Music: Triumph motif reiterated and out.

NARRATOR. And the world citizen did it again in the East Indies, when he got the Netherlands and the Republic of Indonesia to call off their war and negotiate a settlement.
    Three out of three, and in less than a year's time. Not easy; much interrupted; much shot at; but in all the negotiations, nobody trying to change anybody's politics or religion, no plugging for one economic system against another, no taking sides. In fact, partisanship is one of the worst things that can happen to a citizen of the world; so much so that he takes an oath against it when he joins the U.N. staff. Here is Rahat Bokhari of Pakistan taking that oath:
BOKHARI. I solemnly swear to regulate my conduct with the interests of the United Nations only in view, and not to seek or accept instructions in regard to the performance of my duty from any government or authority external to the United Nations.
NARRATOR. The world citizen considers himself no less a patriot for taking on matters outside of his country than a son is any less a son for having interests outside his father's household. Here, for example,

is America's own Admiral Nimitz[17] explaining (especially for this program) his perspective mission to India and Pakistan:

NIMITZ. On the first of last January, the fighting which had raged for fifteen months between India and Pakistan over the question of Jammu and Kashmir came to an end. This resulted from the acceptance of proposals put forward by the United Nations Commission for India and Pakistan. Since that time, the terms of the cease-fire have, substantially, been carried out. This was an outstanding victory for the cause of peace throughout the world, and for the United Nations in particular.

NARRATOR. A national hero becomes an international servant, a working citizen who stands ready to referee a plebiscite. Admiral Nimitz has a low opinion of war as a way to settle an argument; he prefers other means.

NIMITZ. Wars and fighting do not remove differences, they only deepen them. I hate war and I know what I am talking about. But differences can be settled or at least reduced by discussion and agreement. I believe in the United Nations as a means of preventing or reducing fighting. Only good can come in the end from cooperation through the many parts of the United Nations. We have just got to get along together in this world.

NARRATOR. So the Admiral joins the poet, statistician, clerk, economist, veterinarian — the man who's doing the world's work. It's certainly varied work; sometimes it's pleasant, most of the time it's hard work; and once in a while it's dangerous, and the risk is high. It was so in the case of Count Folke Bernadotte of Sweden. He was not the only citizen on world business to lose his life. Many of them died far from home, not for their countries at war, but for a world at peace. None of the dead can speak for himself; here is volunteer, a driver named George Hendricks of New York, who saw a colleague killed in Palestine — had this to say:

HENDRICKS. If I were asked to volunteer again for a dangerous spot, to work for a mission that was working for peace, there isn't much question in my mind whether I'd go or not...I'd go.

Music: Maestoso treatment of motif.

NARRATOR. In the ordinary unassorted jumble of daily life, with its deadlines and taxes and appointments and chores, there may seem little

---

17. Fleet Admiral Chester W. Nimitz, who signed, as the U.S. representative, the Japanese surrender document aboard the USS *Missouri* on September 2, 1945.

connection between the citizen of the world and the people of the world; but there's hardly a man alive who doesn't stand to benefit, some way or another, by the work this citizen has cut out for himself. There are even those who think the citizen is just about the greatest hope on two feet…that he's involved with every one of us whether we know it or not…no matter how unrelated we may be, or how scattered our voices…like these:

WORKER. Hand me the wrench there, Joe.

FARMER. Got twenty percent more yield since I switched to contour plowin'!

MINISTER. "The wolf and the lamb shall feed together, and the lion shall eat straw like the bullock…"

NURSE. The X-ray will take only a second.

READER. Did you see this piece in the *Herald*?

MARY. Darling, it's a wonderful ring.

MOTHER. My baby is due in December.

NARRATOR. These people and what they say may seem as unrelated to the citizen of the world as they are to each other, but when you put together the jigsaw pieces of their lives, they add up to a picture. And in this picture, it's possible to see how all stand to benefit if the citizen of the world comes through…comes through with the answer to their needs. Try that parlay again…

WORKER. Hand me the wrench there, Joe.

NARRATOR. — Comes through with the lucky combination that produces full pay envelopes and steady work.

FARMER. Got twenty percent bigger yield since I started contour plowin'!

NARRATOR. — Comes through with good prices for produce, crops that are free of blight.

MINISTER. "The wolf and the lamb shall feed together."

NARRATOR. — Comes through with rights for the man of faith, whether his symbol be Cross, Crescent, Star of David.

READER. Did you see this piece in the *Herald*?

NARRATOR. — Comes through with a free press and freedom of information.

NURSE. The X-ray will take only a second.

NARRATOR. — Comes through with victory over the big killers; brings bloom to the sickly parts of the earth.

MARY. Darling, it's a wonderful ring.

NARRATOR. — Keeps young couples from being separated by wars for years…or forever.

MOTHER. My baby is due in December.

NARRATOR. — Comes through with assurances to the mother that she is not creating life only to have it starved, impoverished, or slaughtered.

Music: A short phrase, going into a quiet passage under:

NARRATOR. — Comes through for the unborn, who will bear our names and faces, who will carry on our languages and some of our habits, size up the monuments to our accomplishments and mistakes, and weigh our record in a balance between sheer wonder and sheer horror.

Music: A swell, and down behind:

NARRATOR. When, long years from now, the full returns are in and there can be a grand accounting, perhaps someone will place a footnote with a bright star marking it:
FOOTNOTE. Around mid-century came the first citizen of the world to gang up against the terrible Big Five — to take them on.
NARRATOR. Meantime, tomorrow is tomorrow, and the year 2000 is a long way off. There's work ahead: rubble to clean up — quarrels to settle — fears to quell — mouths to feed — a thousand chores to do…And in the doing, the Citizen of the World will be right there pitching with the rest of us who care; for to him and what concerns him, a seed is not too little nor is all humankind too big.

Music: Resolution.

CORWIN ON
CITIZEN OF THE WORLD

This was broadcast over CBS as the third in a series of documentary programs narrated by Lee J. Cobb, who was then starring in the original Broadway production of *Death of a Salesman*. One of the few programs I did not produce myself, for I had left CBS two years earlier. The producer was a longtime friend named Werner Michel.

FROM THE EDITOR

The backdrop of this show was, of course, the deepening divide among nations of the world into East and West spheres of influence, as well as the bleating of Anti-Communism forces in America. In early August, 1949, only weeks after the broadcast of *Citizen of the World*, Senator Pat McCarran of Nevada cited Corwin by name as a "communist and subversive" from the floor of the U.S. Senate. On August 9, 1949, Corwin was quoted in the *New York Times* calling McCarran a "political mad dog" and describing himself as a "vastly better patriot" than the Senator.

Even though the personal attacks would continue, Corwin pressed onward. Having recently traveled around the globe as winner of the Wendell Willkie One World Award, Corwin knew first-hand how high the stakes were in the aftermath of World War II. The United Nations, chartered only four years earlier, could not risk repeating the fate of the League of Nations. These early years were crucial.

Also of note: Though the title of this show comes from a Socrates quote, Corwin felt a strong affinity for the Benjamin Franklin quote: "God grant that not only the love of liberty but a thorough knowledge of the rights of man may pervade all the nations of the earth, so that a philosopher may set his foot anywhere on its surface and say, 'This is my country.'" At age 101, he could still quote it verbatim.

DOCUMENT A/777

The show was produced under the auspices of the United Nations and carried in the United States over the Mutual Broadcasting System on March 26, 1950 from 9–10 p.m. EST. It was the first in a series of documentaries about the United Nations under the collective title, *The Pursuit of Peace*. The show was also broadcast in Europe, Africa, Asia, and the Americas.

The all-star cast included Richard Basehart as Trelawney, Charles Boyer as Émile Zole, Lee J. Cobb as the Swedish Officer, Ronald Coleman as Lord Byron, Joan Crawford as Eliza Lynch, Maurice Evans as Lord Capulet, José Ferrer as Francisco Lopez, Reginald Gardner as de Mandeville, Jean Hersholt as the Swedish Itinerant, Lena Horne as the Singer, Marsha Hunt as Juliet, Alexander Knox as the Contact Man, Charles Laughton as Whitman, Sir Laurence Olivier as the voice of the Preamble, Vincent Price as the Indian Lawmaker, Edward G. Robinson as the Chinese Official, Robert Ryan as the Opening Voice, Hilda Vaughn as Lady Capulet and Emilyn Williams as the Spanish Commandant. Robert Young personified the Document and Van Heflin was the Narrator.

Music was composed and conducted by Lyn Murray. The author directed.

BULLETIN. Ladies and gentlemen:
   There is a man-made force thousands of times greater than the hydrogen bomb.
   It's an instrument of many parts: small, can fit into a handbag; yet it has the power to penetrate to every area of human life.
   Details may be found in Document A/777.

Music: Up brightly and retard maestoso behind:

NARRATOR (*quietly*). You have a rendezvous on the waterfront of New York City. You drive up to a parking lot near a power plant. You leave your car, and meet the contact who is going to put you in touch with Document A/777. Together you walk toward the entrance of a tall building where thousands of documents are on file. On your way, you quietly ask a few questions: (*Up.*) Er — tell me — what is the striking area of this force?
CONTACT. Vastly greater than the H-bomb.
NARRATOR. I see. — What is the pressure at the center?
CONTACT. The conscience of mankind.
NARRATOR (*Down.*) Maybe he can't talk now. You follow him through revolving glass doors into a lobby of marble columns and a checkered stone door. You come to a little bookstore sitting inconspicuously behind a bank of elevators; together you go in and approach a young girl. Her face betrays no emotion. She could be a clerk in any bookstore.
CLERK. Yes, sir?
CONTACT. Document A/777, please.
CLERK. Certainly.
NARRATOR. She moves swiftly to a counter, picks up a small pamphlet, and returns with it.
CLERK. Ten cents, please.
NARRATOR. He pays her ten cents…

Sound of a cash register.

NARRATOR …and turns over the pamphlet to you. You read what it says on the cover…(*Reading.*) "Declaration of Human Rights." (*Up, to contact.*) You mean *this*?
CONTACT. Read what it says inside the cover.
NARRATOR. You come to italicized type: (*Reading.*) "On December 10, 1948, the United Nations adopted and proclaimed the Universal Declaration of Human — "

CONTACT. No, no, below that.

NARRATOR (*reading*). "This is the authorized text as contained in the official Records of the Third Session of the General Assembly, Document A/777."

CONTACT. Well, there it is.

NARRATOR. And *this* is what you mean by a force greater than the hydrogen bomb?

CONTACT (*offhandedly*). Well. If you take the trouble to examine the text, you'll see that the (*Trailing off.*) ideas set forth in the Declaration could, if supported by every country in the world...

NARRATOR (*over him*). But your eye has already caught the word "Preamble"; and under it, Document A/777 begins to explain *itself*...

Music: Sneaks behind:

PREAMBLE. "Whereas recognition of the inherent dignity and of the equal and inalienable rights of all members of the human family is the foundation of freedom, justice and peace in the world; (*Music in.*) Whereas disregard and contempt for human rights have resulted in barbarous acts..."

Music: Up fully now, it obliterates the voice of the Preamble, and subsides to continue behind:

NARRATOR. Sure. That's the way it is in radio. Catch the listener on a fishhook dangled in air — a bright spinner of music — an angle of urgency in the voice; a promise of bombs and spies and secret rendezvous.

But it *is* true, that bulletin cast in the stream:

BULLETIN (*as before*)...a force thousands of times greater than the hydrogen bomb.

NARRATOR. It's true enough if you look at that claim — not as a fish at a fly, or a fly at a fish, but as a man looking at a world of human beings more or less like himself.

"Declaration of Human Rights." Thirty short articles. Before the first Article, appear seven "Whereases," one "Now Therefore," and at least five millenniums of struggle and violence. For, in a sense, this program took five thousand years to prepare.

The story of Human Rights began shortly after the first tenants appeared in Eden; but for practical purposes we pick up the narrative considerably later, on a night in December, 1948...

Music: Paris in the grip of a midnight fog.

NARRATOR. It was getting on toward midnight. A fog spreads over the city, shrouding the Seine, swallowing monuments, paling the lights of Place de la Concorde. Paris is asleep, its theaters and restaurants shut down, its subway trains making their last run before gates closed. Only nightclubs and the United Nations are still open.

Music: Out.

NARRATOR. In the brand new Palais de Chaillot, half a hundred nations are at work on a launching. After two years of meetings, coursing down a long winding river of debate, after hundreds of amendments and a thousand statements, the time of decision has come.
    The President of the Third General Assembly of the United Nations, Herbert Evatt of Australia, leans forward, and speaks into a microphone:
EVATT. The vote is now on the Declaration as a whole.
NARRATOR. Now the roll call begins country by country. Approval or opposition will be expressed by the famously brief words "Yes" or "No." Some countries may neither approve nor oppose. These will answer "Abstain." But all of the countries, whether "Yes," "No," or "Abstain" have already contributed through conference and debate to the cluster of articles being voted on. So here it is coming up. Two billion people have a stake in this. For the first time anywhere on the face of the earth, human rights for all the peoples of the world stand for a vote.
PRESIDENT (*off perspective*). Afghanistan?
AFGHANISTAN. Yes.
PRESIDENT. Argentina?
ARGENTINA. Sí.
PRESIDENT. Australia?
NARRATOR. Wait. Hold the roll call. This is the birth of a Bill of Rights, whose first article speaks of birth itself.

Music: Document motif.

DOCUMENT (*on echo*). Article One. All human beings are born free and equal in dignity and rights.

Music: Fade quickly for:

PRESIDENT. Australia?

AUSTRALIA. Yes.
PRESIDENT. Belgium?
BELGIUM. Oui.
PRESIDENT. Bolivia?
NARRATOR. Bolivia! Step away from the meeting a moment and look behind you. Look as far behind as the year 1780, when Bolivia was still a part of Peru.

Music: Bolivian theme in.

NARRATOR. Go back to a dusty village, to a prison in the village, to a cell in the prison. Túpac Amaru, an Incan, descended of royal blood, lies chained in the cell for leading a rebellion against the Spanish occupation. A commandant arrives, stands for a moment outside the cell door, looks down his Castilian nose at the prisoner, then goes in leaving the door ajar.

Opening of iron cell door.

SPANIARD. One last time, Indian: who are your accomplices? (*No answer.*) Who are the other conspirators?
AMARU. The only conspirators are you and myself. You for oppressing the country and I for trying to liberate it.
SPANIARD (*quietly*). I see. One of the clever ones. When will your kind learn to behave?
AMARU. One of *your* kind beheaded my ancestor in Cuzco two hundred years ago. If we haven't learned to behave in two hundred years, I can promise you we *never* will.
SPANIARD. I find you tiresome. But as you seem to enjoy a show of unbroken spirit, you may be interested to know what's intended for you.
AMARU. I can imagine. Don't bother.
SPANIARD. No bother: on the contrary, a pleasure. There is the matter first of ripping out your tongue. Then for you and your colleagues, an iron collar. In the middle, I'm afraid, will be three sharp spikes, red hot, which, under pressure, will come out through your mouth. Somehow I have an idea you won't take the affair so coolly at that point. — Shall I go on? (*There is no answer.*) In whatever condition you may be in after this — ah — shall we say experience — you will then be put on public show for a whole day. After that you'll be drawn and quartered, and your remains scattered to dogs outside the city.
AMARU. Rather dead among dogs than living among you Spaniards.

SPANIARD (*going off*). Yes, yes, of course, of course. Well — a very good night to you, what little remains of it. Oh, and one other thing — I have the honor to tell you that along with the forty captains and the men in prison, there will be hanged before your eyes, your wife and children.

The cell door slams.

Music: It comes down behind:

NARRATOR. Not fiction. Nothing in this program is fiction. Túpac Amaru in Bolivia; before and after him, thousands of men like him, tortured in other countries, for other causes, at other times, right up through Germany, 1945. All of which, Document A/777 takes into account...

Music: Document motif behind:

DOCUMENT. Article Five. No one shall be subjected to torture, or to cruel, inhuman or degrading treatment or punishment...

Music: Flashes up and out.

Atmosphere of Assembly Hall.

PRESIDENT. Bolivia?
BOLIVIA. Sí.
PRESIDENT. Brazil?
BRAZIL. Sí.
PRESIDENT. Burma?
BURMA. Yes.
PRESIDENT. Byelorussia?
BYELORUSSIA. Abstain.
PRESIDENT. Canada?
CANADA. Yes.
PRESIDENT. Chile?
CHILE. Sí.
PRESIDENT. China?
NARRATOR. Stop for China. Go back to a time 213 years before Christ — the time of the Emperor Shih Huang-ti, warrior, conqueror, builder of the Great Wall. He is tough, brilliant, powerful and vain; he thinks so highly of his own regime that he doesn't want it compared to anything that ever went before. Between Shi's Great Wall and the

distant sea, sprawls a nation already ancient in the arts, a people who have inherited, among other things, the freedom to think and speak.

One day, in the year 213 B.C., in a teahouse in Shensi Province, a scholar rises to recite a poem that is already three hundred years old. He is among friends who enjoy the old and common Chinese custom of writing, speaking, listening to poetry...

SCHOLAR. The locusts' wings say "Throng, Throng";
> Well may your sons and grandsons
> Be a host innumerable.

> The locusts' wings say "Join, Join";
> Well may your sons and grandsons
> Be forever at one.

> The locusts' wings —

OFFICER *(off)*. STOP! Stop, I say!
SCHOLAR. What's the matter? What are you doing?
OFFICER. You are under arrest for violating an imperial edict.
SCHOLAR. What imperial edict?
OFFICER. The order that all people who recite poetry are to be executed.
SCHOLAR. But that's ridiculous.
OFFICER. Yes, exactly. Too many of you scholars think the Emperor's laws are ridiculous. Come along.
SCHOLAR. Just a moment. Take your hands off me. I refuse to believe that any such stupid and vicious order exists under the Imperial seal. You will either produce such an order —
OFFICER. You will not threaten one of his Majesty's officers! And I caution the rest of you to stand back. (*More quietly.*) Since you have apparently not heard of the Decree of the Grand Councilor, though ignorance of the law does not in any case reduce your crime — I will read it to you:

Unrolling of parchment.

OFFICER. "Whereas scholars, instead of learning the present laws, are studying ancient dynasties, and as a result seeking to criticize by comparison the present government and poison the minds of the people, THEREFORE:

 1. All historical records, save those of the present dynasty will be burned.

 2. All libraries of literature and philosophy, except those under the custody of the Imperial Doctors, will be destroyed.

3. All people who recite poetry or discuss history will be executed.

4. All those who raise their voices against the present government in the name of antiquity, will be beheaded, together with their families."

Music: A stinging comment, subsides for:

NARRATOR. And the scholar of the locust wings was buried alive, along with 459 others in the same year.

Music: Document motif, behind:

DOCUMENT. Article Nineteen. Everyone has the right to freedom of opinion and expression...freedom to hold opinions without interference and to seek, receive and impart information and ideas...

Music: Flash up and out.

PRESIDENT. China?
CHINA. Yes.
PRESIDENT. Columbia?
COLUMBIA. Sí.
PRESIDENT. Costa Rica?
COSTA RICA. Yes.
PRESIDENT. Cuba?
CUBA. Sí.
PRESIDENT. Czechoslovakia?
CZECHOSLOVAKIA. Abstain.
PRESIDENT. Denmark?
DENMARK. Yes.
PRESIDENT. Dominican Republic?
DOMINICAN REPUBLIC. Yes.
PRESIDENT. Ecuador?
ECUADOR. Sí.
PRESIDENT. Egypt?
NARRATOR. Wait. Spin the globe in reverse until you are back three thousand five hundred years, back to a time when the Great Pyramids had been standing for only a few centuries...

Music: Fading up under the foregoing is the melody of "Go Down Moses."

SINGER. When Israel was in Egypt's land
    Let my people go
    Oppressed so hard they could not stand
    Let my people go
    Go down Moses, way down in Egypt's land
    Tell old Pharaoh to
    Let my people go.

(Continue under:)

NARRATOR. Oppression is a burden heavier than mountains, and only a great force can lift it — sometimes revolution, sometimes war, sometimes even the striking of the firstborn dead. When Israel was in Egypt's land it took the wrath of Jehovah himself, to pry the people free of oppression.

Music: Up in the clear.

NARRATOR. The Bible itself bears witness:
BIBLE. Thus saith the Lord, "Let my people go."

Music: Up and under, continuing behind:

NARRATOR. And the people were let go; and three thousand years after them, another people, also oppressed so hard they could not stand, identified themselves with the ancient Israelites of Egypt's land. Out of a new bondage half a world removed from where they were born, out of the anguish of their suffering, great spirituals of freedom came welling up…

Music: In the clear again.

NARRATOR. And again, Song, as many times before and since, spoke on the side of Human Rights, crying this time for the right of a man to get up and go…

Music: The spiritual soars now, briefly, but is soon smothered in an upsurge of the Document motif, which then sustains behind:

DOCUMENT. Article Thirteen. Everyone has the right to leave any country, including his own…

Music: Flash up and out.

PRESIDENT. Egypt?
EGYPT. Yes.
PRESIDENT. El Salvador?
EL SALVADOR. Sí.
PRESIDENT. Ethiopia?
ETHIOPIA. Oui.
PRESIDENT. France?
NARRATOR. France! The country outside the wall of this Palais, the country of painters, poets and champagnes, with all its pageantry of kings and queens and guillotines, its Joan at the stake, its headstrong emperors, its religious massacres, its Voltaire, its own bold Declaration of the Rights of Man.

Music: Faintly, a pastoral coloring of the Marseilles.

NARRATOR. As in other countries on and beyond her borders, France has many a wronged right to explain to the God of Nations on Judgment Day; but also she has many a righted wrong. And none more stirring than the righting of the wrong done to an obscure Army captain[1].

Framed, smeared, convicted, disgraced, exiled — and innocent — such was the victim. And in a time of cowardice and treachery, when even in the face of new evidence the press violently opposed recalling the convict from Devil's Island, one newspaper had the courage to speak out, and it spoke with the thunderous voice of Émile Zola.

ZOLA. (*fading up under the last of the foregoing*)...continued to defend his deadly work by machinations as ridiculous as they are guilty.

I accuse General Mercier of having made himself an accomplice in one of the greatest crimes of history...

I accuse General Billot of having had in his hands the decisive proofs of the innocence of Dreyfus and of having concealed them out of political motives...

I accuse the War Office of having led a vile campaign in the press in order to misdirect public opinion and cover up its sins...

I accuse, lastly, the first court martial of having violated all human rights on condemning a prisoner on testimony kept secret from him...

Making these accusations, I am aware that I render myself liable to laws which punish acts of defamation...I expose myself voluntarily...

---

1. Refers to The Dreyfuss Affair, the treason conviction of Captain Alfred Dreyfuss in 1894. He was finally exonerated in 1906.

As to the men I accuse, I do not know them, I have never seen them, I feel neither resentment nor hatred against them...

I have one passion only: for light, in the name of humanity, which has borne so much and has a right to happiness...

Mr. President, I beg you to accept the assurances of my deepest respect.

NARRATOR. As the world well knows, he won. Won, after being himself slandered, tried, convicted of libel for those accusations. Years later, when the thunder was stilled, when Zola lay dead in state in the Pantheon, with Dreyfuss free among the mourners, the gifted Anatole France stood above the coffin and reminded his nation of one man's struggle for the rights of another...

FRANCE (*on echo*). Look upon him! He has honored his country and the world...Look upon him! He was a moment of the conscience of mankind!

Music: Sweep up, then segue into Document motif under:

DOCUMENT. Article Ten. Everyone is entitled to a fair and public hearing by an independent and impartial tribunal...

Music: Flash up and out.

PRESIDENT. France?
FRANCE. Oui.
PRESIDENT. Greece?
GREECE. Yes.
PRESIDENT. Guatemala?
GUATEMALA. Sí.
PRESIDENT. Haiti?
HAITI. Oui.
PRESIDENT. Honduras?...Honduras?
CLERK. Absent.
PRESIDENT. Iceland?
ICELAND. Yes.
PRESIDENT. India?
NARRATOR. Hold it. Look below there. Do you see the little white-haired woman sitting among the Indian representatives of the General Assembly here in the Palais de Chaillot? That is Mrs. Vijaya Lakshmi Pandit, chairman of her nation's delegation. A woman. Bear this in mind, because —

PRESIDENT. India?

NARRATOR. Please hold it. History has been long enough at the job in India, to permit a few moments of reminiscence here. Remember — a *woman* chairing India's group at the United Nations! Now fan through the pages of India's past, through the millenniums of this massive sub-continent, past the wars, the mutinies, the famines, the droughts, the floods, all the way back to ancient law. Listen now to the duties, mark the position of Woman as prescribed in the early Ordinances:

ORDINANCES. One should not eat with his wife, nor look at her eating, sneezing, yawning, or sitting at her ease.

No act is to be done according to her will by a young girl, a young woman, or even by an old woman, though in her own houses.

The good wife of a husband, be he living or dead, must never do anything disagreeable to him. But she may at will, when his is dead, emaciate her body. She may not, however, when her husband is dead, mention even the name of another man. She must be till death subdued, intent, chaste.

A man...may marry again.

Music: Document motif, behind:

DOCUMENT. Article Two. Everyone is entitled to all the rights and freedoms set forth in this Declaration, without distinction of any kind, such as race, color, *sex*...

Music: Flash up and out.

PRESIDENT. India?
INDIA. Yes.
PRESIDENT. Iran?
IRAN. Yes.
PRESIDENT. Iraq?
IRAQ. Yes.
PRESIDENT. Lebanon?
LEBANON. Yes.
PRESIDENT. Liberia?
NARRATOR. What a bright name for a country — Liberia, for Liberty! Yet north and south of its palmy shores, in times not so remote, the export of these parts was just the opposite of Liberty — it was the marketable, perishable commodity of enslaved human beings.

The trade flourished along this coast; there was money in it, as there is today in cattle. It actually was figured in percentages.

INGRAM (*dryly*). Exclusive of the slaves who died before they sailed from Africa, twelve-and-a-half percent were lost during the passage to the West Indies; at Jamaica, four-and-a-half percent died whilst in the harbors or before the sale; and one third more in the "seasoning." Thus, out of every lot of one hundred shipped from Africa, seventeen died in about nine weeks, and not more than fifty lived to be effective laborers in the islands.

NARRATOR. "The seasoning." One third more died in the seasoning. What seasoning meant, only a slave could know. Once, across the continent from Liberia, out in the Indian Ocean, a Briton named Trelawney, adventurer, pirate, later to be the friend of Byron and Shelley, landed on the Island of Mauritius. No South Sea Isle has ever had a better billing. It was called...

TRELAWNEY. A fairy island, conjured up out of the sea by a genie for the delight of mankind...

NARRATOR. Now Trelawney is no dilettante. He is tough. He has killed men in brawls and battle — with knives, bullets and his naked hands. He is hardly one to squirm at the sight of blood. Yet listen to what he has to say on the treatment of slaves on that very island conjured up for the delight of mankind...

TRELAWNEY. I saw them lash the bare and festered back of an overloaded female slave, her tender nature one animated mass of ulcers and cancers, half-consumed alive by flies and maggots, death her only hope...I have seen men with their spines knotted like pine trees and their skins as scaled and callous, the flesh cracked into chasms from which the blood oozed like gum...The pity and pain I felt at the sight of these poor slaves could only be equaled by the deep and overwhelming damnation I invoked on the heads of their oppressors forever. Surely such monsters are annihilated, they cannot be immortal! Yet they should have an eternity to torture them! What they have done to others, should be done to them, and I defy the invention of Hell's demons to be more cunning in cruelty than themselves!

Music: Up passionately and into Document motif, behind:

DOCUMENT. Article Four. No one shall be held in slavery or servitude; slavery and the slave trade shall be prohibited in all their forms.

Music: Flash up and out.

PRESIDENT. Liberia?
LIBERIA. Yes.
PRESIDENT. Luxembourg?
LUXEMBOURG. Yes.
PRESIDENT. Mexico?
MEXICO. Sí.
PRESIDENT. Netherlands?
NETHERLANDS. Yes.
PRESIDENT. New Zealand?
NARRATOR. Now how do you suppose modest, quiet New Zealand is going to vote? New Zealand, down there toward the South Pole, out of the way of everything but the weather? What would a remote Dominion in the Tasman Sea know about Human Rights?

Here is the Number One citizen to answer that: the Prime Minister, Sidney G. Holland, especially addressing this program by shortwave:

PRIME MINISTER HOLLAND. It is a matter of pride to every New Zealander that this country, one of the youngest in the world, was the first to give women the right to vote; the first to give an old-age pension to its citizens; and among the first to introduce a full system of social security; and benefits for widows, orphans, and the sick...

Music: Document motif, interlaced with the theme of the New Zealand anthem, behind:

DOCUMENT. Article Twenty-One...Periodic and genuine elections...by universal and equal suffrage...

Music: Flourish.

DOCUMENT. Article Twenty-Two. Everyone, as a member of society, has the right to social security...

Music: Flourish.

DOCUMENT. Article Twenty-Five...Everyone has the right to...security in the event of unemployment, sickness, disability, or other lack of livelihood in circumstances beyond his control...

Music: Flash up and out.

PRESIDENT. New Zealand?
NEW ZEALAND. Yes.
PRESIDENT. Nicaragua?
NICARAGUA. Sí.
PRESIDENT. Norway?
NORWAY. Yes.
PRESIDENT. Pakistan?
PAKISTAN. Yes.
PRESIDENT. Panama?
PANAMA. Yes.
PRESIDENT. Paraguay?
NARRATOR. Paraguay! Eighty-eight years ago…Asunción…the capital city…night…Down the street rides a man on horseback…

Hoof beats on pavement; steady, unhurried, under:

NARRATOR. He is Francisco Solano López, whose father, the first president of the republic has just died. On both sides of the street long aisles of men stand at attention, his guard of honor.

This man on a horse is one of the big "I-AMs" of history. One of the supreme fatheads whom circumstance, accident, and fate too often thrust into power. Because of this fellow, not a single soldier in these long ranks of silent Paraguayans will be alive seven years from this moment. The short, stocky, strutting peacock, an ardent admirer of Napoleon, rides up now to a woman sitting on horseback awaiting him. This is his mistress, Madame Eliza Lynch. El Supremo López reins his horse and stops in front of her.

Hoof beats up and stop.

LOPEZ. Madame, I am Paraguay!
LYNCH. Long live the Emperor!
NARRATOR. Emperor? He's the son of a president, who has just died, that's all. Nobody elected him to be anything. But that doesn't matter. Nothing matters when you are dealing with his species. In almost every country, at some time or another, despots of this sort have risen, held sway, and been put down at great inconvenience either by their own countrymen, or by other countries' men, or by both.
LOPEZ. Madame, I am Paraguay!
NARRATOR. Alexander the Great, for example. When Darius offered to share the Persian Empire with him, the young Macedonian responded:

ALEXANDER. Heaven cannot support two suns, nor earth two masters.

NARRATOR. France had its share. King Louis XIV, announcing to one of his court:

LOUIS XIV. I am the state.

NARRATOR. Russia, too, was well represented. Ivan the Terrible had this to say:

IVAN. The sovereign is above the empire. No Russian Sovereign need ever give account of his actions to anyone on earth.

NARRATOR. And somewhat further along, here is Napoleon Bonaparte, speaking to the Austrian statesman, Metternich:

NAPOLEON. I was brought up on the battlefield, and a man like me does not concern much about the lives of a million men...

NARRATOR. But back to Francisco Solano López of Paraguay...He is breakfasting with is mistress on a day in the fourth year of the six-year war he started against three neighboring countries.[2] An orderly arrives with the message that one of Paraguay's forts, Humaitá, has been surrendered by Colonel Martinez, after a long battle against crushing odds. Lopez receives the news with a sweeping gesture...

The crashing of dishes and cutlery as a table is overturned.

LYNCH. Francisco, what are you doing?

LOPEZ. The swine! The man has surrendered Humaitá!

LYNCH. But didn't you expect that? You sent him no reinforcements.

LOPEZ. Shut up! I am going to arrest the wife of that yellow, gutless Martinez. Before I'm through with her she'll be something no traitor will ever forget.

LYNCH. Martinez a traitor? He defended that fort for months...bravely, and even if he did give up, how can you blame his wife?

LOPEZ. When a country is fighting for its life, cowardice is a knife in the back. I will see to it the name Martinez is drenched in blood.

LYNCH. His wife is blameless!...Francisco, you can't do that to an innocent woman!

LOPEZ. Don't tell me what I can't do! Her husband handed a fort of mine to the enemy! He surrendered two thousand of my men! Do you hear? — Two thousand men!

LYNCH (*angrily*). But *she* didn't surrender them! For God's sake, have some pity!

---

2. The Paraguayan War with Argentina, Brazil and Uruguay 1864–1870. Also known as The War of the Triple Alliance.

LOPEZ. Pity! I will make her an example for all of Paraguay. No officer of mine who has a wife or a sister or a mother will surrender any of my men after they see what I do to her.

LYNCH. You're not going to do anything to her. You've done more to people than I care to remember. But you're not going to kill that woman!

Whiplash, successively striking under the following:

NARRATOR. Promptly the next morning, the wife of Colonel Martinez, who had not seen her husband for a year, was flogged to death.

Whiplash, successively striking under the following:

NARRATOR. And the lash was kept busy in Asunción...falling impartially on men and women. Even Francisco López' own mother, his sixty-year-old mother, was flogged at the order of her son...having been charged with "conspiracy."

More whiplashes.

NARRATOR. And his two sisters...The whip fell on them as well...

More whiplashes.

NARRATOR. And his brother Benigno, whom he had put to death after a brutal flogging.

(*Over fading whiplashes:*) And thanks to El Supremo, the senseless war of vanity and ambition, dragged on: Men of sixty and boys of twelve were drafted into the army. Women dug trenches and carried ammunition. The supreme one ordered his soldiers to massacre all the wounded on the battlefield. His own as well as the enemy's. At the start of this madness Paraguay had a population of one million, three hundred thousand. At the end, only two hundred thousand. Eleven out of every thirteen people in the country were dead of single man's ambition...of a depot's will...

LOPEZ. Madame, I am Paraguay.

Music: A violent upsurge, going straight into Document motif, behind:

DOCUMENT. Article Twenty-One. The will of the *people* shall be the basis of the authority of government.

Music: Flash up and out.

PRESIDENT. Paraguay?
PARAGUAY. Sí.
PRESIDENT. Peru?
PERU. Sí.
PRESIDENT. Philippines?
PHILIPPINES. Yes.
PRESIDENT. Poland?
POLAND. Abstain!
PRESIDENT. Saudi Arabia?
SAUDI ARABIA. Abstain!
PRESIDENT. Siam[3]?
SIAM. Yes.
PRESIDENT. Sweden?
NARRATOR. Sweden. Even Sweden! Comb the continents and the islands, anatomize the history of humankind, and there will turn up very few times and domains where injustice has not done its work. Sweden, then: 1723. A country road. A man walking down the road is overtaken by an officer of the Crown.
CROWN. You there.
MAN. Yes, sir?
CROWN. Let me see your certificate.
MAN. What certificate?
CROWN. Showing that you attend services and receive instruction in the Christian faith.
MAN. I didn't know I had to have one. When did this law…?
CROWN. Act of Parliament…Are you a thread maker?
MAN. No, sir.
CROWN. Are you a hook-and-eye maker?
MAN. No.
CROWN. Are you a vagabond?
MAN. Certainly not.
CROWN. Are you a Jew?
MAN. No, sir. I'm a —
CROWN. A Gypsy?
MAN. No, heavens, no — I'm a Christian! I'm from Sigtuna. I go to church regularly. I use all prescribed means to be saved.
CROWN. Well… (*Pause.*) You look to me like a good Swede, therefore I'll take your name and let you go. But see that you get a certificate from

---

3. Now Thailand.

your parson immediately, otherwise you are liable to be seized and put to public work. This is done to all inferior types until they show serious desire to be instructed in the knowledge of God.
MAN. Yes, and well they should be. Especially the Jews and Gypsies.
CROWN. Gypsies we now exile altogether. As for Jews...parliament is going to take stern measures with them.
MAN. Ah, good; the sooner the better.
CROWN. Yes...Now, your name?

Music: A somber Hebraic motif, behind:

NARRATOR. Including the Scandinavian! Even Sweden at one time picked on the Wandering Scapegoat, who for two thousand years was scattered in every clime and under every flag except his own.
    Babylon, Jericho and Persia; Greece and Rome and the Dispersion; Spain, Russia, England, Poland; pogrom, ghetto, inquisition; Haman and Hitler; the rack and the gas chamber;...all too well, these people who were let out of Egypt-Land knew what it was to be deprived of Human Rights...Of *every* Human Right...even in Sweden...

Music: Up to resolution in Document motif, and behind:

DOCUMENT. Article Two. Everyone is entitled to all the rights and freedoms without distinction of any kind, such as race...religion, national origin, property, birth...

Music: Punctuation.

DOCUMENT. Article Fifteen. Everyone has the right to a nationality.

Music: Punctuation.

DOCUMENT. Article Eighteen. Everyone has the right to freedom of thought, conscience and religion.

Music: Flash up and out.

PRESIDENT. Sweden?
SWEDEN. Yes.
PRESIDENT. Syria?
SYRIA. Yes.

PRESIDENT. Turkey?
TURKEY. Yes.
PRESIDENT. Ukraine?
UKRAINE. Abstain.
PRESIDENT. South Africa?
SOUTH AFRICA. Abstain.
PRESIDENT. Soviet Union?
SOVIET UNION. Abstain.
PRESIDENT. United Kingdom?

Music: A compound of "Green Sleeves" and "Brittania," largo, behind:

NARRATOR. United Kingdom! Tight, little, stubborn, sceptered Isles that alone stood off the Fascinator of the Masses, together with his Luftwaffe, his intuition, and his allies.

And just as the Blitz on London has dissolved in the slipstream of time, so the longer and equally gallant struggle for Human Rights recedes past the Magna Carta, past the Dark Ages, past the Roman massacres, back, back to the dimmest beginnings of English history.

And nowhere such a breed of genius ranged on the side of the Rights of Man!...Milton, Tennyson, Keats, Byron, Shelley, Wordsworth, Wells, Shaw — and of course, the genius of geniuses...

In *Romeo and Juliet*, Shakespeare took up an injustice that was almost universal. Midway in the play, we come upon Lord and Lady Capulet reprimanding their daughter Juliet for failing to appreciate a noble named Paris, whom they have picked to be her husband.

Capulet speaks to his wife in front of the girl:

CAPULET. How now, wife!
Have you deliver'd to her our decree?
LADY CAPULET. Ay, sir; but she will none, she gives you thanks.
I would the fool were married to her grave.
CAPULET. How! Will she none? doth she not give us thanks?
Is she not proud? doth she not count her blest,
Unworthy as she is, that we have wrought
So worthy a gentleman to be her bridegroom?
JULIET. Not proud, you have; but thankful, that you have:
Proud I can never be of what I hate;
But thankful even for hate, that is meant love.

CAPULET. How now, how now, chop-logic! What is this?
    'Proud,' and 'I thank you,' and 'I thank you not;'
    And yet 'not proud:' mistress minion, you,
    Thank me no thankings, nor proud me no prouds,
    But fettle your fine joints 'gainst Thursday next,
    To go with Paris to Saint Peter's Church,
    Or I will drag thee on a hurdle thither.
    Out, you green-sickness carrion! out, you baggage!
LADY CAPULET. Fie, fie! what, are you mad?
JULIET. Good father, I beseech you on my knees,
    Hear me with patience but to speak a word.
CAPULET. Hang thee, young baggage! disobedient wretch!
    I tell thee what: get thee to church o' Thursday,
    Or never after look me in the face:
    Speak not, reply not, do not answer me;
    My fingers itch. Wife, we scarce thought us blest
    That God had lent us but this only child;
    But now I see this one is one too much.
LADY CAPULET. You are too hot.
CAPULET. God's bread! It makes me mad:
    Day, night, hour, tide, time, work, play,
    Alone, in company, still my care hath been
    To have her match'd: and having now provided
    A gentleman of noble parentage,
    Of fair demesnes, youthful and nobly train'd…
    And then to have a wretched puling fool,
    To answer 'I'll not wed; I cannot love,
    I am too young; I pray you, pardon me.'
    But, an you will not wed, I'll pardon you:
    Graze where you will, you shall not house with me:
    Thursday is near; lay hand on heart, advise:
    An you be mine, I'll give you to my friend;
    An you be not, hang, beg, starve, die in the streets,
    For, by my soul, I'll ne'er acknowledge thee…
JULIET. Is there no pity sitting in the clouds,
    That sees into the bottom of my grief?
    O, sweet my mother, cast me not away!
    Delay this marriage for a month, a week;
    Or, if you do not, make the bridal bed
    In that dim monument where Tybalt lies.

LADY CAPULET. Talk not to me, for I'll not speak a word: Do as thou wilt, for I have done with thee.[4]

Music: Document motif comes up powerfully.

DOCUMENT. Article Sixteen. Marriage shall be entered into only with the free and full consent of the intending spouses...

Music: Flash up, but not into resolution: moderate, and sustain behind:

NARRATOR. But every age and every country has its Capulets, its Francisco López, its body of contempt for human blood or human rights. In this same England, Baron de Mandeville, a man of wit and charm — whom Benjamin Franklin once met and called the life of the party — came up with a formula for making wealth. It was simple...

DE MANDEVILLE. In my view the surest wealth consists in a multitude of laborious poor. To make society happy and people easy, it is requisite that great numbers of them be ignorant as well as poor. I'm convinced the knowledge of the working poor should be confined within their occupations. The more a shepherd, a plowman or any other peasant knows of the world, the less fit he'll be to go through the fatigues and hardships of it with cheerfulness and content.[5]

Music: Document motif, under:

DOCUMENT. Article Twenty-Six. Everyone has the right to education... Elementary education shall be compulsory...Higher education shall be equally accessible to all on the basis of merit.

Music: Again up but not to resolution: moderate, and under:

NARRATOR. Notwithstanding the de Mandevilles, there was a ceaseless fight for betterment of the worker's lot in England. The people of Britain themselves did the bitterest fighting, but they were helped, sometimes, by men of high position. Here is Lord Byron, the poet, the aristocrat, addressing the House of Lords — his first and only speech to the House — against a bill to punish by death the destruction of machinery by jobless workers...

---

4. *Romeo and Juliet*, Act III, Scene v. (1594-5)
5. Bernard de Mandeville from his 1714 book *The Fable of the Bees*.

BYRON. These men never destroyed their looms till they were become useless. These men were willing to dig, but the spade was in other hands. Their means of subsistence were cut off: all other employments preoccupied; and their excesses, however to be deplored or condemned, can hardly be the matter of surprise.

And what are your remedies? After months of inaction, at length comes forth the grand specific, the never-failing nostrum of all state-physicians! After feeling the pulse, and shaking your head over the patient, you decide these convulsions must terminate in death!

Is there not blood enough upon your penal code? Can you commit a whole country to their own prisons?

Are these the remedies for a starving and desperate populace?

When a proposal is made to emancipate or relieve, you hesitate, you deliberate for years, you temporize and tamper with the minds of men; but a death-bill must be passed off-hand!

Music: Up into Document motif.

DOCUMENT. Article Twenty-Three. Everyone has the right to work, to free choice of employment, to just and favorable conditions of work and to protection against unemployment...

Music: Flash up, this time for keeps, and resolve.

PRESIDENT. United Kingdom?
UNITED KINGDOM. Yes.
PRESIDENT. United States?
NARRATOR. The United States of America! First country in the world to produce a constitutional guarantee of freedom, first to call it by its proper name:
NAME. Bill of Rights.
NARRATOR. Take a moment here in the Assembly Hall in Paris, and look down there. Note that tall woman sitting among the American delegation there in the Assembly — she is chairman of the U.N.'s Commission of Human Rights — the group which has framed the very articles now being voted on. She is the widow of a President of the United States — the thirty-first.[6]

All right, take your eyes off the meeting now, and fade back with us to a time of the *third* president of the United States — Jefferson. A man who has always had a passionate concern for men's rights. It

---

6. Eleanor Roosevelt.

was he who wrote the Declaration of Independence, who introduced a plan for the gradual emancipation of slaves; he who battled for the Bill of Rights itself. All who personally knew Jefferson agree that he's sweet-tempered, honest, frank and dedicated to his country. Also that he's a highly moral man. Hear him on that:

JEFFERSON. I am a Christian in the only sense in which Jesus wished anyone to be; I am sincerely attached to His doctrines in preference to all others.

NARRATOR. Unquestionably this president, so respectful of the rights of all men, is honored and respected by all men.

Listen to these tributes from all quarters of the republic.

Here is a Mr. William Smith of South Carolina, writing in the *Press*:

SMITH. Mr. Jefferson's political principles are subversive!

NARRATOR. And the Rev. Mr. Parish of Boston, in the course of a Thanksgiving sermon:

PARISH. It is out misfortune to live in an age when the chief magistrate of the nation, has wantonly assaulted the religion of our fathers…a baleful influence…

NARRATOR. And the *Portfolio*, published in Philadelphia:

PORTFOLIO. We protest the reading of the Declaration of Independence on July Fourth! It is a false and flatulent and foolish paper, written by a man of unskilled style, and of questionable honesty.

NARRATOR. A minister in Southington, Connecticut:

MINISTER. The president is a debauchee, an infidel, a liar…

NARRATOR. The *New England Palladium*, warning the people of what will happen under Jefferson's administration:

PALLADIUM. The seal of death will be set on our holy religion. Our churches will be prostrated, and some famous prostitute, under the title of the Goddess of Reason, will preside in the sanctuaries now devoted to the worship of the Most High!

NARRATOR. Some of Jefferson's appointees are hounded as subversive; as disloyal; unfit to work in the manufacture of war materiel. And a toast is proposed to the President, at a banquet of Federalists in Middletown, Connecticut:

BANQUETEER. May he receive from his fellow citizens the reward of his merit — a noose!

Music: A stern statement, modulating into the Document motif, under:

DOCUMENT. Article Twelve. No one shall be subjected to…attacks upon his honor and reputation. Everyone has the right to the protection of the law against such attacks.

Music: Flash up but not out; sustain andante maestoso, and American theme behind:

NARRATOR. The people of the young United States thought better of this champion of their rights than did those sections of the press and clergy. The people twice elected him to the highest office. And from the day Jefferson died, to this one, his name is revered across his country; his face is on the stamps and coins of America. They are his hundred million daily memorials.

From Jefferson onward, constant, gallant, and sometimes bloody conflicts to preserve human rights. Not even stopping at civil war. And through it all, the people, the artists, the great leaders, lining up on the side of the Individual and his Rights.

Playwrights, poets — Longfellow, Whittier, Emerson, Thoreau, Walt Whitman:

WHITMAN. This America is only you and me,
Its power, weapons, testimony, are you and me,
The officers, capitols, armies, ships, are you and me,
Past, present, future, are you and me.
I swear nothing is good to me now that ignores individuals.
The American compact is altogether with individuals;
The whole theory of the universe is directed unerringly
to one single individual — namely, to YOU.[7]

Music: American theme segues to Document motif, and sweeps over the verse, to retard and sustain under:

PREAMBLE. Whereas the peoples of the United Nations have reaffirmed their faith in the dignity and worth of the human person...

Music: Flash up and out.

PRESIDENT. United States?
UNITED STATES. Yes.
PRESIDENT. Uruguay?
URUGUAY. Sí.
PRESIDENT. Venezuela?
VENEZUELA. Sí.
PRESIDENT. Yemen?...Yemen?
CLERK. Absent.

7. Excerpt from the Whitman poem "By Blue Ontario's Shore" published in *Leaves of Grass*.

PRESIDENT. Yugoslavia?[8]
YUGOSLAVIA. Abstain.

Slight pause; room tone.

NARRATOR (*with an air of a big job finished*). The roll call is completed... The vote?
EVATT. In favor of adoption, forty-eight; against adoption, none; abstentions, eight...So now we reach the stage at which by an enormous vote, and without any direct opposition, this Assembly has adopted this very important Declaration...

The voice of Herbert Evatt fades under the following:

NARRATOR...without any direct opposition, he says. Some countries have abstained because they think the declaration goes too far. Others because they don't think it's gone far enough, but no direct opposition. No noes, nons, nays or nyets.
    The President of the Assembly makes a little speech reminding the nations that though this Declaration of Human Rights does not yet have the force of law, it is the all-important first step toward that end. Here is Evatt of Australia, speaking in that Palais in Paris, at the end of a long day, the clock now reading almost midnight...
EVATT (*faded up*)...nor does it provide for enforcement. Still, it is the first step in a great evolutionary process. It is the first occasion on which the organized community of nations has made a Declaration of Human Rights and fundamental freedoms, and it has the authority of the body of opinion of the United Nations as a whole; and millions of people, men and women and children all over the world, many miles from Paris and New York, will turn for hope, and guidance, and inspiration, to this document. (*Fading.*) I must congratulate, and I do congratulate, those who have worked so zealously to achieve this result, and for so long.
NARRATOR (*over the fading Evatt*). It is midnight now in foggy Paris, and the bells of the nearby Notre Dame de Grace de Passy strike the hour.

Sound of bells.

NARRATOR. And as the sound pulses toward the outskirts of Chaillot, so do the mighty overtones of Document A/777. (*Bells fade.*) Radiating

---

8. Yugoslavia existed as a country from 1918-1941 and 1945-1992 before splitting up into smaller nations.

from the city of Voltaire, the first vibrations of world conscience... eastward from Paris, over the freezing heartland of Europe, down the plains of Asia, out into the Pacific...

DOCUMENT. Everyone...without distinction of any kind...

NARRATOR. Westward from Paris, over the farms and villages, past the stormy Channel, out across the Atlantic, all the way around to the New World, to the City of Towers, through its griddle of streets and avenues shimmering magnetically over the very ground where America's Bill of Rights was composed...

DOCUMENT (*in a whisper*)...free and equal in dignity and rights...

NARRATOR...inundating the byways and back-alleys of every town, lapping around factories and schools, swarming into office buildings, swirling around the altar of a country church, throbbing in the pipes of a cathedral organ.

Music: Church organ up briefly, then down and behind:

NARRATOR. Freedom, freedom, articles of human rights, running like quicksilver through homes, stores, offices, public buildings, city halls, marriage bureaus...

HE (GROOM). We'd like to apply for a marriage license, please.

SHE. All right, fill out the forms.

Music: Document motif, just a moment of it.

DOCUMENT. Article Sixteen. Men and women of full age, without any limitation due to race, nationality, or religion, have the right to marry and to found a family...

Music: Another short fillip.

NARRATOR. Wavelengths of freedom, flashing through the union hall, the courtroom, the polling booth, the hospital, bouncing off the walls of the maternity ward, the nursery...

Crying infant, behind:

DOCUMENT. Article Twenty-Five. Motherhood and childhood are entitled to special care and assistance. All children, whether born in or out of wedlock, shall enjoy the same social protection...

Infant fades under:

NARRATOR. Vibrations of freedom, fluttering in the wings of the theater, riding down the shaft of light from the film projector in the movie house…

Music: In.

NARRATOR…weaving around the feet of the ballerina at the opera; harmonizing with the musical instruments as they speak the universal language in the concert hall…

Music: Symphonic passage up in the clear, then down behind:

DOCUMENT. Article Twenty-Seven. Everyone has the right freely to participate in the cultural life of the community, to enjoy the arts…

Music: Fade under:

NARRATOR. Signals, cycles, voltages of world conscience, dancing along the radio antenna on your roof, running like fire through the condensers and tubes of your receiver in your room as you sit and listen at leisure…

DOCUMENT. Article Twenty-Four. Everyone has the right to rest and leisure, including reasonable limitation of working hours and periodic holidays with pay.

NARRATOR. Ripples spreading around the world from Paris, roiling the waters of the East River as it passes the United Nations complex, circulating in the conference chambers, the committee rooms, the delegates' lounge, the Assembly Hall…

DOCUMENT. Whereas it is essential to promote friendly relations among nations…

Music: Sneak curtain cue.

NARRATOR. The endless transmission…the ceaseless, silent broadcast…the man-made force thousands of times more powerful than the most fearsome bomb…the force that radiates not poison and disintegration, but life and hope, liberty and love…the hard-won, blood-bought, glittering articles of freedom in the simple paper known as:

DOCUMENT. Document A/777...Universal Declaration of Human Rights, Adopted and Proclaimed by the General Assembly of the United Nations.

Music: Up and sweeping to a finale.

CORWIN ON *DOCUMENT A/777*

Document A/777 was a broadcast under the auspices of the United Nations, carried in the United States over the Mutual Broadcasting System, from 9:00 to 10:00 p.m. Eastern Standard Time on March 26, 1950. A recording of the program was played to the full United Nations Assembly after being introduced by Mrs. Eleanor Roosevelt, who had been Chairman of the United Nations Commission on Human Rights.

FROM THE EDITOR

Corwin is often credited with two George F. Peabody medals. The first one was in his name for the landmark four-network broadcast of *We Hold These Truths* in 1941, only the second year of the award. The other Peabody, given to the Mutual Broadcasting System and United Nations Radio in 1950, is directly related to this broadcast.

Here is the citation for that Peabody Medal: "A Citation to the Mutual Broadcasting System and United Nations Radio for the significant series of hour-long documentary programs, *The Pursuit of Peace*, which delineated to listeners the world-wide scope of man's international undertakings for the benefit of his fellowmen, and particularly, for the premiere program, *Document A/777*, which dramatized the historical background and implications of the United Nations declaration on human rights."

Corwin was, at this time, Chief of Special Projects for United Nations Radio and was directly responsible for producing these shows.

THE STRANGE AFFLICTION

Written at the invitation of Fletcher Markel and Elliott Lewis for the *Sears Radio Theater*, the program was broadcast over CBS Radio on May 29, 1979. The cast: Nanette Fabray (Jane), Steve Franken (Ned), Fletcher Markle (Therapist, Publisher, Cytologist), Byron Kane (Garmisch, Headline, Endocrinologist), Parley Baer (Healer, Kestenbaum, Traumatologist), Mel Welles (Witch Doctor, Cop, Doctor), True Boardman (Calvin Fox, Teratologist), Richard Erdman (Harry, Repogle, Hematologist, Network Exec), Mary Jane Croft (Woman Executive, Interviewer, Nurse) and Janet Waldo (Girl, Nutritionist, Lady Poet). Hosted by Andy Griffith. Music by Nelson Riddle and Art Gilmore was the Announcer. The author directed.

In 1994, the script was slightly revised by Norman Corwin for a production by the California Artists Radio Theater (CART) at the Roosevelt Hotel in Hollywood, produced by Peggy Webber and under the direction of the author. The CART show starred Samantha Eggar (Jane), David Warner (Ned), Norman Lloyd (Replagle, Garmisch, Network Executive), Jeanette Nolan (Dr. Nolan, Woman Poet), William Windom (Harry, The Healer, Hematologist), Kathleen Freeman (Speech Therapist), John Astin (Interviewer), Linda Henning (Girl, Woman Executive), Marvin Kaplan (Kestenbaum, Traumatologist, Publisher), Ashby Adams (Headline, Endocrinologist, Doctor), Elliott Reid (Witch Doctor), Shay Duffin (Cop, Teratologist) and John Harlan (Announcer for CART, Cytologist). Ray Erlenborn performed the sound effects and Marty Halperin engineered. The show aired nationally on NPR *Playhouse*.

The following script is the 1994 revision.

DR. NOLAN. Good evening. I am Dr. Jeanette Nolan, Director of the National Dysphemia Foundation. And I am happy to announce that we have something of a revelation for you today. Because here in this studio of KIII in Tustin, California, is the one person best able to tell, at long last, the complete story of the first recorded case of Dysphemia Glossopoesis. Now don't be alarmed by that term — it will be fully explained by Mr. Ned Kesey, the gentleman I'm speaking of. And here he is!

NED. Thank you, doctor. I am the husband of Jane Kesey, who is at the center of this story, so to speak. We'd been happily married for eleven years, when suddenly we had an experience that was, well, bizarre, to say the least. I'm sure there are many worse things than what we went through, but when it's happening, you feel you're in the power of a strange and, at times, even contagious affliction that will never let go of you.

It began one April morning. My alarm clock went off, as usual, at 7 a.m. We got up, dressed, and went down and had breakfast. It was kind of an unsettled morning — you know how it is in early spring. Jane made herself some cereal, and I was eating pancakes with molasses on them, and reading the sports page, while Jane was reading the comics.

JANE. More coffee?
NED. Thanks.

Coffee pouring in a cup.

NED. I've got a feeling it's going to rain.
JANE. Here, or on the plain in Spain?
NED (*narrating*). I didn't pay any special attention to that answer, because she was obviously quoting from the song in *My Fair Lady*. (*Up.*) What does the weather report say?
JANE. About today?
NED. I'm not asking about yesterday.
JANE. Probability of rain.
NED. Then I'd better take an umbrella.
JANE. That's my fella.
NED. Wait a minute. Are you playing some kind of game?
JANE. A game?
NED. The way you link —
JANE. What makes you think — ?
NED. Why are you replying to everything I say with a rhyme?
JANE. Every time?
NED. Yes.
JANE. Well, even if I were, is that a crime?

NED. Are you mocking me?
JANE. No.
NED. Just don't pursue it.
JANE. But I didn't intend to do it.
NED (*raising his voice*). Come on, now, will you *cut that out*?
JANE (*raising hers*). PLEASE — DON'T SHOUT!
NED. All right, already! Enough, enough!
JANE. My, you're *really* in a huff!
NED. Do that once more, and you'll regret it!
JANE. See here: if you — oh, well, forget it.
NED. No, finish what you started to say.
JANE. Very well. I'll put it just this way:
Threaten me once more, I will leave you flat.
NED. But, dammit, you must realize that
You cannot treat me like a child!
I don't begin to be beguiled
By silly games, like when you play
At rhyming everything I say.
There is a moment of silence.
JANE. Oh, my poor dear Ned —
Do you know what you just said?
NED (*shaken*). See what you made me do?
JANE. Why blame *me*? *You're* the one who
Spoke in rhyme just now, not I!
NED. But you *induced* it! I don't deny
That I'm upset! — Where are my glasses?
JANE. You're wearing them. — You've spilled molasses
On your vest.
NED. You've messed
My morning up. I've got to go. I'm late.
I'll call you from the office. (*Going off.*) Oh, great!
We sound like a pair of teenage bards,
Like a couple of idiot greeting cards!
JANE. I'm sure there's some explanation why —
NED. Well, *you* find out what it is! — Goodbye!

Door opens, closes with a slam.

Music: Echoes the slam with a percussive bridge.

Interior of an automobile.

NED (*narrating*). As I drove to work, I could hardly keep my mind on the road —

Screeching tires, angry auto horn.

NED. I was afraid to think in *words*, lest they *rhyme* — but after a few miles, the sense of alarm wore off and I felt free of any compulsion to rhyme. And suddenly, you know, the whole thing seemed to me comic. I figured that Jane, who really has a great sense of humor, had just been pulling my leg — that maybe she had *practiced* that routine, had worked it up into a sort of production...Anyway, when I reached the office...
GIRL. Good morning, Mr. Kesey.
NED. Morning.
KESTENBAUM. Morning, Kesey.
NED. Morning, Mr. Kestenbaum. (*Narrating.*) The first thing I did when I got to my desk was to call Jane...

Phone rings through the receiver. Two rings and the other receiver comes off the cradle.

JANE (*filter*). Hello?
NED. Jane — listen — I'm sorry about losing my cool this morning. Y'u know, I really didn't have enough sleep; and when I was dressing I couldn't find my wallet; and then you started to make rhymes of everything I said, I thought you were playing some kind of silly *mocking* game —
JANE. But just the same —
NED. No, let me finish. I should have realized that you were just exercising your sense of humor, right? Your sense of *play*, really, which at times can be frightening, you know, and —
JANE. *Frightening*?
NED. Yes...I mean —
JANE. Well, *that's* enlightening!
NED. No, what I mean is that it's sometimes *scary* how *clever* you can be... and what I should have done, instead of getting all worked up and everything, was to relax, and roll with the punches, so to speak — and I should have *enjoyed* your mimicking — I mean, you were giving me the hotfoot, and so what? I reacted like a fool, when I should have appreciated your humor, and realized that you were poking —
JANE. Just a minute, Ned. (*Pause.*) I wasn't joking.
NED. What?
JANE. You heard me.

NED. You were serious?
JANE. I was in my right mind. I was not delirious.
NED. Now wait a minute, baby —
JANE. After you left, I thought that maybe
   It would leave me. I had to speak to *some*one,
   And so I, like a dumb one,
   Picked up the telephone and called
   The market to order food. I was *appalled!*
NED. Appalled? What happened?
JANE. When I started to read the shopping list,
   The words all took a crazy twist —
   They came together in a sort of jing-a-ling!
   The clerk, I'm sure, thought, "Who's this ding-a-ling?"
NED. Why, what did you order?
JANE. You really want to know?
NED. Yes.
JANE. Well...(*Taking the plunge.*) I said to that jerk, I said —
NED. What jerk?
JANE. The *clerk!* — I said:
   "I want a tin of salmon, a pound of brie,
   A stalk of winter celery,
   A can of clams, a bag of yams,
   And, if you have some devilled hams
   From Poland, I'll take *two* — "
NED. And did he —
JANE. No, wait, I'm not yet through —
   "A pound of peppers — red —
   A loaf of pumpernickel bread,
   A bunch of parsley, a box of-er-whatsis —
   — Oh, what d'you call it? — Matzos!
   A pack of Oriental teas,
   Black olives and some feta cheese,
   A jar of marinated herring — "
   At which point he started *swearing!*
NED. He swore at you?
JANE. Yes! (*Starting to cry.*) Oh, Ned, I'm really getting scared.
   The way that everything I say — gets — paired!
NED (*alarmed by her tears*). Darling, something's very wrong. Stay right
   where you are. I'm coming home...

   Music: In and under:

NED (*narrating*). I excused myself to the boss…told him it was an emergency…(*Up.*) It's an emergency, Mr. Replogle.
REPLOGLE. Yeah.
NED (*narrating*). And I left the office and sped back home over the freeway. And I mean sped. I must have been going seventy-five when —

Motorcycle cop's siren. Car slows down and stops.

COP (*approaching*). Okay, what's the rush?
NED. Emergency at home.
COP. What kind of emergency?
NED. Illness.
COP. What kind of illness?
NED. My wife can't stop rhyming!
COP. Say that again?
NED. My wife can't stop rhyming.
COP. Your wife can't stop rhyming.
NED. That's right.
COP. Did you call an ambulance?
NED. No, officer, it's not the kind of thing you call an ambulance for.
COP. That's what I was thinking, too. Let's see your license, please.
NED. Yessir. It happened only this morning. It just came right out of the blue. It's so weird! I mean, whenever I said something, she'd answer with a rhyme. Anything like that ever happen to you? I don't know what you'd *call* it!
COP. Would you please take your license out of your wallet?
NED. See? See? "Call it / wallet." *You're* doing it! It was just like that!
COP. See your registration, please?
NED. Yep.
COP. You still at this address?
NED. Yessir. (*Narrating.*) So I got a ticket for speeding. That was all I needed. But the time I reached home, I was as rattled as Jane was.

Door opens and closes.

NED (*calling*). Jane? *Jane!* JANE! (*Narrating.*) I found Jane sitting in the den, staring at the wall. (*Up.*) Jane! Are you all right?
JANE. No. (*Pause.*) I'm a fright!
NED. Now don't worry. Whatever it is that's disturbing you, we'll track it down. In the meantime, just remember that it's *bearable*. — How do you feel?

JANE. Terrible.
NED. Do you have any idea of what triggered it?
JANE. No. This morning I figured it
   Was just a passing flurry
   Of rhymes. But now I worry
   That I'm *stuck* with it.
NED. Have you tried deliberately *not* to rhyme?
JANE. Yes, but I had no luck with it.
NED. You know what I think? Maybe a shock would stop it.
JANE. Drop it. I don't fancy being electrocuted.
NED. No, I don't mean a jolt of electric power —
JANE. Oh, you mean like a cold shower?
NED. Exactly.
JANE. I hate cold showers!
NED. But you won't be under it for *hours*. — Isn't it worth at least a try?
JANE. Well…all right…But why me? That's the question: why?

Shower running.

NED (*shouting to top the sound of the water*). Do you feel any better?
JANE (*shouting also*). No — only wetter.
NED. Well, stay under it some more! (*After a moment.*) Is it easing?
JANE. No, dammit — I'm freezing.
NED. Just give it a little more time!
JANE. No!
   The water is shut off. Shower door slides open.
JANE. I'd rather *rhyme*!
   Than freeze to death! — Here, dry me!
   (*As he does.*) It's so easy for you to *try* me
   Under the cold tap! I feel like ice!
   Rub me harder. — There, that's nice.
NED. Well, so it didn't work.
JANE. No dice.

Patting and drying.

JANE. I'm really — beginning to — despair. (*Crying again.*)
NED. Oh come now, Janie. Come. There, there. We've only just *begun* to fight!
JANE. Do you think I'll *ever* be all right?
NED. Of course! There are all *kinds* of ways out!

JANE. We've got to find one before the day's out.
NED. We'll soon discover just what goes on.
JANE. But first — suppose I get my clothes on.
NED (*narrating*). We tried other things. Jane stood on her head for ten minutes at a time. She didn't speak for a whole day. We jogged. We swam. We abstained. We lifted weights. We tried fasting. Nothing worked. Then I suggested putting marbles in her mouth. I had read somewhere that a great orator did that to cure himself of stuttering.[1] So I fed her a dozen little glass aggies.
JANE (*speaking with marbles in her mouth*). Wait — or heaven's sake! That's all I can take!
NED (*laughing*). It makes you sound — (*Searches for the word and doesn't find it.*) — uncouth!
JANE. What's so funny? I could break a tooth!
Why are you wearing that silly grin?
How long do I have to keep these in?
NED. Give them a chance to help their case. (*Laughs.*)

She blows the marbles out of her mouth.

NED (*stung*). Was that nice, to spit them in my face?
JANE (*grumbling*). All while my jaw was *buckling*,
You stood there *chuckling!*
NED. I'm sorry. You just looked so *funny*, Jane.
JANE. I did, did I? (*Going off.*) You give me a *pain!*

Door slams.

NED (*narrating*). Well, it took her quite a while to get over my having laughed at her discomfiture. (*Up, calling.*) Can't you find it in your heart to forgive?
JANE (*off*). Not as long as I live!
NED. What can I do or say?
JANE. Nothing. Just go away.
NED (*narrating*). But after a spell she calmed down, and went back to feeling miserable full time about her problem. She was right to blame me for laughing — but who could blame her for crying?
JANE (*crying again*). By now — it can be — assumed —
That I — am doomed!
NED. Oh no no no no no no! This *has* to be only a passing affliction!
JANE (*grimly*). An affliction of my diction!

---

1. Ancient Greek orator Demosthenes.

NED. Yes. (*Gets an idea.*) You know, that gives me an idea! I think what you should do is, go to a speech therapist. I imagine it's the sort of thing a therapist deals with all the time. Maybe I can find one in the Yellow Book.

JANE (*resigned*). Oh, well…anything. — Go ahead. Look.

Music: A little trip across town.

THERAPIST. Well, it's really not a matter for a speech therapist, Mrs. Kesey. You seem to *speak* without impediment, but in a pattern that seems, to say the least, very curious.

JANE. Oh, I'm so *angry* with myself! I'm *furious*!

THERAPIST. No, you mustn't blame yourself. Whatever else it may be, it's — uh —

JANE. Involuntary?

THERAPIST. Correct. — I couldn't begin to hazard a guess as to the *cause* of your — uh — complaint — but I *would* suggest that you see a psychiatrist. The problem lies more in that field, I should think.

JANE. You're suggesting I should see a shrink?

THERAPIST. A psychiatrist. The investigation may have to be extensive.

JANE. But wouldn't that be expensive?

THERAPIST. Very possibly — but can you afford to go around, indefinitely, speaking verse?

JANE. No. Nothing could be worse.

THERAPIST. As a suggestion, have you tried *trapping* yourself into words or phrases or sentences that would be difficult, if not impossible, to rhyme?

JANE. Time after time.

THERAPIST. That's hard to believe. I should think that by just slowing down your speech and carefully *avoiding* rhymes, you would soon get over this malady. It's worth a try.

JANE (*vexed*). That's what *you'd* do, but you're not *I*!
It isn't that I won't or I shan't —
I would if I could, but I CAN'T!

THERAPIST. Well, I'm more certain now than ever, that
You should see
Someone in psychiatry.
The problem's bigger than it looks —
There's nothing like it in the books.

JANE (*after another one of those pregnant pauses*). Did you hear yourself just now?

THERAPIST. Hear what?

JANE. You spoke in rhymes!
THERAPIST (*afraid to admit it*). Oh, come. Nothing of the sort!
I'm afraid your time's
Up. — I'm sorry. — I wish you the best,
And hope it's not too long a quest
Before you find relief. — *Good grief!*
JANE. Why, what's the matter?
THERAPIST. Suddenly I feel quite dizzy!
JANE. Well, now that'll keep *you* busy...
My husband caught it this very same way.
But he got *over* his. — Good day.

She walks to the door and goes out.

THERAPIST (*to himself*). Oy, vay!

Music: Anything but the Beethoven Ninth.

NED (*narrating*). Well, when Jane told me what happened to the therapist, I began to worry all over again. You see I had sort of blocked out that *I* had caught Jane's trouble from her — I had convinced myself that it never happened. But after the therapist, there was no guarantee that I might not catch it again, and get a relapse, so to speak. And if that happened, how could I show my face at the office? Now, unlike the speech therapist, I didn't pick the *psychiatrist* out of the yellow pages. I made an appointment for Jane with Dr. Ludwig Garmisch, one of the top men in town.
GARMISCH (*German accent*). *Most* interesting. I have of course seen many cases of dysphemia, vich is a neurotic disorder of speech, but nothing vich fits this description. I once treated two patients who spoke in *reverse* — one of them Dr. Furbish sent me, the other a quack sent.
JANE. Do all psychiatrists speak with an *acc*ent?
GARMISCH. Mostly in radio plays, my dear. However, yours is a most *peculiar* case! I vould first like to make a little test, yes? I give you vords, you answer quvickly before you can think. There is something I will know by this.
JANE. What do you hope to show by this?
GARMISCH. Vell, rhyming is not that easy, you see. Most people, ven you ask them quvick to give a rhyme for a vord, they have to search for it. Now, it's vun thing to end a sentence mit a rhyme, but another to give right avay, vidout *thinking*, a rhyme. Do you follow? So you are ready, yes?

JANE. More or less.
GARMISCH. Remember, answer quvick. Now, first vord: Army.
JANE. Pastrami.
GARMISCH. Dimple.
JANE. Simple, pimple, Jakob Gimpel.
GARMISCH. Just vun vord is enough — Christmas.
JANE. Isthmus.
GARMISCH. Cough and sneeze.
JANE. Aristophanes.
GARMISCH. Putt-putt.
JANE. Scuttlebutt.
GARMISCH. Radio.
JANE. Hey-di-ho.
GARMISCH. Appeal.
JANE. Schlemiel.
GARMISCH. Lostock.
JANE. Vladivostok.
GARMISCH. Nicholas.
JANE. Tickle us.
GARMISCH. Bursitis.
JANE. Worse itis.
GARMISCH. Au gratin.
JANE. Latin.
GARMISCH. No, it's French.
JANE. Wench.
GARMISCH. Tally.
JANE. Finale.
GARMISCH. Vell, I guess finale is a good vord to end on. Okay. Remarkable! Tell me, vas your mother ever infatuated by some doggerel?
JANE. Oh, she never knew a dog that well.
GARMISCH. I see. Vas your father, by any chance, a poet?
JANE. Not that you'd know it.
GARMISCH. Vas your childhood happy?
JANE. No, rather scrappy.
GARMISCH. Did you enjoy to skip mit rope?
JANE. Nope.
GARMISCH. Did you like to play mit boys?
JANE. Not as much as I liked toys.
GARMISCH. Vere you an impatient virgin?
JANE. No, I needed urgin'.
GARMISCH. Vere you very fond of petting?

JANE. Dr. Garmisch! Where is this getting?
GARMISCH. Vell, let me be frank. You are suffering from an acute form of dysphemia vich is unprecedented, so I am going to *give* it the name Dysphemia Glossopoesis — from the Greek "glosso," meaning tongue, and "poesis," meaning poetry. You *see*? (*Proudly.*) I have given a new vord to the language!
JANE. So I have *glossopoesis*?
GARMISCH. At least, that's my thesis —
Now rhythm, you see, if you'll bear with me,
Rhythm is part of the natural order,
But sometimes it gets very close to the border
Of angst, or anxiety, should there be such of it
As you have been having, and having too much of it —
Now I'm fully aware that whatever you *do* do
Mit rhymes, *I'm* now doing as *you* do!
To laymen, of course, this may seem outrageous,
But scientifically, you're *contagious*!
I think for this reason, you should be *confined*
Until ve can find what goes on in your mind!
JANE. *Confined*, Dr. Garmisch? You must be kidding!
GARMISCH. Then you're not *serious* about ridding
Yourself, by whatever degrees,
Of your disease?
JANE. Please —
GARMISCH. Let me call up your husband. Where does he vork?
JANE. Replogle, Kestenbaum, Grackle and Burke.

Music: Anything but the Brahms Second, going into:

NED (*narrating*). Dr. Garmisch persuaded Jane to go to a psychiatric institute for tests. He had gotten over his glossopoesis almost as quickly as I had, although every now and then I thought I detected a little relapse, like when he asked whether I had tried ways of getting rid of Jane's rhyming, and I answered, "Yes, I tried *many* things, but all in vain, man."
GARMISCH. One of the first things we must do is a brain scan.
NED (*narrating again*). You see what I mean? "Vain, man" and "brain scan." But these lapses were few and far between. Anyway, Jane, who was getting pretty depressed by now, agreed to enter the Harold G. Squamous Institute of Neurological Symptomatology. Well, let me tell you, they gave Jane every test known to science, and a

few that weren't. It seemed like every branch of medicine ran right through her room. Besides a squadron of psychiatrists, there was a teratologist:

TERATOLOGIST. Everything checks out fine, right down to your feet.

JANE. So now I can eat?

NED (*narrating*). And a hematologist:

HEMATOLOGIST. You red count's normal. So's the white.

JANE (*cynically*). Uncontrollable delight.

NED (*narrating*). And a traumatologist:

TRAUMATOLOGIST. We can find no precipitating cause.

JANE. Applause, applause!

NED (*narrating*). And a cytologist:

CYTOLOGIST. We can't fault a single cell.

JANE. Swell.

NED (*narrating*). And an endocrinologist:

ENDOCRINOLOGIST. Everything checks out. Every last gland!

JANE (*dourly*). Strike up the band!

NED (*narrating*). You couldn't blame Jane for feeling bitter. Here she was, a sort of prisoner in this institute, being treated like a guinea pig. She got tired of them trying all kinds of things on her, and she finally rebelled:

NURSE. Here's some sodium amytal.

JANE. I won't take it, dammit all.

DOCTOR. You are to get daily steam baths in a sauna.

JANE. Well, I'm not gonna.

NUTRITIONIST. We propose to put you on a liquid diet.

JANE. I don't buy it.

NED. Why not try it?

JANE. *Quiet!*

NED (*narrating*). After a while she got tired of resisting, especially since she wasn't making any progress, and so they resumed experimenting. They tried sedatives, tranquilizers, narcosynthesis, anti-histamines, hot compresses, cold compresses...but nothing made the slightest difference.

GARMISCH. Do you feel any change?

JANE. No, just strange.

NED. How are you today?

JANE. Go away.

NED (*narrating*). And when none of those things worked, we tried brining in various people outside of medicine and psychiatry. There was this faith healer, the Reverend Vocal Richards, who came with a small choir that sang a few numbers, and then the Reverend went to work on her:

HEALER. Dear one, dwell not upon the affliction of words that hath afflicted thee, but look up to heaven, and trust in the *Word*, and thy name will be wrote in the Book of Life! Hallelujah!

    And all that man uttereth, yea, and that goes for woman, too; all that they uttereth is but VANITY, praise the Lord, and all the words that are uttereth by man that are born of woman, all of them are as the dust of the field — yea, verily they are as the sands of the desert, HALLELUJAH! And they are like unto the words that cometh from out of the mouths of babes and sucklings, hallelujah, and they are as drops of water in the sea!

JANE. But what has that got to do with *me*?

NED. When the Reverend didn't get to first base, someone suggested a witch doctor, who happened to be in the city because he was part of a touring dance group from Africa; and this witch doctor came in with a lot of feathers and stuff, and he went into his magic chant:

Music: Bongo drums, not too loud, behind:

WITCH DOCTOR. ArrAMaagong barraBOOKa Ngumbu YorrabaLINGah!
TorroWANGie cooLONGalook DurranDURRA!
WarrabaHINI!
Tuombolong, wallamolo!
Turranbulla, yurrambi. And also nelungaloo.
Kamgoloola jeril-derie iluka kurajong!
    — I have spoke. — Now I sing:
(*Sings.*) Ulla, wagulla,
Gumboola, Kokoukou,
Bomdouki, Pangako,
Mokoukay, bou*m*ako! (*Stops singing.*)
    That is end of song. Do you feel of some change?

JANE. No. — Can you sing "Home on the Range?"

NED (*narrating*). Well, so nothing seemed to be of the slightest help. The Institute kept giving us a lot of double-talk, and, because it was so expensive being a patient there, Jane insisted on going home. — By now the fear of contagion had passed, because although some of us, like the speech therapist and Dr. Garmisch and I myself had caught the symptoms, we soon got over it. But not poor Jane. She began to think of herself as a sort of Typhoid Mary.

JANE. I'm just a jinx.

    This whole thing stinks.

NED (*narrating*). Of course we couldn't keep it from the neighbors forever, and I must say people were nice about it — they made various suggestions, none of them of any use — until Jane's brother blew in from Seattle to spend a few days with us. His name is Harry Krill, and he runs a diner that he calls Krill's Grill, which is worse than anything that ever came from Jane, I just have to say that. I was listening to the radio one evening...

Music: Filter, as on radio. Muzak-type earwash.

NED. ...when Harry came up with a notion that stunned us...
HARRY. Ned, will you turn off the radio? There's something I want to ask you.
NED. Okay, Harry, so what's your question?
HARRY. Has there been any publicity on Jane?
NED. Hell, no — we've done everything we can do to keep this *out* of the papers. That's all we need — people calling us up to hear Jane speak in rhymes.
HARRY. Don't you know you've been missing out on a *bonanza*?
NED. What d'ye mean, a bonanza?
HARRY. Why, you've both been looking at this thing *entirely* the wrong way. It's a *talent*, not a liability that Jane has! How many people in this whole world can go around rhyming *spontaneously*?
NED (*considering*). Yeah...Garmisch said there's never been a case like it. He even had to invent the name for it — glossopoesis.
HARRY. Well, there you are. Instead of getting Jane all kinds of doctors, you should have gotten her an *agent*!
NED. Well, what could *he* do?
HARRY. Line up interviews! Line up some guest appearances! Advise and consent! Maybe even get Jane her own TV show!
NED. Are you out of your head? Jane has never *been* on TV.
HARRY. So what of it? How about those people on game shows — they've never been on TV either, and look what *they* get.
NED. What *do* they get?
HARRY. Rich!
NED. Well...I don't know...it seems so...well —
HARRY. Whyncha let me handle it?
NED. You'd have to persuade Jane, to begin with.
HARRY. Listen, she's the most sensible girl in the world. I know my sister. If she understands that she can be *respected* for a special talent, and get well *paid* for it instead of being looked on as a weirdo, or avoided for fear of contamination, do you think she'll hesitate for a second?

NED. Well...you ask her. (*Narrating.*) And he did ask her. He persuaded her. And the first thing you know, there she was on the front page of the *Times*, under a big headline:

HEADLINE.
> RHYME COMES EASY
> FOR MRS. KESEY

NED. ...followed by an interview with a reporter who came to the house — a *long* interview just chock full of Jane Kesey rhymes:

INTERVIEWER. And now a final question, Mrs. Kesey: Do you find that the prospect of spending the rest of your life automatically making jingles — do you find this depressing?

JANE. I did once, but I think of it now as a blessing.

INTERVIEWER. Ah! Well, then, I'm glad for you!

JANE. I am, too.

INTERVIEWER. Thank you, Mrs. Kesey, for letting me call.

JANE. Not at all, not at all.

NED (*narrating*). Well, that interview really stirred things up. We got calls from all over, including *The Poetry Society*, *The Guinness Book of Records*, *People* magazine, *Scientific American*, *Psychology Today*, and *Verbal Quarterly*. — Every mail brought a new proposition...

PUBLISHER. Dear Mrs. Kesey...Would you like to write a book about your experience? We would pay you an advance against royalties, and furnish you with a qualified ghostwriter. We have had very good success with ghostwritten books; in fact, this company proudly boasts —

JANE. No; I don't believe in ghosts. — Next!

WOMAN POET. Dear Mrs. Casey: Enclosed please find in these two crates, an epic poem which I have written about the March of Womankind since the dawn of civilization. It is called *Forward, Daughters of Eve*. I would like to have your opinion of it. It now runs 4,291 pages, but I am thinking of trimming fifteen or twenty pages to tighten it up. As I wish to send this off to a publisher real soon, I would appreciate your writing something immediately that I could quote on the back of the jacket. Perhaps you could point out how my handling of the subject is comprehensive, lyrical, majestic, moving, inspiring, and even tender —

JANE. Return to sender.

NED (*narrating*). There were nibbles from TV and radio news programs, wanting to come to the house and talk to Jane and me...(*Up.*) Look at this, Jane! From CBS!

JANE. Is it better than the one from PBS?

NED. I don't know yet. — And here's one from the BBC.

JANE. As well as Canada! See? The CBC!
NED. Gee!
JANE. NBC
Asks do we
Wish to be interviewed.
But isn't it rude
Not to mention a fee?
Don't you agree?
Or isn't it their policy?
NED. No, it's not. — By the way, the mail is piling up. You've got to begin answering soon, because this pile *grows* so!
JANE. Yes, I suppose so.
NED (*narrating*). And then, of all things — Dr. Garmisch asked us for a percentage of whatever action might develop, as a reward for having invented the term Glossopoesis. When he proposed this, I said to him, (*Up.*) "Aren't you being a little greedy, Doctor?"
JANE. You've not exactly needy, Doctor.
GARMISCH. Ah, but have you never heard of the importance of *packaging*? Once you give a *name* to something, it has identity. It takes on a whole new life. You know vot is a logo?
NED. Yes.
JANE. No go.
GARMISCH. It can be very influential. Listen how beautiful it sounds: "Dysphemia Glossopoesis." — Even if people are not interested in the phenomenon of a lady who can't stop rhyming, they vill find themselves attracted by the unusualness of those vords. They vill say to each other, they vill say, "Did you see that program about Dysphemia Glossopoesis last night?" And they vill be proud to be able to *pronounce* it, let alone to know vot it means! In this vay, my dear Mr. and Mrs. Kesey, the condition of vich you have the distinction to be the first known case, vill become famous throughout the vorld, as svine flu, athlete's foot, tennis elbow —
JANE. But as you well know,
All of those names are simple to spell,
Without having to go through hell,
And more than that, what *really* counts
Is that they're easy to pronounce,
Whereas Dysphemia —
GARMISCH (*haughtily*). Are you telling me that you vould be villing to change Glossopoesis to something vulgar, something common, like Stiff Neck, or Vater-on-the-Knees — something ordinary, and even cheap?

JANE (*losing patience*). Oh, for heaven's sake, why don't you keep —
GARMISCH (*going right on*). Something vich has no style, no cadence, no euphony —
JANE. You know what you can do for me?
  Leave me alone! I've earned the right to profit
  From my talent! To make money off it.
GARMISCH. If money's to be made.
JANE. Besides, you've already been paid!
GARMISCH (*sadly*). Ned — Jane — have you no loyalties?
JANE. Not when it comes to royalties.

Music: In and under:

NED (*narrating*). It got bigger and bigger. There were gifts, requests for Jane to lecture, invitations to attend the opening of supermarkets, requests that she serve on various committees. None of which she accepted, of course, because we didn't want to overexpose her; we wanted things to *build*. And they did build. She got to enjoy all the excitement — she thrived on her celebrity, so to speak. And then she was asked to meet with some top network executives, the big brass, about a program series to be built around her. And she met with them, and charmed them all with her wit and rhyming ability...
NETWORK MAN. Now in order to get the whole country alerted and excited about you, we're going to start you off with an appearance on Marvin Smith's program.[2] It's before a big studio audience, and everybody watches it.
WOMAN EXECUTIVE. Yes, Mrs. Kesey, we at first thought that people would think it was all too much of a gag, so we took a poll, and we were all more than gratified when we saw the results of the gag poll.
JANE. In other words, you ran it up the flagpole?

All laugh. Ad libs: "very good, you're terrific, what a sense of rhyme."

NED (*narrating*). And so it was arranged. A contract was drawn up — a wonderful deal. Great money, great residuals, all kinds of extras that I won't go into. And to kick things off, came the interview with Marvin Smith. We were all there in the studio on the big night — Garmisch, my brother-in-law Harry, and even the witch doctor. After the usual blizzard of commercials, Marvin introduced Jane...

---

2. It was called Calvin Fox's program in the 1979 version.

SMITH. And now, as our very special guest, the woman who has attracted so many headlines and aroused so much curiosity among scholars, scientists and laymen, both in this country and abroad…the little woman who has taken over the headlines from inflation, energy, and politics — JANE KESEY!

Audience applause, whistling, etc.

SMITH. Welcome, Jane. Good of you come. Welcome to our show.
JANE (*joking*). Thank you. There was nowhere else to go.
SMITH (*laughing*). Well, apparently the reports are true, about your sense of humor.
JANE. Oh? Was that the rumor?
SMITH. That was one of them. — Is it true, Jane, that you've been rhyming like this, non-stop, for some months now?
JANE. And how.
SMITH. And that at first you were distressed about your inability to stop rhyming so persistently and, well, wildly?
JANE. To put it mildly.
SMITH. What did you do to try to stop?
JANE. Well, suppose we begin at the very top.
SMITH. All right, let's go back to the beginning. When did you first notice that you were replying to everything said to you, in the form of rhyme-endings to sentences?
JANE. It happened at breakfast one morning. My husband asked if the weather report called for rain, and I said that it did.
SMITH. Go on.
JANE. He noticed that every time he said anything, and I replied, it was with a rhyming *partner* to what *he* had just said. And he thought I was mocking him, so he resented it, naturally.
SMITH. And you started to quarrel?
JANE. Yes. As a matter of fact, he got quite angry, and I tried to explain that I was not doing it *intentionally*.
SMITH. Mrs. Kesey — are you conscious of the fact that you haven't spoken a single rhyme since you started to explain what happened?
JANE (*stunned*). I haven't?
SMITH. You were not aware of that?
JANE (*flustered*). Why, I — I — no, I —
SMITH. Are you kidding me, now?
JANE (*nearing panic*). No, I — I really wasn't aware that I had stopped rhyming —

Some in the audience start to boo and whistle.

SMITH (*to audience*). Now hold it! Hold it right there! I must say to those in the audience who booed just now, that Mrs. Kesey is not faking — I can see that she's very disturbed, and I'm sure it's only a momentary aberration. (*To Jane.*) Surely, Jane, after all these *months* in which you have been unable to speak *without* rhyming, the ability hasn't suddenly abandoned you, has it?

JANE. Well, I don't know. I —

SMITH. Perhaps it's just that you've never been in front of cameras and a studio audience before. Perhaps all it will take is a little priming to get you back in the rhythm of things. May I give you a few lines to get you started again?

JANE (*nervously*). Yes.

SMITH. "Listen my children, and you shall hear
Of the midnight ride of — " (*He waits.*)

JANE (*groping*). Mario Andretti?

Laughter from the audience.

SMITH. No, no, Jane. Let's try another:
"A diller, a dollar,
A ten o'clock scholar,
What makes you come so soon?
You used to come at ten o'clock
And now you come at — " (*Waits.*)

JANE (*tentatively; in tears*). Twelve?

Derisive laughter, now mixed with boos. It increases until it is wiped out by:

Music: A passage feeling sorry for Jane.

NED (*narrating*). Well, there went the whole ball game. They cancelled the contract. People called Jane a fraud, and they made jokes about her. It was disgusting!

GARMISCH. I now believe I can explain what happened, Mrs. Kesey.

JANE. Don't bother.

GARMISCH. You see, there is in the multiphasic personality, a phenomenon in which the hypoglossal impulse is stimulated within the infundibulum of the pituitary, and —

NED. She really doesn't want to hear this, you know.

GARMISCH. But there is no charge for vat I am telling you.

NED. Thanks just the same.

GAERMISCH (*going off*). Vell, all right...

NED (*narrating*). Jane took it hard for a while, but then we realized that only a short time before, we both had been *praying* that she'd be able to stop rhyming. And we realized also that although we no longer had that great contract, and a career in show business to look forward to, we had each other. — And so, Dr. Nolan, when all is said and done, I guess the way it came out could really be called a happy ending, couldn't it?

DR. NOLAN. Oh yes, Mr. Kesey, it certainly could. I must confess that I listened to your story with the greatest sympathy and appreciation for both you and Mrs. Kesey.

NED. Thank you.

DR. NOLAN. I admired the way, from day to day,
You stayed at her side, and when she cried,
You tried and tried to ease her mind,
And through it all you were so *kind*.
And — (*Pause.*) — well, I see that *I've* been hit.

NED. Oh, you'll recover. Bit by bit. But just don't try to hurry it.

DR. NOLAN. Thanks a lot. I hope you're right.

NED. I know I am. Good night.

DR. NOLAN. Good night.

Music: Curtain.

CORWIN ON
THE STRANGE AFFLICTION

In 2007, it was performed as a fund-raiser for the Thousand Oaks Library Foundation, which houses the Corwin Collection. Jokingly, I offered a package of Fig Newtons free to anybody who pledged a million dollars — and one turned up: the family of Edgar Bergen, the comedian whose home was in Thousand Oaks. Samantha Eggar, film actress, appeared on the program — a comedy also starring the comedian Carl Reiner. The million-dollar contribution was warm to the touch, but forty or fifty more millions would have to be added before the new archives could be built. The program was introduced by Steve Brogden, director of the library, and was the last of its kind.

FROM THE EDITOR

With the goal of constructing a new two-story facility to house the American Radio Archives on the grounds of the Thousand Oaks Library, Corwin directed *The Strange Affliction* as a "coming out party" for the project, with Peggy Webber again producing. In addition to Samantha Eggar as Jane and Carl Reiner as Ned, the cast included Norman Lloyd, Nanette Fabray (star of the 1979 version), Janet Waldo, Linda Henning, Shay Duffin, and film historian Leonard Maltin. The Bergen Foundation provided the one million dollar grant mentioned above.

Also of note: Handwritten at the end of the broadcast script for the *Sears Radio Theater*, Corwin wrote the following ending to pad time before segueing back to announcer Art Gilmore:

NORMAN CORWIN. Uh, forgive the intrusion, my dear Mr. Gilmore,
    But — if you don't mind — I have still more
    Rhymes — Just a few at the close
    So we can end this program right on the nose.
    I am the author, Norman Corwin,
    And I wouldn't have had to be doin' this jawin'
    If I'd written it to exact dimensions —
    But you know how it is with good intentions.
    Well, now I see that I don't have to kill more
    Time — so back to you, Mr. Gilmore.

NATIONAL HOLIDAYS SERIES

This six-episode series was commissioned by National Public Radio and was broadcast on its network of 270 stations. Under the collective title of *The National Holidays*, Corwin wrote and directed shows for Memorial Day, Independence Day, Labor Day, Columbus Day, Thanksgiving, and New Year's Day. The series aired on these holidays from May 29, 1983 through January 1, 1984.

Two of the plays have been included in this volume: MEMORIAL DAY, broadcast on May 29, 1983 on *All Things Considered* and LABOR DAY, made available to NPR affiliates on August 26, 1983. (This show was distributed as a "Module"; NPR sent the show over its satellite and local stations recorded the live feed for later broadcast.)

Produced by Jay Kernis. The author directed.

MEMORIAL DAY

Music: Trumpet Fanfare.

Deep, sonorous bell. Over its fading reverberation:

NARRATOR. Remembrance is a light sleeper
  No blast of trumpets is needed to awaken it.
  No booming bells.
  No saluting guns.
  They make important sounds, but they
     are for occasions.

Saluting cannon. After three volleys:

NARRATOR. No, none of that.
  No one need carve letters ten feet high
  To remind us in granite that today is —
VOICE (*out of stone; on echo*). Memorial Day.
NARRATOR. All it takes is the slightest memorandum,
  a number on a calendar:
  Day Thirty.
  A day in May, toward the end of Spring,
  The season whose habit is to bloom with
     colors and textures richer than
     anything woven in Persia,
  The month famous for showers left over
     from April, and consequent flowers,
     and mayflies and May wines and May
     Queens and May Day and — highest in
     all the May polls — Day Off.

Music: A pleasant, light-hearted passage, dipping down behind:

NARRATOR. But the merriest of months is not all merry:
  On its last day but one, on the verge of
     June, we turn aside to think of those
  Unable to be with us, for good reason,
  Couched in sleep, the fastest of all sleeps,
  Beyond arousal.

This is their day, wherever they may be,
The men of our big and little wars, who
 fell on hard ground, or in grass, or
 clawed at sand, or stained snow red,
 or stumbled among jungle vines, or
 dropped out of the sky, or went down
 in the drink.
This is their day.

Never entirely, of course.
They wouldn't want the ball game to be
 canceled in their memory
Nor the freeways empty,
Nor the beaches left to gulls and crabs;
They would prefer to sit beside you on a
 blanket, watching waves rise and curl and
 cataract…

The seashore: surf, the piping of birds; it continues behind:

NARRATOR (*no pause in the narration*)…watching sheets of foam surge
 and ebb, smoothing the shore like a
 planetary trowel,
Watching the girls in their scanties, swimming
 and running, or lolling, or tanning
 themselves beneath lotions;
They would rather listen to the bickering of
 birds and the crash of surf, and swig coffee
 from a thermos, or rinse their throats in
 beer, or just sit and soak up sunshine…
 Start to fade, as narration continues unbroken.
NARRATOR. They have only the earth now to keep them warm.
They have been gathered like leaves stripped
 from a tree by a great wind,
And set down gently in serried order in
 green pastures.

They have forgotten Chickamauga and Manassas,
 Antietam and the Wilderness,
 The slaughter below Round Top,
 The siege of the city on the river,

The marches and bivouacs, the bitter campaigns.
They've left that to historians and to
   living memory.

But not all epics are blood and thunder.
   Flowers, too, make history:

HISTORIAN (*a woman*). Two years after the end of the Civil War, some women in a small Mississippi town on the Tombigee, chose May 30 to decorate the graves of soldiers. Not just their own, but their late enemy's as well. Word of this traveled north to the big city on the Hudson, where New York's Chauncey DePew, would recall, later:

DEPEW. The widows and mothers of the Confederate dead went out and strewed their graves with flowers. The women scattered them impartially also over the unmarked resting places of Union soldiers. When news of this touching tribute reached the North it roused, as nothing else could have done, national unity, and allayed sectional passion. Thus out of sorrows common alike to North and South came this beautiful custom.

Music: Reflective passage behind:

NARRATOR. Many a May has come and gone since then,
Many a new danger, new grievance, new cause,
Many a new weapon and new war,
Many a fresh grave dug in many a foreign field,
Many a mourner, many a flower cast...

Fade in airplane engines and sustain behind:

HISTORIAN. Each Memorial Day, in southeast England, an old warplane of the Royal Air Force is loaded with cargo — not ammo, but exactly 3,811 flowers. It takes off and flies over rolling countryside, over towns and villages, over the meandering river Cam and the cloisters and spires of Trinity College, Queen's and King's Colleges, Jesus College, out to pastureland given by Cambridge University to the United States of America as a burial ground for our airmen lost over Europe, sailors lost in the Battle of the Atlantic, infantrymen lost in the invasions of Normandy and North Africa. When the plane reaches airspace over the cemetery, it releases the 3,811 flowers — one for each of the men who have slept their youth and manhood away in this gathering place across an ocean from home. And after the flowers float down, there is a dip of the wings to the Wall of the Missing, a wall covered with the names of another 5,135 of our countrymen, all of them missing in action, never recovered.

Plane engine fades under:

HISTORIAN. And onto the same day denoted by the flower-bearing women in Mississippi — there are remembrances in peaceful valleys, in meadowlands, on the floor of a crater in Hawaii; at Margraten in the Netherlands; in Tunis, North Africa; Manila in the Philippines; in Belgium, in Italy, in Brittany, in France, on the German border; in a hundred and more grounds across the width of our mainland — among them certain acres in Pennsylvania, a short crow's flight from where farmer Getty plowed his fields and gave his name to a burg and a battle and the Gettysburg Address…

LINCOLN…we cannot dedicate, we cannot consecrate, we cannot hallow this ground. The brave men, living and dead, who struggled here, have consecrated it far and above our poor power to add or detract…

HISTORIAN. And in Arlington, Virginia, not far across a river from a shrine to Lincoln, not far from the memorial to the dead of Vietnam, lie the remains of three Unknown Soldiers, one for each of three wars of this century — sharing anonymity and honor…special honors on Memorial Day…

Fade in measured steps on stone, as of a passing Sentry, and sustain under:

HISTORIAN…but measured and unflagging honor on all other days…a *Guard* of Honor, pacing evenly through the hours, perpetually, back and forth, night, dawn, noon, dusk, in calm and storm and the cyclic seasons — relays of sentries, each man honored to do honor to these dead, to attend the inscription on their marble crypt:

INSCRIPTION. "Here rests in honored glory an American soldier known but to God."

Footsteps fade.

HISTORIAN. But not always honor for the fallen. Not everywhere. To the haughty and arrogant nothing is sacred except power and conquest, and blood is deeper than wine. Napoleon Bonaparte, man of war, said with a flourish:

NAPOLEON. I was brought up on the battlefield, and a man like me does not concern much about the lives of a million men.

HISTORIAN. To be measured against the words of another man of war, a General, George Catlett Marshall, coming home after a pilgrimage to American World War II cemeteries abroad:

MARSHALL. I went as an old soldier seeking fallen comrades. The hours I walked among our lost legions were among the most poignant of my life. Each site evoked old memories of decisions made, or battles waged and won, and, above all, of the young men who paid the highest price that war can exact. Yet the tribute I paid these men in my thoughts must remain unwritten ones, for words cannot capture or convey gratitude held so deeply.

NARRATOR. It is his day, it is their day.
   Not that they would want us to turn in our
      tickets to the rock concert or the
      symphony,
   Or stow away the fishing tackle and instead
      stay home and meditate,
   Nor put off until tomorrow the running of
      the Indy 500...

Fade in racing cars roaring around the speedway at Indianapolis, and hold under:

NARRATOR...Not unless it's raining out there in
   Indiana and the track is too wet to
      race on —
   Certainly not for their sake —
   They would rather sit beside us in the stands
      and enjoy the crowd, the spectacle, the
      action, the rasp and whine of the engines,
   Meanwhile shelling a few peanuts maybe,
      ingesting a hot dog or a burger and
      washing it down with Cola,
   Looking for speed and excitement, but no
      accidents —
   They've seen enough men and machines
      smashed up.

Fade engines under:

NARRATOR. No, it is quiet where they are today,
    In a grand muster of crosses and six-pointed
        stars;
    But there are certain ones missing from
        these ranks,
    Gone, having left not a rack behind,
    Swallowed by earth, or bedded in unfathomless
        gulfs…

Fade in the putt-putt of a marine engine, as in a small craft. Sustain behind:

HISTORIAN. Each year, on Memorial Day, from several ports, small crafts set sail carrying wreaths of flowers, and when they are far enough out, they cast on the water the wreaths, in memory of the sailors, merchant mariners and submariners lost at sea in our wars…

The engines stop. Sounds of lapping water behind:

NARRATOR. The restless ocean, cradle of life, is grave
        as well.
    What guide can lead us to these scattered
        catacombs?
    The bones of good men lie like coral under
        the Coral Sea,
    Mingled with urchins and anemones in the
        waters of Midway and the Philippines,
    In shallows and abysses on the floor of the
        hard-used Mediterranean,
    Strung out below the awful run to Murmansk,
    Below pavements of ice in the Arctic Sea,
    On sea mounts, and along the raceways of
        the continental currents…
    Here are garlands for all that wide-strewn
        company,
    Flowers whose speech, like the call of
        dolphins and whales,
    Travels long distances in water.

Music: A gentle passage, almost a barcarole, overtakes the sound, swells, and come down behind:

NARRATOR. There *is* a language spoken by these sweet
 embassies we call by the names of flowers:
They say for us, "We remember you. We take
 our ease in freedom because you
 surrendered yours to the shackles of war."
They say for us, "You commended to our keeping
 the good times and the good things."

Music: In the clear for a moment, then down behind:

NARRATOR. And if the three Unknown Soldiers who rest
 in honored glory there in Arlington,
 could give reply, translated for us by
 the flowers that we lay upon their
 marble coats,
Might they not say:

FIRST UNKNOWN. Listen to me: Old men make wars, and young men die in them. Cool it, all of you. Work it out. Don't fight it out…

SECOND UNKNOWN. You say we died in honor? You want to honor us? Then live in honor…

THIRD UNKNOWN. May there come a time — soon — may it last forever — when the shade of an oak tree will spread wider than the shadow of war!

Music: A passage of quiet strength, holding behind:

NARRATOR. Flowers, gentlemen, are hieroglyphs
 of love.
We send them today on errands of
 remembrance.
May they find the missing,
And tell the known and unknown they
 are not forgotten —
Tell them that their country lives.
That the flag flies.
That the republic stands.

Music: Up to conclusion.

LABOR DAY

NARRATOR. Mr. McGuire, may we have a word with you? (*No answer.*) Peter J. McGuire? (*No answer.*) (*Down.*) It may take a little while for him to respond, ladies and gentlemen. — He's been dead for nearly a century. (*Up.*) Mr. McGuire, sir?

MCGUIRE (*coming on; he speaks with a slight brogue*). You called?

NARRATOR. Welcome back to Labor Day. (*No response.*) After all, you started it.

MCGUIRE (*remembering*). Ah, so I did, so I did.

NARRATOR. New York City. Just over a hundred years ago.

MCGUIRE. A hundred years already! Well, we do lose track of time. — Remind me. Jog my memory.

NARRATOR. You were an officer of the Knights of Labor, so called.

MCGUIRE. That's true.

NARRATOR. Also president of the United Brotherhood of Carpenters and Joiners of America.

MCGUIRE. Ah, yes. — What do you want to know from me?

NARRATOR. How a young Irish-American, one of ten children of immigrants, a worker from the age of eleven, could originate an important national holiday like Labor Day.

MCGUIRE. Well, it was simple. — It just struck me while shaving one day, that all kinds of dignified things and people were honored by holidays — I mean, military victories and birthdays of martyrs and presidents and saints — as well as trees and flags and such — but there was no holiday for the working man. Without labor, you know, *nothing* happens in this world.

NARRATOR. Without labor, nobody's even *born* in this world.

MCGUIRE (*no sense of humor*). So I simply proposed to the Central Labor Union of New York City, that a day be set aside once a year, to be called Labor Day.

NARRATOR. And they took you up on it.

MCGUIRE. They did that. We chose the first week of September because, y'know, it's a nice time of year; and also it's just about midway between the Fourth of July and Thanksgiving, when all of us can *use* a holiday.

NARRATOR. And the first holiday was when?

MCGUIRE. Right after that we got our representatives to talk it up in Washington, and after ten or twelve years or so, Congress warmed to the idea, and voted to make Labor Day a *national* holiday — to be held on the first Monday of September, so's to make it a long weekend, d'ye see?

NARRATOR. What was the first Labor Day like?

Under the following, without interruption in the dialog, sneak in crowd sounds and a marching band, and hold behind:

MCGUIRE. Oh, we had a divil of a good parade in downtown Manhattan. Ten thousand workers. Marched from Union Square — Fourteenth Street — up to Fifth Avenue to Forty-Second Street. Afterwards, there was a picnic in the Park and dancing, and fireworks, and speech-making. It was a hell of a day. — Pardon the expression.
NARRATOR. We want to thank you, Mr. McGuire, for being with us today.
MCGUIRE. Pleasure. — Anytime.

The sound pattern which had been behind him, now fades under:

NARRATOR. Now if we could summon up all the ghosts of Labor's history as conveniently as we did Mr. McGuire, if we had a sort of mysterious reel-to-reel playback machine that, in addition to the usual controls — play, stop, fast-forward, rewind — it could go back to infinity, we might be able to return through the ages to the very first labor holiday, an occasion of cosmic grandeur. Let's press this rewind button and see what happens.

Snap of a switch, followed by high-pitched gibberish of a tape going backward at great speed. When it stops:

Music: Something maestoso out of Handel or Hadyn, which sustains behind:

NARRATOR. We're back to the day after the Creation of the World, when, according to the second verse of the second chapter of the first book of the Bible, there was a break:
GENESIS. "...on the seventh day God ended his work which He had made; and He rested on the seventh day from all His work...and God blessed the seventh day and sanctified it; because in it He had rested from all His work."

Music: Fades.

NARRATOR. In that short opening passage, work is mentioned no less than three times. Based on that, can there be any question, that of all man's activities, labor has the highest credentials? Look at it this way — if the Sabbath is sanctified, then doesn't the labor that *earned* the day of rest, glow in the reflection?

You don't have to answer that — it's best we leave it to the philosophers and theologians while we go on ahead fast-forward on the time machine.

Snap of switch again, and another blur of high-frequency cacophony, followed by:

Music: Slinky Egyptian music, possibly from the ballet score of Aida, dipping behind:

NARRATOR. We have now advanced from the Creation to the building of the Great Pyramid of Cheops — a jump of two or three billion years, give or take a few hundred million. The music is by Verdi, and the labor is by slaves. A hundred thousand slaves, toiling for twenty years in the hot sun of Egypt. Slavery, after all, is a kind of labor policy — a detestable one, that has caused no end of trouble in this world, particularly in our own history. — But whatever the working arrangements were under the Pharaohs, the achievement still stands, after seven thousand years. The work, as we say, was guaranteed to last. — Let's go on ahead...

The same tape pattern as before, except that this time instead of going into music, it yields to:

Noise of stone-dressing, hammering and sawing, which holds behind:

NARRATION (*there has been no interruption*)...past the building, by myriad labors, of enduring landmarks, ancient and modern — Baalbek and Stonehenge, the Acropolis, the Colosseum, the Great Wall of China, the Angkor Wat, the Suez and Panama Canals, the dams and bridges and towers and cathedrals — past all of that, right into our own history of labor — a history made in America. We can stop anywhere — but let's settle on the year 1829.

B.G. out.

NARRATOR. In that year, a small new political party emerged, the Workingmen's Party, nicknamed the Workies. There weren't many of them — maybe seven or eight thousand members — but they made a lot of noise with a very radical program:

WORKIE (*hotly*). We demand a ten-hour day! And no more sending people to jail because they can't pay their debts! And we want a decent public school education for our kids!

NARRATOR. It was the first intrusion of a labor movement into American politics, and it outraged a good many respectables. Typical was a newspaper editorial in the *New York Commercial Advertiser*, which roared:

NEWSPAPER. "The leaders of the Dirty Shirt Party are lost to society, to earth and to heaven…they are godless and hopeless, and they deserve nothing more than to die like ravenous wild beasts, hunted down without pity!"

NARRATOR. To which the Workies roared back:

WORKIE. "Great wealth ought to be taken away from its possessors on the same principle that a pistol should be wrested from a robber!"

NARRATOR. On with the tape: thirty-one years later:

Fade in under the following, band music and crowd noises, with women's voices predominant.

NARRATOR. We are in Lynn, Massachusetts. This is the first state whose supreme court has sanctioned the right of workers to strike; and on this snowy day in March, eight hundred women are striking for higher pay in the shoe factories. They're parading behind a corps of smartly uniformed City Guards carrying rifles on their shoulders, and up ahead there's a band playing. The women are carrying parasols against the snow, and are trying to keep their hoop skirts from trailing in the slush and mud.

WOMAN STRIKER (*shouting*). American ladies will not be slaves! Give us fair compensation and we will labor cheerfully!

Cheers.

NARRATOR. That's the actual wording of a banner they're carrying. — The Chief Marshall of the city is out there marching in the front ranks alongside the women.

SECOND WOMAN (*slightly off mike*). Are you a reporter?

REPORTER. Yes, I'm from the *Boston Globe*.

SECOND WOMAN. Listen, if we're still out on strike next week, we're going to hold an outdoor chowder party, followed by dancing and kissing games! (*Going off.*) Print that in the paper, will you?

NARRATOR. Not all strikes were as genial as that one; gun-toting guards were rarely, if ever, on the side of the workers. Take, for example, the summer of 1877, and the railroad troubles:

Tape at high speed, followed by crowd noises in B.G. This is a more menacing sound.

FIRST RAILWAY WORKER (*fuming*). The Baltimore & Ohio has cut our wages *again*! By another ten percent!
SECOND RAILWAY WORKER. That's the third cut in three years, and we're not going to stand for it! The bastards!
THIRD RAILWAY WORKER. Three other roads are also cutting wages. The workers are gonna go out in Pittsburgh!
FOURTH RAILWAY WORKER. They've called in the Sixth Maryland Militia, to try and break us!
NARRATOR. The strikers face double opposition — management and militia. Inevitably, confrontation. Tempers flare.

Gunfire, continuing under:

NARRATOR. Killed — fifty-seven strikers, soldiers, and rioters. Destroyed — three million dollars' worth of locomotives and other property...
  Oh, we can tick them off — a terrible rundown of numbers and names, a terrible log of inequities, struggles and brute force.
LAWRENCE. Lawrence, Massachusetts, 1882. Mill hands here work a thirteen-hour day, 5 a.m. to 7 p.m., with two half-hours off to eat.
HAYMARKET. Chicago, 1886. Three thousand union men hold an outdoor meeting in Haymarket Square to protest police killing of a picket who was agitating for the eight-hour day. Someone throws a dynamite bomb into a crowd of one hundred eighty advancing policemen. Eight of them are killed, along with a dozen workers. The bomb-thrower is never caught, but four anarchists accused of arousing passions are hanged.
HOMESTEAD. Homestead, Pennsylvania, 1892. Carnegie Steel orders an eighteen percent wage cut. Thirty-eight hundred workers go on strike. The company hires private police — the Pinkertons — specialists in strikebreaking.

Shooting.

NARRATOR. Killed, three Pinkerton men, ten strikers. The Governor calls out the entire state militia, eight thousand strong, to reopen the mills. The strike fails.

A year later. George M. Pullman, inventor of the Pullman car and president of the company that makes them, has built a model town near Chicago, for his fifty-five hundred employees, and named the town after himself. He calls the work force his "children" but the rent he charges them for housing is twenty percent higher than the going rate for comparable housing nearby. And though his company enjoys a surplus of twenty-five million dollars, he lays off workers and then hires them back for twenty-five percent less than what they were making. Yet at the same time he refuses to reduce his rents to match the cuts. His workers try to negotiate with him:

WORKER. We feel, Mr. Pullman, that —

PULLMAN. Workers have nothing to do with the amount of wages they shall receive.

WORKER. But your company has just paid shareholders two and half million dollars in dividends!

PULLMAN (*dismissal*). We have nothing to negotiate.

NARRATOR. His children go out on strike. The national railway union boycotts all railroads using Pullman cars. A federal court issues an injunction against the strikers. President Grover Cleveland orders a regiment of regular army troops to enforce the court order. Then, not surprisingly:

Shooting.

NARRATOR. Twelve men are killed, the strike is broken.

Sound fades under:

NARRATOR. It is not the last strike, nor the last bloodshed.

In the chronicles of American industry — the world's most successful — labor fights many battles on many fronts; it wins and loses; it fights giants, and becomes one itself; it tangles with police, soldiers, goons, fights the courts, fights the government, fights within its own ranks; it is hounded and does hounding of its own; it forms massive combinations, gathers strength, goes deep into politics; is tainted by rackets and corruption every now and then, and has to clean house; is held in affection or contempt by partisans on both sides. Like, for example, the Baron de Mandeville:

DE MANDEVILLE. The surest wealth consists of a multitude of laborious poor. To make society, it is requisite that great numbers of them be ignorant as well as poor. Knowledge in the working poor should be kept within their occupations. The more a plowman or any other peasant knows of the world, the less fit he'll be to go through the fatigues and hardships of it with cheerfulness and content.[1]

NARRATOR. J.P. Morgan, American financier, is asked a question during a Congressional hearing on industrial relations:

QUESTIONER. Mr. Morgan, do you consider ten dollars a week enough for a longshoreman with a family to support?

MORGAN. If that's all he can get, and he takes it, I should say it's enough.

NARRATOR. And on the other hand, Abraham Lincoln:

LINCOLN. If the Almighty had ever made a set of men that should do all of the eating and none of the work, he would have made them with mouths only, and no hands.

NARRATOR. And a Lincoln biographer, Carl Sandburg:

WOMAN. Stocks are property?

MAN. Yes.

WOMAN. Bonds are property?

MAN. Yes.

WOMAN. Machines, land, buildings, are property?

MAN. Yes.

WOMAN. A job is property?

MAN. No, nix, nah, nah![2]

NARRATOR. Whichever side you're on, this day — Labor Day — Peter McGuire's pet holiday — is a good time to take into account, along with the ball scores and weather forecast and the end of vacations, and school coming up, and the drift of the market, the undeniable facts about work in our lives. Ask the demographers and statisticians:

STATISTICIAN. Normally most of us spend more time at work, and at getting to and from it, than on any other activity including eating, sleeping, entertaining or being entertained, reading, watching television, traveling, playing, loving or idling. Moreover —

NARRATOR. Moreover, there is nothing that we wear, use, eat, drink, nothing on our shelves, in our closets, files, vaults, nothing that we read or even *know*, that does not represent the work of people living and dead. Ask any educator:

EDUCATOR. All that we have learned has come to us through the work of workers immemorial; education is the filtration of billions of hours

---

1. Bernard de Mandeville from his 1714 book *The Fable of the Bees*.
2. Excerpt from Poem #38 of Carl Sandburg's *The People, Yes.* (1936)

and study and labor in the arts and sciences. We communicate by words that were minted, jointed, conjugated, inflected by workers in language. The sublimest music, the grandest sculptures and canvases, the brightest efflorescence of the human spirit, trace back to work, to prodigies of work.

NARRATOR. Ask any plumber:

PLUMBER. The faucet water that washes the dinner dishes had to be tapped, impounded, purified, pumped, and piped.

NARRATOR. Ask any writer:

WRITER. The pen in hand, the paper on the desk, the desk on the floor, the floor on the foundation…

NARRATOR. Ask any farmer:

FARMER. The oldest labor of all is agriculture. As long as we remain an arable planet, the sun will never set on sowing, reaping, threshing, harvesting. We've made working gardens out of the steppe and upland, the desert, the swamp, the terraced mountain, the weed-beds of the sea…

NARRATOR. Ask the architect:

ARCHITECT. Next in scale to the mantle of the globe itself, are the works that cover it, for our Earth is an inexpressibly huge monument to work — to outpourings of thought and energy preserved in the forms of cities: in fulfilled architecture, actualized engineering, consolidations and agglomerations of the lifting and hauling and straining of multitudes of laborers, present everywhere we turn — increments and profusions of labor in every pavement, vehicle, house, store, church, depot, skyscraper, revealed in each inch of fabric, every pane of glass, in every ray of artificial light, in every coil of wire —

NARRATOR. And in this microphone and in the transmitters and in the radio receiver on which you are hearing this, and in the network of stations banded together on this Labor Day, as on other days, and known to you and us (as we come to the end of a modest labor of love) as —

ANNOUNCER. National Public Radio, which has just brought you the third in a series of broadcasts on the National Holidays.

FROM THE EDITOR

In 1982, Corwin was approached to write and direct a series of ten-to-twelve-minute radio plays for National Public Radio "about the celebration of American holidays." The series began under the working title of *Eight by Corwin* before airing as *The National Holidays* on NPR programs such as *Morning Edition* and *All Things Considered*. In the end, the total number of shows was only six, not the eight originally proposed.

The series was produced by Jay Kernis, then the senior producer of *Morning Edition*. Mr. Kernis later became senior vice president of programming at NPR. In television, Kernis served as a producer for *60 Minutes* on CBS, followed by three years as CNN Managing Editor. He is currently producing *Rock Center with Brian Williams* for NBC.

FIFTY YEARS AFTER 14 AUGUST

This show commemorated the fiftieth anniversary of the Japanese surrender on August 14, 1945, bringing an end to the Second World War. On that date, Corwin had quickly put together a fifteen-minute special program at the request of CBS called *14 August*. It was a single voice piece (performed by Orson Welles) and contained only one sound effect.

Rather than expand or merely update the original script, Corwin wrote an entirely new piece for NPR. Several lines from the original script are resurrected.

The show aired on National Public Radio (NPR) in August 1995. Charles Kuralt narrated and Pat Carroll served as the Historian. The program was co-produced by Mary Beth Kirchner and Dan Gediman, and was directed by the author.

For this production, Norman Corwin was awarded The Alfred I. duPont — Columbia University Award, Silver Baton, in 1997.

Music: Establish and hold under:

VOICE. Fourteen August.

Music: Up to conclusion.

NARRATOR. Slaughter on a grand scale is always appalling, but World War II was the most abominable blood purge of them all.
    Exactly fifty years ago, the second global war to be known by a number, came to an end.
    Today, after half a century of unstable peace and intermittent lesser wars, we commemorate the surrender, on 14 August 1945, of the most powerful and haughty Asian empire that ever was.

Music: Punctuation.

NARRATOR. Congratulations on being alive and listening. Millions didn't make it.
    The course was long and winding — tank tracks, vapor trails, the frothing wakes of warships, skies pocked by ack-ack, landscapes of unmitigated ruin, mountains of ordinance, warheads homing to living targets, never bothering to ask which way to the barracks or the ammo depot.
    And, as in every war, new ways of killing. And a new way, too, of instigating war — by gathering a fleet of carriers and hiding them in the mists of the North Pacific, and plotting and rehearsing deception and surprise, then steaming south to strike on a Sunday, a good day to strike, a day off, a church day, a tennis and golf day. It's all in the record.
HISTORIAN. They came in over Oahu in two waves, and expertly, surgically, loosed bombs and torpedoes that successfully surprised, killed, and maimed 3,507 people, destroyed or damaged eighteen warships and 188 planes, and, task accomplished, flew back exultant to their hives. It was a triumph of sleazy criminal grandeur.
NARRATOR. We have seen pictures of that attack, seen them many times, tableaus at once shocking and beautiful, like a painted masterpiece of a massacre. And we have heard, or heard of, the President's address to Congress the next day, starting with:
VOICE OF FDR. Yesterday, December 7, 1941 — a date which will live in infamy...
NARRATOR. But most of us may not remember what the President added moments later:

VOICE OF FDR. Yesterday the Japanese Government also launched an attack against Malaya.
Last night Japanese forces attacked Hong Kong.
Last night Japanese forces attacked Guam.
Last night Japanese forces attacked the Philippine Islands.
Last night Japanese forces attacked Wake Island.
And this morning the Japanese attacked Midway Island.

HISTORIAN. Overnight, war had uncoiled the tentacles of a monstrous octopus, fouling waters now Pacific in name only…a shock-list of islands, atolls and archipelagos whose soft names and hard battles would soon fill a hideous atlas: Guadalcanal, Palau, Kwajalein, Tassafaronga, Mindanao, Saipan, Tarawa, Eniwetok, Tinian, Okinawa, Iwo Jima — their beaches raked by cannon, their jungles shredded, their caves and tunnels scorched by flaming napalm…

NARRATOR. What did they want, those gentlemen of Japan? Why did they lavish yen and men on arms and armies, carriers, planes, the ponderous baggage of the arts of war? Why rape Nanking and bang up Mukden and Korea, and, when censured for it, storm out of the League of Nations? Why an elaborate flimflam of duplicitous diplomacy, bowing from the waist, then hitting below the belt? What did the peers and barons, counts and princes, admirals, and generals expect to gain?

HISTORIAN. A lot. Great expectations. They minted a logo to blazon on the marquee of history, a label for an enterprise they called *The Greater East Asia Co-Prosperity Sphere*.

NARRATOR. Translated from the humbug, it meant Manifest Destiny, Far East Division. The announced intention of the Sphere was to establish a so-called "new order," an era of good deals for everyone around the rim of the western Pacific. The unannounced intention, the one they carried out, was to seize other people's land and property in order to make room for Japan's expanding population, and to ensure that the riches of Asia, the oil, rubber, tin and coal so scant at home, would be in perpetual good supply.

A polite government might have negotiated for all such needs, but politeness in the ministries of Tokyo was rarer even than resources in the ground. The few moderates who raised objection, who said, "Wait a minute, let's think of consequences," were barked at and grunted into silence, and the warrior creed of Bushido, gleaming and polished as a ceremonial sword, took over.

Armageddon is too refined a name for all-out modern war. Atrocities of the past, and fresh ones waiting to be exercised, multiplied like casualties of battle. Though there was no room for armies in the Solomons, the Gilberts and the Marianas, it was never just a scrimmage or a tangle of patrols.

HISTORIAN. Of seven thousand four hundred Japanese defenders on Tarawa, only seventeen, all of them wounded, were taken alive.

On a runt of an island, Iwo Jima, only two-and-a-half miles wide, 6,821 Americans died.

Do you remember the photograph of six marines planting the American flag atop Mount Surabachi? — Three of them were killed in the next few days.

In nine weeks of action on Okinawa — bombardments, salients, banzai charges, hand-to-hand combat, the reckoning was nearly two hundred thousand casualties, of which one hundred and twenty thousand died.

NARRATOR. Numbers. The stuff of astronomy, commerce, and body counts: A thousand — a hundred thousand — a million — ten million — thirty million — tidy figures, simple to write, easy to say, but hard to understand or even to conceive when dealing with authorized murder.

Odds in battle are at best ridiculous, like rolling warped dice on a lumpy table. The ultimate risk of the gamble is of course loss of everything, with no chance to recoup — known, metaphorically, as Death.

HISTORIAN. When the British cruiser *Hood*, bunking 1,338, was struck by a shell that pierced its magazine, three men were left alive.

When our submarine *Queenfish* torpedoed the Japanese transport *Awa Maru*, carrying 2,004 passengers, one survived. — One.

NARRATOR. Charity toward the enemy in war is less common than tap-dancing on quicksand, but there are never any bounds to cruelty. All it takes to excel at it, is power, opportunity and vileness. The Nazis, colleagues of Japan in the vaunted Axis, at Malmedy lined up 129 American prisoners of war and shot them.

HISTORIAN. On Wake Island, Admiral Sigematsu ordered a hundred more prisoners to be killed. On Makin atoll, and again on Honshu, Japanese beheaded captive American flyers. Beheaded them.

Music: Bleak Shostakovich behind:

NARRATOR. War has the voice of a million muzzles, and where it speaks, dust hangs in the air for weeks. Violence is consummate, no worm is safe; the bomb digs deeper than the mole. All creatures living in earth and air, entire censuses of seas, feel the shock. The twin screws of the dreadnought scatter plankton in luminous waters; depth bombs blow up whole nations of schooling fish; not even the sky is the limit of the shedding of blood. Every leaf and every frond knows the score, and so do neutral mountains a hemisphere distant, for the crust of the globe is sensitive, and will instantly relay a jolt in Micronesia to the jittery seismographs of Pasadena.

Music: Under the following, a sweetly harmonious South Sea melody, sung or played.

NARRATOR. Ah, Micronesia! Melanesia! Polynesia! — Benign, enchanting, outskirts of paradise, pretty as an operetta set, dowered with tender climates, caressing breezes, languorous waters, and plant life welling up like green geysers. But no storied island, however ornamental, enjoys immunity if it turns out useful as an unsinkable aircraft carrier, a rooted submarine tender, a passage to a bastion of a foe.

Music: Out.

HISTORIAN. Coral and volcanic Edens, toy-like in the immensity of surrounding seas, for eons reconciled to their own beauty, were in a single generation twice transformed — first by Japanese invasion, into forts and battlements, and then by Americans invading the invaders. We displaced them in stepping-stone victories, victories won by blood and guts, moxie and marksmanship.

Music: A different strain; lull in the fighting. Hold behind:

NARRATOR. War is not only hell, but waiting and monotony, too. In the smelting heat of Aden, in the clammy Pribilovs, on sodden ground where rains come down like Niagara every afternoon at three, troops assigned to hardship and hazard, try to stay clear of mildew, bugs, and enemy raiders, and are forever short on sleep. They chafe, they itch, they have no warranty of safe access even to a latrine; moreover, they miss everything called home, especially the comfort of a loved one.

And the word goes out among the vine-ropes of New Guinea to jungle fighters from Boston, Spokane, and points between, that a singer from the USO, a living female, uniformed, but of a shape distinct and recognizable as that of Woman, has arrived and may be gandered for a short time only, before she flies on to the Marianas. And in the hothouse evening, through the strangling green of tropic bush, soldiers, grizzled, sweaty, hike for miles down to the airstrip just to gaze in silence from fifty feet away, upon the constellation of a single girl — a flash of golden hair, a sparkle of white teeth, and trim American ankles. And in this shining symbol, conspicuous and jeweled as a meteor in a moonless sky, the G.I. sees his wife, his honey, and his hope. And the vision stands for all things ever said and done between the two — the walking on the beach, evenings at the movies, the first kiss, enfolding arms, awakening at dawn — and flowers on occasion; and an evening gown packed in mothballs in a trunk, waiting for the goddam war to end.

Music: Concludes.

NARRATOR. At last an invisible snare began to tighten around Japan, especially now that her accessories before the fact, the powerhouses of Germany and Italy, were already down — Hitler a dustpan of cinders swept up with other trash in a suicide bunker, Mussolini hung up by his heels at a gas station in Milan. Now the object all sublime to be achieved in the shortest possible time, was the seat of the Greater East Asia Co-Prosperity Sphere itself, where it all got started four years ago.

HISTORIAN. Many stratagems were yet pondered, among them the logistics of siegecraft, but one thing was for sure — it would be no cinch to land and to sustain ground forces on the home islands of Japan, where two-and-a-half million troops remained, ready for suicidal defense, where civilian militias, of twenty-eight millions more, had mines and grenades to work with, and where ten thousand aircraft were available for kamikaze strikes against Allied craft, a tactic used successfully against some of the biggest warships on the seas.

How many more Okinawas, Guadalcanals, Wakes, Guams, Midways, and Manilas, would it take?

The answer came sooner than expected.

Crackling transmission under:

NARRATOR. *Little Boy*, it was called. A two billion dollar city-crusher. Its core was constructed out of secret ingredients in Tennessee, its plumbing and shell devised by laboratories in New Mexico. By the authority vested in the American high command, it was disassembled, shipped by road to an airbase, flown to San Francisco, and loaded aboard the heavy cruiser *Indianapolis* for delivery to an island in the Marianas, there to be reassembled for transport to a site in Japan not yet selected.

The *Indianapolis* was a great lady who had carried FDR to South America and elsewhere, had convoyed ships to Australia, bombarded Japanese positions in the Aleutians, fought enemy warships off the Philippines, supported landings in the Gilberts and at Iwo Jima, and earned, so far, ten of the honors known in naval etiquette as battle stars.

And then, having safely offloaded the working parts of *Little Boy* on Tinian, the *Indianapolis* raised anchor and set out for Leyte in the Philippines. On the third day, at a quarter past midnight in a tranquil sea, she was torpedoed, and 881 of her crew went down.

Music: A stern passage, under:

HISTORIAN. Retribution had not long to wait. There would come towering reprisals in behalf of the *Indianapolis* and the ghosts of her sunken sisters; in behalf of sailors entombed in the *Arizona* at Pearl Harbor, in behalf of holdouts in the tunnels of Corregidor, the death-marchers out of Bataan, and the stacked corpses of the killing fields.

Messages went off to whom it concerned in Tokyo — warning of an offstage weapon capable of inflicting unparalleled destruction. And along with that warning, a demand for prompt surrender. Unconditional surrender.

Both messages went unanswered.

Washington resolved to wait no longer. A point on the map was picked. It was Hiroshima. The rest you know.

Music and sound: The Bomb. When it subsides:

NARRATOR. Fate and fission were on our side. The wrath of the atom fell like a commandment, and the very planet quivered with implications.

In the same chambers where not long before, warlords had gourmandized on intrigue and menus of invasion, now there was consternation. What to do about the shocking new Executioner, the behemoth, the fireball ten times brighter than the sun, so fierce it blistered granite, and startled steel and masonry into a state of shrapnel, and cremated on the instant, ninety thousand Japanese?

What to do? Surrender? *Japan* surrender? Never had that happened. Never *could* it happen. To raise a white flag, to give up and give in, were not in the language of Shinto. What of the thousands, the tens of thousands warriors — soldiers, sailors, airmen of the Rising Sun, who had fought to the death — who, if taken at all, had to be taken wounded?

More delay, now, in those exalted chambers, in those cold calculation-rooms, hesitation by the same hawks who had hastened to make war.

A ticking clock; hold under:

NARRATOR. A day passed. No response to the call for surrender. Day two. Still no answer. On day three, Bomb Number Two, named *Fat Man* for its bulging waist, was assigned to double the force of persuasion. *Fat Man* was *Little Boy* grown up — more complex, more vehement, and — new wrinkle — seasoned with plutonium. The city of Kokura was elected to receive him; but when the B-29 on which *Fat Man* rode, reached its target, Kokura was socked in, so Pilot Sweeney veered off to an alternate goal — Nagasaki.

Bomb Number Two. When it subsides:

HISTORIAN. The burst at the impact point was blunted by moderating hills around the city, but still seventy thousand people were obliterated in a blinding instant. And that was enough for the rest of the nation to sue, at last, for peace, even though a Japanese general, still unconvinced, said, "We must fight the war through to the end no matter how great the odds against us."

Japan surrendered on the fourteenth of August.

Music: Morse code motifs.

HISTORIAN. The news was fragmented, coming in spurts from Tokyo, from Washington, from London, Guam, Manila, Moscow, from New York. In a Manhattan radio station at eleven seconds after seven in the morning, Robert Trout, broadcaster, announced:

TROUT. Seven p.m., Eastern War Time. Bob Trout reporting. The Japanese have accepted our terms fully. That's the word we have just received from the White House in Washington...This, ladies and gentlemen, is the end of the Second World War...The United Nations on land, on the sea, in the air, and to the four corners of the earth, are united and are victorious...We take you now to London...

Music: A good thumping fanfare; then, unexpectedly, a pastoral theme, with overtones of poignance. It sustains under:

NARRATOR. Fourteen August.

Fourteen August to the gun turret and the turret lathe.

Fourteen August to the tractor in the wheat field, to the flag on Surabachi, to the mother of the five Sullivan brothers of Iowa, brothers who died together when their cruiser was blown apart in a battle off the Marianas.

Fourteen August to Anne Frank, diarist, to partisans and patriots, to Jews and Gypsies, priests and Poles, torched in the ovens of the death camps.

Fourteen August to the code-named infantry campaigns that slugged it out on plains, mountains, valleys, deserts — *Hellcat, Battle Axe, Cyclone, Lucky Seventh, Thundering Herd, Red Bull, Jersey Blues, Screaming Eagle, Winged Victory...*

Music: A change of color as it continues.

NARRATOR. Now homecoming. Now the future can begin. Dog tags exchanged for civil names. Ranks converging from outlandish zones of time, from secret somewheres known only to postmasters.

Buddies will write letters to each other for a while, then drop out of touch. The mess halls, where the meals were on the house, will be forgotten between Jim's Diner and home cooking.

Beaches without beachheads. Jobs without sergeants. Gunners who tilted the guns of battleships and stoked them in epic combat, will ride the level ferries of bay and river.

The tankman will drive a powered lawn mower while his father watches. The pilot with many missions will do errands for some civilian company. The bombardier, who crushed a city in a blinding instant, will help his wife dry dishes in the kitchen sink.

Fourteen August.

Say it tonight, as fifty years ago, with saluting guns, with psalms, with champagne and with laughter, but let's never forget the fields beyond, the names and faces beyond.

Here in this August the grass is hearty, the sky friendly, the wind in the windsock, birds are competitive, the hills of home are in their accustomed places. All is accounted for except the farmer's boy and the mill hand who lived near the canal, and the young men from the city block where the gutters fry in summer.

One of them sleeps with sand in his eyes, where he fell on a beach in Palau.

The bones of the fisherman rest in clay far from the rocks of Maine.

The cricket sings in the summer night, but the grocer's clerk says nothing.

The fawn leaps in the wolf-proof wood, but jungle roots twine the postman's feet.

The turtle is young as sixty-one, but the flyer is dead at eighteen.

Remember them when July comes round and the shimmer of noon excites the locusts, when the pretty girls bounce as they walk in the park, and the moth is in love with the fifty-watt bulb, and the tar on the road is blistered.

They've given their noons to their country. They've trusted their girls to you. They lie very still in alien earth, for a bunch of tomorrows.

Remember them in the fall of the year when frost airbrushes the withering leaf, and the silo is fat as a bearing woman, and the cleats of the backfield dig up gains to the praise of the stadium, when the number one goose says it's time to go, and the flock points a V to the south.

They gave their seed to fifty states, their football tickets to you. The shirt on their back is a worm-cut rag, for a bunch of tomorrows.

Remember them in the sleeting months when the sap stands still in the veins of the tree, when the skating girls eddy like snow on the rink, and the storm window hooked on the prairie farmhouse mutters in the gale out of Idaho.

They're dead as clay for our right to live, for people the likes of us.

Music: Transfiguration theme, behind:

NARRATOR. If in the millennium that did not wait for them there were to happen a miracle the size of all Creation in which the dead of the war awakened from their dreamless sleep, their eyes reopened and their tongues restored, what would they say to us? Would they curse us, would they warn us, would they bless us?

Would they ask us to work it out, not fight it out?

Would they ask us to honor what they died for, by *living* in honor?

Would they propose, perhaps, and ratify, perhaps, a simple benediction for the lot of us — for black, for white, for yellow and red — for us and our posterity? And might it be something like this?

(*Slight echo; slowly.*) May tribes of trees descend with your children to a time when the shade of the oak spreads wider than the shadow of war.

Amen to the notion.

Music: Curtain.

CORWIN ON
FIFTY YEARS AFTER 14 AUGUST

On the fiftieth anniversary of the surrender of Japan, NPR broadcast my commemorative program, titled as above. It was narrated by Charles Kuralt.

Timing breakdowns relate to the music, which was selected and edited by me. The score consisted mostly of passages from *Uirapuru*, by Villa-Lobos. The production gave credit in its closing announcement, to Everest Records, which on the very week of the broadcast had issued the first CD of that composition.

While there were few reviews of the program, the public's response was immediate and prolonged. More than two thousand copies of the script and/or the audiocassette of the program were sold by the Lodestone Catalog. A review by Dorothy Rabinowitz in the *Wall Street Journal* of August 10, 1995, was eloquent in its praise, concluding with, "No one writing for broadcasting today has, needless to say, anything approaching Mr. Corwin's rhetorical voice, the blend of passion and elegance that informed this work."

FROM THE EDITOR

Corwin was conflicted about the original program and was more than happy to reinvent it fifty years later. The news of the Japanese surrender arrived so quickly that Corwin had to write his commemorative program overnight. Orson Welles had been up all night reading breaking news bulletins on Los Angeles radio station KFWB prior to stepping before the CBS mike at KNX for *14 August*. After the broadcast, Corwin expanded the fifteen-minute original into a thirty-minute version pairing Orson Welles and Olivia de Havilland, broadcast five days later on Sunday, August 19, 1945, under the new title *God and Uranium*. Unknown to Corwin at that time, Welles and de Havilland were not on speaking terms. Still, they did not turn him down and shared the microphone for this show.

Whereas Corwin crafted his piece with typically superb language, there was one line at the beginning that he later regretted from the original (and its immediate follow up):

WELLES. God and uranium were on our side.
    The wrath of the atom fell like a commandment,
    And the very planet quivered with implications.

It appears, modified, in the middle of the 1995 show as:

NARRATOR. Fate and fission were on our side. The wrath of the atom fell like a commandment, and the very planet quivered with implications.

Corwin later said he very much regretted associating God with a weapon of mass destruction.

NO LOVE LOST

The first of six radio plays commissioned by the Corporation for Public Broadcasting under the series title *More By Corwin*. This program was recorded before a live audience at the Beverly Hills Museum of Television and Radio on the evening of August 6, 1996 and broadcast over NPR on November 2, 1996. Starring Lloyd Bridges as Alexander Hamilton, Jack Lemmon as Aaron Burr, William Shatner as Thomas Jefferson and Martin Landau as Mr. Lennox. Public radio host Bonnie Grice served as the Narrator.

Technical direction was by Marty Halperin and Warren Dewey.

Mary Beth Kirchner produced. The author directed.

Music: Establish and hold briefly under:

NARRATOR. You are invited to do what you've done countless times — suspend your disbelief. But not all the way, because most of what you will hear in the next hour, was actually said or done by three great American Revolutionaries. The events and conditions they deal with, their feelings about each other, their positions, their arguments, are all matters of record. The only license taken is that of the occasion that brings them together before a public audience, on an evening in the fall of 1799.

Under the foregoing, fade in a background people settling in their seats as they await the start of an event. They grow quiet under approaching footsteps on a wooden platform.

LENOX. Good evening, ladies and gentlemen. I am John Lenox of the Open View Society, which has arranged this presentation.

I want to thank you for having come through the rain, to this hall whose roof must rank among the leakiest in Philadelphia. But at least it's a roof under which we're fortunate to be able to bring together, in this troubled hour, three men whose contribution to our successful Revolution, and to the fortunes of our country in the twenty-three years since we declared ourselves a nation in this very city, have been as singular as they are distinguished.

Today, when many of us fear we'll have to go to war against our recent ally, France, one could not ask for a more illustrious panel. Two of our three guests are leading candidates, respectively, for Vice President and President of the United States. The third has been a General in the Army, chief aide to George Washington, and was until recently, our first Secretary of the Treasury.

At dinner tonight, we discussed the plan of the evening, and our guests agreed that they should be free to take up not only the quasi-war with France that has been going on for some time now, but any other matters of present concern.

The procedure will be informal. Each discussant may direct questions to any other. My function is to listen, like yourselves, with the privilege added, that in the event of pitched battle, I may act as truce negotiator.

I have first the honor to present a man considered by many the most likely to be elected next Vice President of the United States — a man who fought with distinction in our War of Independence, who participated in the attack on Québec, a brave and resourceful soldier who returned from battle to become Attorney General of the state of New York, and now its Senator — Colonel Aaron Burr!

Applause, as Burr enters. Over the applause:

NARRATOR (*low voice*). As becomes an officer, Colonel Burr, who is now entering, carries himself with dignity and self-command. He's handsome, short, slim, partly balding. He looks younger than his forty-nine years.

LENOX. Next it's my privilege to introduce a man who has but lately retired to the private practice of law, after serving many of the pressing needs of our country almost from the day he arrived, at the age of sixteen, from his native island of Nevis in the West Indies. His military career and his administration of the Treasury under Presidents Washington and Adams, have made him a legend among legends. — Ladies and gentlemen, General Alexander Hamilton.

Applause. Speaking over it again:

NARRATOR. The General, who like Senator Burr has kept a trim figure, is still very handsome in his forties. Also, like Mr. Burr, he dresses impeccably — a long blue coat with bright buttons, a white waistcoat, black smallclothes. And now he settles into one of the four chairs on the platform.

LENOX (*again as applause subsides*). And our third guest, a gentleman from Virginia, once Governor of that state, author of the Declaration of Independence, Ambassador to France, and for the past three years, Vice President of the United States — Mr. Thomas Jefferson.

Applause. Once again it comes down behind:

NARRATOR. At fifty-six, Mr. Jefferson is the oldest of the three, but you'd hardly know it. He has very little gray in his reddish hair. In contrast to the others, he's almost casually dressed. He nods in acknowledgment of the applause and goes straight to his chair.

LENOX. And now, if our guests are comfortably ensconced —

BURR. Mr. Lenox?

LENOX. Colonel Burr?

BURR. Do I understand correctly that we appear on this platform as *discussants*?

LENOX. Yes. We had for a time contemplated calling ourselves The Discussant Company, but settled for Open View Society, as being more euphonious.

BURR. Well, I'm glad you changed the name. I'd be uneasy about being a discussant, because words that end in "ant" bother me — they seem to working for no good cause — like supplicant, mendicant, miscreant, defendant...

HAMILTON. ...Sycophant, pollutant, expectorant...

JEFFERSON. I suppose the only ant-word that has any grandeur to speak of, is elephant — and that would no doubt disappear as soon as the meaning became "one who elephs."

LENOX (*chuckling*). Now that we've had a meeting of three great American minds on the demeaning power of the suffix "ant," I make bold to suggest that we move on to some slightly more substantive issue — like, say, our troubles with France.

BURR. Oh not yet, sir. The effect of the wine at dinner is still with us. Give us another round of persiflage before we attack or defend President Adams for keeping us — so far — out of a hot war with France.

LENOX. There is a motion before the house for another round of persiflage. Do I hear a second?

VOICE FROM AUDIENCE (*shouting*). Second!

General laughter.

LENOX. Adopted by acclamation.

JEFFERSON. All right, Mr. Lenox, suggest a point of small consequence.

LENOX. I don't know how small its consequence may be, but may I propose that General Hamilton tell you about the time he was stoned.

JEFFERSON. You were stoned?

HAMILTON. It was at a public meeting on Wall Street. Someone threw a stone and hit me in the head. One of my friends said the Republicans were trying to knock out my brains out to reduce me to equality with them.

BURR. Perhaps no stones are being thrown, but has there ever been a time when people called each other so many foul names? Men of Jefferson's persuasion are infidels, anarchists, tools of France, jackals, skunks, and cannibals. At the same time, Mr. Hamilton's party consists of pettifoggers, British bootlickers, and wretches who'd sell our their Lord for thirty glasses of rum. I've seen every one of those terms in the press.

HAMILTON. No one can say we don't live in raucous times.

JEFFERSON. Well, freedom is *always* raucous. It's despotism that seems calm...because under it no one *dares* to make any noise.

Cries of approval and "hear, hear" from the audience.

LENOX. Gentlemen, let's get to the matter of the undeclared war that has generated so much noise lately.

JEFFERSON. May I begin by saying that although I've had many occasions to differ with President John Adams, I give him full credit for having resisted — so far — the pressure of the hawks in his Federalists constituency, to plunge us into war against the one country in the world that stood by us in our own revolution.

HAMILTON (*aghast*). You don't think France should be punished for raiding American ships? For insulting our envoys? For threatening to hang American sailors?

JEFFERSON. I just think it would be criminal to declare war against an old friend who has temporarily gotten out of sorts because of her troubles with England. The French may bluster, but they've not yet hanged any American sailor, and they're not going to.

BURR. I don't hold with you there, Mr. Vice President. Three hundred and forty American ships were seized by French privateers last year, and property losses ran very high. General Hamilton would know the figures, I'm sure.

HAMILTON. Fifty-five million dollars, and growing.

BURR. And what about that recent battle between French and American frigates in the West Indies?

JEFFERSON. Well, the French ship surrendered. That should satisfy our hawks for a while.

BURR (*testily*). I confess to a certain agitation when excuses are made for effrontery of the French. Let's not forget that our diplomats were not even given a hearing by them. Instead we were confronted by three agents identified only by the letters X, Y, and Z, and made to understand that unless we came across with a quarter of a million dollars, we might as well turn around and go home.[1] Really, now, with whom do they think they're dealing with? Some weak, vacillating, pusillanimous state in the backwaters of Europe? Any why are they sulking? Because we refuse to get roped into their war with Britain!

JEFFERSON. I'm sure the French remember, if you don't, that they did not refuse to get involved in *our* war with Britain.

---

1. Occurred in 1797 and began the undeclared Quasi War with France.

HAMILTON. Must we be eternally grateful for that? They helped us not so much out of love of us, as out of hatred for England!

BURR. Besides, France has no business carping because we signed a treaty with the British five years ago — as though we haven't the right as a sovereign nation, to settle our affairs in our own way and to our advantage, without asking their leave.

JEFFERSON. Just a moment. It's through the help of France that we *exist* as a nation. If — God forefend — we go to war against her, it would be like a son fighting against his father.

BURR. That's a touching thought, but this is no time for sentiment.

JEFFERSON. So what do you propose to do about it? How do you rid us of worms?

BURR. If France will not conciliate, then peace is to be had not by negotiation, but by the sword. I agree with General Hamilton's announced recommendations.

JEFFERSON. Perhaps the general would be good enough to state for this audience what those recommendations are.

HAMILTON. To increase our army from its present strength of three thousand five hundred men to fifty thousand. And to double the size of the navy.

JEFFERSON. Is it true you've also proposed that any militiamen who refuse service shall be put in prison?

HAMILTON. That's correct.

JEFFERSON. Well, well, well. What a wicked use is made of the XYZ business, cooked up as it was by well-off patrons in Mr. Hamilton's party who are even now arousing the country against the terrible French. It seems there's not been quite the same notice given to the fact that the French government is *sincere* in its disposition for peace, that it does *not* want us to break the British treaty, and is willing to arrange a liberal one with us. I believe the American people will soon realize they've been duped. The truth of the matter is that a scandalous war between the only two republics on this earth, has been avoided principally by the *restraint* France has shown.

BURR. I'm not at all persuaded. Indeed I'm compelled to ask you bluntly, Mr. Jefferson — are you for peace at any price?

HAMILTON. I ask the same question.

JEFFERSON. You both know very well I'm not. But war — all war — it too high-priced. There are other ways of punishing injuries, than by war. Because war punishes the *punisher* as much as the punished.

HAMILTON. Are you saying we were "punished" by our victory over England? A great many members of Congress believe it's in our best interest to go to war *right now*, and the sooner the better.

JEFFERSON. What a lot of false arithmetic is used to persuade people that it's in their "interest" to go to war! If the money it costs to satisfy an insult, or gain a little territory, of the right to cut wood here, or catch fish there — if this money were spent making roads, opening rivers, building ports, improving the arts, and finding employment for the jobless poor — then all nations would be much stronger, richer, and happier.

HAMILTON. Apparently, Mr. Jefferson, nothing can awaken you from your famous dream of a perfectible world.

BURR. I'm with General Hamilton in urging the strongest possible military buildup. I'm for preparation at all costs!

LENOX. It seems, Colonel, that your zeal for arming has not gone unnoticed. You've been criticized by some Congressmen for capitulating to what they call Federalist war fever.

BURR. I don't care what they say. I'm proud to be serving on a committee for the defense of New York. General Hamilton is a fellow member.

HAMILTON. That's true. Indeed, I nominated Colonel Burr to be superintendent of fortifications.

LENOX. The writer James Cheetham, Mr. Burr, has described your attitude as a turnabout — as a bid for high rank in the growing military buildup.

BURR. Is Mr. Cheetham always that entertaining?

JEFFERSON. Are you and Mr. Hamilton always this compatible?

BURR (*lightly*). Well, nobody could possibly mistake us for Damon and Pythias. I don't think the General has ever quite forgiven me for defeating his father-in-law, General Schuyler, for the Senatorship of New York.

HAMILTON (*also lightly*). And I never will. Actually, Colonel Burr and I have been associated from time to time, once in the practice of law as co-counsel; and you may ask the Colonel whether differences in our point of view have in way affected the cordiality of our mutual regard.

BURR. Not once.

HAMILTON. Do you remember the case of The People versus Levi Weeks?[2]

BURR. Never forget it.

JEFFERSON. What case was that?

BURR. We were retained together as defense counsel in a case of the murder of a woman. A young man named Weeks was charged with the murder. There was a great deal of popular sentiment aroused against our client, but we got him off.

HAMILTON. Thanks in largest part to your work.

2. The trial actually occurred in 1800, one year after this play's fictional setting.

BURR. You're much too modest.

HAMILTON. I suppose I must have contributed *something* to the acquittal, because a relative of the murder victim came up to me after the trial and said, "If thee dies a natural death, there is no justice in Heaven!" (*Laughs.*)

JEFFERSON. Well! It is the privilege of this audience to witness the greatest show of amity ever displayed publicly by Messrs. Hamilton and Burr. Strange and wonderful are the forces that bring adversaries together. — Would you have thought this possible, Mr. Lenox?

LENOX. Oh, yes, anything is possible in love, war, and politics. — General Hamilton, you were first thrust into prominence by your appointment to be the right hand, so to speak, of the late George Washington. How did it happen, at age twenty, that Alexander Hamilton was picked as next man to the Commander-in-Chief?

HAMILTON. Well, in the fighting around Princeton, I apparently came to the personal notice of the General. Later, when he needed help in drafting documents and executing orders, he looked for someone who knew military tactics and who, like himself, was a disciplinarian. So he offered me the post of his aide.

JEFFERSON. Of course you jumped at it?

HAMILTON. No, not quite. It was enormously flattering, naturally, but I preferred the smell of powder to the smell of ink.

BURR. Still, one could hardly be cavalier about an invitation from the Commander-in-Chief to be his aide.

HAMILTON. I was not cavalier. Just young.

JEFFERSON. General, concerning your preference for the smell of powder, some of your critics say you were — and are — over-fond of war.

HAMILTON (*coldly*). Do they now?

BURR. I must say, I've heard that too, General — it's even been suggested that you were at times careless with the lives of men under your command.

HAMILTON. Now that, sir, is a serious charge. I insist you be specific.

BURR. I would rather not. We've been getting along fairly well up to this point.

HAMILTON. Repeating a canard in public is not my idea of an anxiety to get along well. I cannot let such a statement rest.

BURR. Well, I don't have any evidence before me —

HAMILTON. I thought not.

BURR. But wasn't there some incident involving troops under your command at the Battle of Yorktown?

HAMILTON. In battle, there tend to be *many* incidents involving troops.

JEFFERSON. I see Mr. Lenox is searching feverishly through his papers. Perhaps he has in his hands, amongst what I presume to be sheaves of documents on *all* our nefarious activities, something that could illuminate us on this point.

LENOX. As a matter of fact, I do have — permit me —

NARRATOR (*sotto voce*). Mr. Lenox has risen from his chair to hand a piece of paper to Mr. Hamilton. — The General, who seems quite annoyed, refuses to accept it...

HAMILTON. I didn't ask for it. Perhaps Mr. Burr would like to read it.

BURR. I defer to Mr. Jefferson, who after all raised the possibility that the document could be with us.

JEFFERSON. And I defer to Mr. Lenox, since he *realized* the possibility.

LENOX. Well, since, I didn't bring up the matter, and since no one —

BURR. Aren't we all being terribly coy? Why don't you read it out loud, Mr. Lenox?

LENOX. There being no objection?

There is none.

LENOX. It seems that a certain Captain James Duncan —

HAMILTON. Duncan?

LENOX (*continuing*). Yes...indicates he served under you, Sir, in the Battle of Yorktown. Claims that after a successful action in the field, you called for an extraordinary maneuver.

HAMILTON. Oh? And what was that?

LENOX. He wrote that you advanced your men to a parapet, where you commanded them to go through the whole soldier's manual, presenting and grounding arms, in full sight of the enemy.

HAMILTON. Then why didn't the British fire on us?

LENOX. According to the Captain — I quote him — "Although the enemy had been firing a little before, they did not now give us a single shot. I suppose their astonishment at our conduct must have prevented them, for I can assign no other reason. Colonel Hamilton gave those orders; and although I esteem him highly, I must beg leave in this instance to think he wantonly exposed the lives of his men."[3]

HAMILTON (*stung*). The operative phrases in the Captain's comments are "I suppose," and "I beg leave to think." You have quoted an opinion of a recollected event, and the author is entitled to think whatever he begs leave to think. But while we're on the subject of an officer's

3. *Diary of Captain James Duncan* (1781)

concern for his troops, I have heard the story, Colonel Burr, that you nearly cut off the arm of one of your own soldiers.

BURR. That is true, General.

JEFFERSON (*after a moment's silence*). Somehow, Colonel, I don't think you can quite leave the story there.

BURR. During the days of Valley Forge, you may recall, there was poor morale in the Army. There were desertions, there were soldiers whose terms of enlistment had expired and who refused to re-enlist. Now around that time, a detachment of militia was ordered to protect a pass ten miles from Valley Forge. Perhaps out of boredom, or bitterness, or malicious humor, they took to sending back frequent false alerts — word that the British were on the march. This would arouse the sleeping main camp; it was very disruptive, as you can imagine. Well, since I had become known, like General Hamilton, as a disciplinarian, I was assigned to straighten out that militia. I took over command of it, and issued very strict orders. This didn't sit well with the thugs and mischief-makers in the force. As a result, they planned to get rid of me.

JEFFERSON. What do you mean, get rid of you?

BURR. Just that.

JEFFERSON. Kill you?

BURR. Yes. Luckily for me, I found out about it, and devised a plan of my own. Unknown to them, I had all the bullets removed from their weapons, and one midnight — it was a very cold, moonlit night — I had the company awakened and mustered for a roll call.

HAMILTON. Carrying their arms?

BURR. Yes.

HAMILTON. But you knew their arms were not loaded?

BURR. I just said that.

JEFFERSON. Were *you* armed?

BURR. Only with a saber. — May I go on?

JEFFERSON. By all means.

BURR. As I inspected the troops, I stopped in front of each man. When I came to the ringleader, he raised his gun, leveled it at me, and shouted "Now is the time, boys!" Instantly, I came down hard with my saber, and slashed his arm; I all but cut if off; I then dismissed the men. That was the end of it.

JEFFERSON. And what about the arm?

BURR. Amputated next morning.

JEFFERSON. You don't mind telling that story?

BURR. You seem to forget I was asked to do so. May I add, after that there were no more false alarms.

HAMILTON. Excellent. I believe our friend from Virginia never had any problems with matters such as troop discipline. — Am I mistaken?

JEFFERSON. No General, that is right. I was never in uniform, having been engaged in other matters. My closest brush with enemy soldiers, was being *pursued* by them during my days as Governor of Virginia. Perhaps I anticipate you General, in bringing up that incident.

HAMILTON. Oh no. I daresay it is sufficiently well-known without my bringing it up. Your flight before enemy troops has been characterized, in terms I, of course, do not support, as a show of cowardice by a state leader.

JEFFERSON. I'm not sure about you, Mr. Lenox, but the rest of us on this platform are more or less accustomed to calumny. The event of which Mr. Hamilton speaks, has been interpreted in some quarters to suggest that I, ignoring the noble example of Don Quixote and his windmill, declined single combat in my doorway, against an entire force of British dragoons.[4]

LENOX. Let's get back to George Washington. Mr. Burr, you knew him, did you not?

BURR. I did. I found him a rather cold and haughty man.

JEFFERSON. He could be that, on occasion.

HAMILTON. We can all be that, on occasion. But usually the occasion is inspired by something. Colonel, did you not have some difference with the Commander?

BURR. "Difference" depends on who does the differing, and why. My first relation to General Washington came soon after I volunteered for service. He had received two letters strongly proposing that I be given a commission in the Army. One of them was from John Hancock. Mr. Washington did not see fit to honor those requests.

HAMILTON. Isn't it true at that time, commissions were given only by the *states*? That the General did not have the authority to appoint you?

BURR. That may have been a factor then, but it would not explain his denial several times, of later commissions. He found it convenient each time to obstruct my progress by withholding promotions and assignments. — Perhaps he had some help on that from close advisors.

JEFFERSON. Did you ever actually meet General Washington?

BURR. Oh yes. Several times.

HAMILTON. Once, I heard, under strained circumstances.

BURR. Any meeting with George Washington was a strained circumstance.

---

4. January 1781, with British forces attacking, Governor Jefferson ordered the state government relocated from Richmond to Charlottesville, Virginia. In May 1781, Jefferson barely escaped capture by the British in Charlottesville.

HAMILTON. I believe you know to what I refer.

BURR (*coldly*). I think not.

HAMILTON. The letter on his desk?

BURR. Oh, well, I have no compunction about telling that story. The General had sent for me. When I entered the room, he was at his desk, writing. He made a sign for me to be seated, kept on writing for a little, and then excused himself and went out of the room. I was burning with curiosity to see what a letter from the great man looked like, so I sidled up to his desk and peeked. Once I'd gone that far, I got interested in what we had written, and started to read it. At which point the General suddenly returned, and caught me at it. He exploded. He was livid. He gave me the tongue-lashing of my life! (*Laughs*.)

HAMILTON. But wasn't that unbecoming conduct on your part?

BURR (*still laughing*). Not unbecoming. Just young. I daresay I deserved what I got. But I don't think it should have put me on his enemy list from that time forward.

JEFFERSON. Oh, I wouldn't agree with you on that designation. The General seemed to me not the grudge-holding type. Obviously you didn't like him, but what did you think of him as a General? Militarily speaking?

BURR. Would you like to withdraw that question?

JEFFERSON. No.

BURR. I'm afraid I must answer frankly. He was not a good General. In his whole career he was associated almost entirely with defeat. He had nothing to do with our one important victory before Yorktown, which was Saratoga, where General Gates was in command. As for Yorktown, where would Washington have been without the guns of the French fleet?

JEFFERSON. I perceive, Colonel, that nothing could possibly change your estimate of the man.

BURR. Nor yours, I'm sure.

LENOX. Mr. Jefferson, I feel secure in the presumption that if you had done nothing else but compose the Declaration of Independence, your prospects for the esteem of posterity would be secure.

JEFFERSON. Thank you.

LENOX. How did you feel when you crossed the last "t" and set down the last period of the Declaration?

JEFFERSON. Tired. (*The others laugh*.) Actually I felt tentative about what I'd set down, because I was convinced that the draft would be revamped by Congress — resisted, haggled about, picked apart. And that's what happened. It was attacked from the first sentence.

BURR. By who in particular?

JEFFERSON. Just about everyone. Including a Congressman from my own state, Mr. Nicholson. He berated the assertion that all men are created equal as *vehement*, as an open invitation to civil convulsion, said all men are *not* born free and equal and that we should not weaken our first national pronouncement to the world, by so stating.

BURR. Wasn't there also a ruckus over your calling for abolition of the slave trade?

JEFFERSON. Yes. Even some who, like myself, wanted to get *rid* of slavery, argued that if we insisted on it in the Declaration, the southern colonies might split from the rest of us even before we got started, right there and then.

HAMILTON. How much of your original text was dropped?

JEFFERSON. Four hundred and eighty words — eighty-six changes.

LENOX. How many words *unchanged*?

JEFFERSON. One thousand three hundred and thirty-seven.

BURR. Very tidy bookkeeping.

JEFFERSON. Since I was not accustomed to being rewritten by a roomful of men, I kept careful and grudging account. — But the framing of the Declaration is a long story, Mr. Lenox, and I assume that you'd like to steer us back to more recent events.

LENOX. You read my mind. — Gentlemen, among the problems facing our country today, other than that of France, which do you consider the sorest?

BURR. The Alien and Sedition Acts,[5] by a wide margin. The trend toward conformity, the putting down of dissent, the existence on the statute books of a series of gross, unworkable, and unjust laws.

JEFFERSON. I agree. The Acts are intrusive, excessive, and altogether repressive.

HAMILTON. What evidence do you have of that?

JEFFERSON. Will personal evidence do? My mail has been opened in Philadelphia. Some of my supporters have been threatened. Others have been shadowed on the streets and their movements recorded.

BURR. And not a word of protests from the Federalists?

JEFFERSON. None.

LENOX. How does this sit with you, Mr. Hamilton?

HAMILTON. I had, and still have, some reservations about those Acts. But then I never expect to see perfection in a creature as imperfect as man.

JEFFERSON. I am not speaking of perfectibility. I'm speaking about a threat to our rights. Under these laws the President can, at any time, *deport* such aliens as he — HE — judges to be dangerous.

---

5. Enacted by Congress in 1798.

BURR. And if an alien returns after deportation, he can be imprisoned and kept there for as long as the President likes. The whole thing is obviously aimed at the foreign-born.

HAMILTON. Well, sir, I am foreign-born.

BURR. Oh, come now, Mr. Hamilton, you know very well why you Federalists are against the foreign-born. It's because as a rule they're against you Federalists.

HAMILTON. Now why should that be, unless they've been assiduously educated by Mr. Jefferson's faction, to be hostile?

JEFFERSON. No education has been necessary. They're against your faction because most of them came to this country to escape the tyranny of crowned heads and mischief-making aristocrats, and they're fully aware —

HAMILTON. Sir, it was not aristocrats who made all the misery in the France you so slavishly admire. Was it aristocrats who invented the guillotine and kept it busy decapitating former friends of yours among the aristocracy? Friends who had been very kind to you when you were Ambassador to France?

LENOX. I'm afraid we're straying somewhat afield of —

BURR. Mr. Hamilton, let me ask your opinion about the sentencing to prison of Congressman Lyon of Vermont, for criticizing President Adams.

HAMILTON. A very rough specimen of democracy is Mr. Lyon. Any Congressman who would *spit* in the face of a colleague on the floor of Congress —

BURR. He had been slandered by Senator Griswold on that same floor — and moreover Griswold followed him and kept plucking at his coat. Small wonder —

JEFFERSON. Congressman Lyon was not jailed for spitting, but for criticizing the President. Four months in prison and a fine of a thousand dollars!

HAMILTON. Which fine you helped to pay, I believe.

JEFFERSON. That is correct.

HAMILTON. Did you not, Mr. Burr, also support a gentleman accused of seditious libel? One Mr. Burk?

BURR. I certainly did. I contributed to his bail of two thousand dollars.

HAMILTON. Wasn't he the same Mr. Burk who escaped from Ireland disguised as a woman?

BURR. Yes. And he was the same Mr. Burk who wrote a very popular play about Bunker Hill, and dedicated it to me.[6] I hope you've seen the play, Mr. Hamilton. It is still performed.

HAMILTON. I've not yet had the pleasure. — I believe Mr. Burk is in hiding somewhere now, is he not?

6. The play *Bunker-Hill* by John Daly Burk, first performed in 1797.

BURR. I don't keep the same watch on private citizens that the Adams administration seems to do. I don't know *where* the man is.

LENOX. Perhaps in view of the time left, we should mine some other vein. — Mr. Jefferson, you were Secretary of State and Mr. Hamilton was Secretary of Treasury in the cabinet of President Washington. It's well known that relations between your Departments were strained. Was there personal animosity between the two of you?

JEFFERSON. Not personal, but I must say there were some rather pronounced administrative differences.

LENOX. What were the differences?

HAMILTON. Since candor seems rampant tonight, let me just say that the State Department tried to persuade Mr. Washington to remove the Post Office from the control of Treasury. Friend Jefferson did not succeed there, but he did manage to get the *Mint* under his control, which certainly astonished us at the Treasury.

JEFFERSON. I'm sorry to be compelled to reply that Mr. Hamilton, as Secretary of the Treasury, performed more like a Prime Minister in that he became involved in every aspect of government including foreign affairs, which was the exclusive province of the State Department. He met unilaterally with foreign representatives, especially British diplomats, without my knowledge.

HAMILTON. I'm afraid you misapprehend —

JEFFERSON. You had a staff of over a hundred. I was obliged to operate with a staff of only *five*. After a while I began to think that Treasury possessed so much influence as to swallow up the whole of the government's executive powers.

HAMILTON. I have no apology to make for the fact that Treasury, under my charge, was the most vital of the federal departments.

JEFFERSON. It still is. Besides management of revenue, it runs the lighthouse service, regulates aid to navigation, conducts land surveys, controls certain medical programs —

HAMILTON. The only legitimate complaint to all this activity would be if any of these things were done badly. And those complaints have never been made.

BURR. What was your total budget in the State Department, Mr. Jefferson?

JEFFERSON. Sixty-six hundred dollars a year.

BURR. Surely you are joking.

JEFFERSON. Mr. Hamilton can verify that.

BURR. And what did that cover?

JEFFERSON. The operating expenses of the State Department, including the salaries of myself and my staff.

BURR. For a year?

JEFFERSON. For a year.

BURR. That wasn't much money to run a government department.

HAMILTON. You must remember that we were a poor country. Before we even got started, we were eighty-five million dollars in debt.

LENOX. All the more credit to you, Mr. Hamilton, for so swiftly putting the country on solid ground.

HAMILTON. At last, a kind word.

BURR. May I ask you a candid question, Sir?

HAMILTON. I hadn't noticed that any of the questions asked heretofore were exactly veiled. But go ahead.

BURR. Is it possible that, since your foreign birth made you ineligible for the presidency, you may have, without being altogether aware of it, tried to acquire as much power as you could manage, short of the highest seat itself?

HAMILTON (*below zero*). I have been perfectly aware at all times, of the goals for which I have striven, and personal power was not one of them. If you are speaking of acquiring power for the *nation*, then I cheerfully confess to that ambition. I hope that answers your question with as much candor as went into the asking of it.

BURR. I have no way of measuring, but thank you.

LENOX. Speaking of candor, Mr. Hamilton, I have another question, involving a matter you yourself made public. It occurred during your administration of the Treasury. I refer to the Reynolds affair.

A silence. A pregnant silence. The Narrator steps in:

NARRATOR (*hushed, as before*). Oh-oh. It's as though a bomb has dropped. General Hamilton's face is flushed. He's obviously very angry. He seems to be counting before he answers…

Under the following, a series of audience reactions:

HAMILTON (*sharply*). I had thought you might have the good taste not to bring that up.

LENOX. But nobody could have cast more intense light on it than you yourself, by writing and publishing this pamphlet which I hold in my hand, entitled, "Observations on Certain Documents in which the Charge of Speculation Against Alexander Hamilton, is Fully Refuted."[7]

---

7. Published in 1796.

NARRATOR (*barely above a whisper*). General Hamilton is now on his feet...

HAMILTON. Mr. Lenox, I have apparently been deceived as to the nature of this event. You carry a small library of documents with you, and so far I see you have taken pains to include an attack on me by an obscure Army Captain, based on an incident more than twenty years ago. And now the pamphlet. If I had understood this was going to be a kangaroo court...

LENOX. But General, we are dealing with history; and it is to your honor, that both your personal and public life interact with the past and ongoing history of the United States. I felt that since —

HAMILTON. I see no reason to go on.

NARRATOR (*astonished*). General Hamilton is starting to leave the platform...the others remain in their chairs...a bit uncomfortably, I think...especially Mr. Lenox...

JEFFERSON (*placatingly*). I can understand Mr. Hamilton taking offense at what might be construed under the circumstances, as an invasion of his privacy. I think we should try to understand that.

HAMILTON (*from halfway to the wings*). I am no more in need of special understanding, than I am of special dispensation. What I do need is to cool an anger for which I make no apology.

NARRATOR. Mr. Hamilton has left, and Mr. Lenox seems undecided what to do. He looks at Colonel Burr and Mr. Jefferson for some cue, but both are silent. Mr. Lenox is getting up and now comes forward to address the audience.

LENOX. I assure you, it was not my intention —

Some in the audience do not approve of what Lenox did, and there are a few scattered cries: "You were wrong!"... "That was uncalled for!"... "You should apologize!"... "Call him back!"

LENOX (*flustered*). Perhaps we could all profit from a recess.

BURR. A General, absent without leave?

JEFFERSON (*with some surprise*). Hold on...I think the General is coming back...

NARRATOR (*also with surprise*). Yes, here is Mr. Hamilton, back on the platform. He's coming forward to speak, as Mr. Lenox returns to his seat.

HAMILTON. Ladies and gentlemen, I felt the need to cool my anger, and that has been done. I had thought this presentation was one in which the public could hear our views on issues of abiding interest to the nation. God knows there are enough such issues. But no — there was brought up without warning, reference to an indiscretion I committed involving a woman whose husband attempted to blackmail me. Just how this relates to the past or future of the United States, how it interacts with history, as the moderator put it, escapes me. Now while I may be loath to respond to some things, I'm not *afraid* to, which is a different matter entirely. I will not evade any question asked of me, even one as tasteless as that of Mr. Lenox. — Perhaps he will be kind enough to tell us just what he wishes to know about the pamphlet.

LENOX. Why did you expose to the whole country, the circumstances of a protracted adulterous affair with a woman of low character? — Why did you choose to publish so much about it, including semi-illiterate letters you received from her, and sordid details of how her husband practiced extortion?[8]

HAMILTON. Is that the end of the question?

LENOX. Was it necessary to turn all that into the glare of publicity? *Anybody* could buy your pamphlet — and many did. — I did.

HAMILTON. It was necessary, Sir, because my enemies in Mr. Jefferson's party, having invented venomous and highly prejudiced reports, deliberately raised the suspicion that I used my cabinet office and public funds to pay blackmail monies to an extortioner. I was willing to endure the humiliation of opening confessing injury to my private honor, rather than suffer the imputation of wrongdoing in my exercise of the Treasury Department. — Does my answer satisfy you?

LENOX. I was not seeking satisfaction, only information.

HAMILTON. Is it now your intention to ask Mr. Jefferson and Mr. Burr about reports of their liaisons? By your standard, all three of us are public figures who interact with history.

LENOX. I don't believe either gentleman has *published* any confessions. That was the sole ground of my inquiry. — Do you have any comment, Mr. Jefferson?

JEFFERSON. Only that perhaps we might profit by moving on to some broader, less personal subject.

BURR. Discretion being the better part of procedure, Mr. Vice President?

JEFFERSON. Since I do respect discretion, I'd rather not be pressed to say anything on the matter you have been entertaining.

HAMILTON. I understand you had a good *deal* to say about the matter.

JEFFERSON. Not publicly.

HAMILTON. Things that are said privately have a way of *becoming* public.

---

8. Referring to James Reynolds and his wife Maria.

JEFFERSON. You seem eager to expedite that process. — What I did say privately, was that self-exposure of an affair in order to allay suspicion of wrongdoing in office, suggested to me that pleading guilty to one offense, is not a select way of establishing innocence of any other.

HAMILTON (*angrily*). Are you implying, Sir, that I —

JEFFERSON. Nothing of the kind. I know, and the world knows, that you are a man of the highest integrity and honesty. My comment was addressed merely to the method of your disavowal, and in that respect it was no more ill-intended than Mr. Lenox's original question.

NARRATOR. General Hamilton seems not too happy about any of this, but he's returned to his seat and it apparently ready to —

BURR. I've been silent up to now because Mr. Jefferson and the General seemed deeply fascinated in what each other had to say; but I cannot dismiss the implication made by Mr. Hamilton that his confreres on this platform have had liaisons which are perhaps subject to scrutiny, or at least to comment. I invite Mr. Hamilton to particularize, if he feels that by doing so, it will contribute to fair play.

HAMILTON. Very well, Mr. Burr. It has been grist to the tireless mills of gossip that you, Sir, have had many affairs with women, some of them of tender age; that your intrigues have been without number.

BURR. My intrigues were not exactly without number, but I will say that the number was high. And, I would say that in each instance, discreteness about the particular arrangement was honored more than it is being honored here.

HAMILTON. I see. — Do you, from experience, have any comment to make about the principle of fatherhood outside of wedlock?

BURR. When a lady does me the honor to name me as the father of her child, I trust I shall always be too gallant to show myself ungrateful for the favor.

HAMILTON. I have heard it said that on the march to Québec with troops under Benedict Arnold, you were accompanied by an Indian maiden.

BURR. Only part of the way. She was delectable — and ornament to her race and womankind in general. I happen to think Woman is a glorious species; that contrary to the fiction held by many men, women are man's intellectual *equals*; and if it were not for discrimination in education and by custom, they would match us in every endeavor except perhaps war. I see no reason why we should continue to value grace, allure, frivolity, and vanity in a woman, above skill, acumen and intellect.

Genteel applause.

HAMILTON. More essay than memoir, Mr. Burr, but I'm sure that your preachment will win you many supporters among women in this audience. — And Mr. Vice President, Sir, how do you manage to cope with the ugly rumors that arise from time to time, concerning your relationship to a member of your household of slaves on the one hand, and with the wife of a friend of your youth, on the other?

JEFFERSON. I have made it a point never to reply to calumnies, for while I should be answering one, twenty new ones would be invented.

LENOX. Excuse me, Mr. Jefferson, Mr. Burr. I should like to make clear to you and to our audience that I regret asking a question which caused offense, and which generated this last exchange. If my judgment miscarried, then I am at fault and I apologize. I am particularly sorry if I caused General Hamilton distress, for I have always regarded him with esteem as the man who put our government on its feet. Out of a period of intense turmoil, he succeeded in securing our national credit at home and abroad; his reports are famous for their clarity, scope and penetration.

HAMILTON (*not pleased*). Really, this is not necessary.

LENOX. It is to me, Sir. — He showed us how to raise and collect revenue, he established a mint and a national bank.

BURR. Not altogether unopposed —

LENOX. — He regulated our currency, and laid down vital guides for industry. And it is to him that a lion's share of the credit must go for ratification of our Constitution.

JEFFERSON. All very true. But as regards to the Constitution, General, is it fair to say you've had, and *still* have, many reservations about it?

HAMILTON. I just don't think it will endure as it stands — but it's *necessary*. It's a vital compromise between those who, like myself, believe a strong central government is absolutely indispensable, and others who tremble at the idea of a state surrendering the slightest bit of sovereignty to federal authority.

BURR. You see no chance of an eventual conciliation of the two positions?

HAMILTON. No. I think there'll always be controversy over the interpretation and application of the Constitution. It will be open to amendments, and amendments to amendments.

LENOX. This subject is long, wide and deep, and we could go on all night with it, but there are one or two other questions that it might be derelict not to ask while we have the opportunity. First — do any of you doubt that liberty and democracy are compatible?

JEFFERSON. I have no doubt whatsoever.

HAMILTON. I do. I'm afraid democracy has a way of degenerating into mobocracy. Take what happened in France. The majority sometimes gets drunk with its own power, and when that happens, everything becomes chaotic. I long ago advocated that only landowners be permitted to vote for Senator. A wealthy Senate and President would tend by their natural conservatism, to check the tendency of the lower House to carry liberty to unhealthy excesses.

JEFFERSON. What you're saying, in effect, is that you're in favor of a perpetual aristocracy.

HAMILTON. That's what you say I'm saying. It narrows down to a belief in the rule of gentlemen. In the rule of the rich, the good, and the wise.

BURR. We can tell how rich a man is by his property and credit, but how do you measure goodness and wisdom?

HAMILTON. Oh, those qualities are not so obscure as all that! Hasn't it been your experience that they have a way of shining out? You see, when a man has a certain position, when he has *prestige* to maintain, then he values honor; he stands above vulgar striving for advantage. Aristocracy, I submit, is not a bad word.

JEFFERSON. It depends on the kind of aristocracy. There are two kinds — the natural one of virtue and talent, and the artificial one of money and title. I've known the latter to do very great mischief in government. And when the rich get too rich and poor get too poor, there can be a terrible explosion.

HAMILTON. Sound no alarms. There are natural balances. You and I come from different schools, Mr. Jefferson. Man will always be ambitious and vindictive — a monster at times.

JEFFERSON. Well, it'll take more than your pessimism to shake my faith in man's ability to *think* this way out of his troubles. I make allowance for such a thing as *progress*.

HAMILTON. I have very strong feelings about the incentive to progress, and they may surprise you all.

BURR. I'm gripping my chair.

HAMILTON. Among the greatest incentives is avarice.

JEFFERSON (*with a shrug*). Well — I rest my case.

BURR. Avarice? Do you say that with regret?

HAMILTON. Not at all. Far from being a deadly sin, avarice is an integral part of the order of nature. The average man's instinct to make money — his *love* of money — are the main motive forces of the economic machine. When harnessed to the service of the state, avarice can carry a nation to power and opulence. I think we should *encourage* a spirit of avarice!

JEFFERSON. I happen to place a much higher premium on the spirit of charity and altruism.
HAMILTON. That sounds very pious, but isn't altruism usually a disguised form of selfishness? How many acts of charity are done out of purity of heart? How many because it soothes the giver's conscience, or expiates some guilt or other?
JEFFERSON. I have never made count, but I think it's cynical to believe that guilt is a kind of Muse that inspires the best in man.
LENOX. Gentlemen: all about us in the world are old and powerful nations. Do you believe we shall ultimately take our place among the greatest?
HAMILTON. Beyond any doubt. We are a Hercules in a cradle.
BURR. No question about it.
JEFFERSON. I share that view. But we must not assume our greatness is inevitable. If we're not careful we could blunder and forfeit our chance for greatness. If needs are ignored, and rights disregarded, people could forget themselves except for the sole faculty of making money.
BURR. Ah, but then General Hamilton's theory of avarice would come to the rescue!
HAMILTON. I find it refreshing that Mr. Jefferson at last admits people are as capable of being corrupted as they are of being perfected.
JEFFERSON. I have never denied that bad leadership can subvert. In fact, I wish our government could depend less and less on the character of its leaders. Bad men will sometimes get in, and on the strength of immense patronage they can make a great deal of progress toward corrupting the public mind. To me the whole art of government consists of being honest.
BURR. How simple! How pure!
HAMILTON. And how naive!
JEFFERSON. Scoff as you please, but to me the sum of good government is to leave men free to regulate their own pursuits and never take from the mouth of labor the bread it has earned.
BURR. Mr. Jefferson, I've come to believe you were endowed with a gift for large abstractions. This talent worked to the benefit of us all, to be sure, in your Declaration of Independence, but your formula for good government is somewhat wanting in particulars.
JEFFERSON. Particulars? It's late, but will you settle for two?
BURR. Try them on us.
JEFFERSON. One: I believe there should be a limit to the number of terms of a President. If that limit is not fixed by the Constitution, or set by practice, the office could become lifelong, and degenerate into a kind of royal succession.

Two: I would exempt from taxation everyone below a certain level, and tax the wealthy in geometrical progression as their wealth increases.

BURR. Don't frighten your audience, this is late at night.

HAMILTON. As a point of interest, Mr. Burr, may I ask you the same question as you put to Mr. Jefferson, concerning advocacies on your agenda?

BURR. I invite you to judge from what is already in the log. I advocated doing away with secrecy in the Senate. I introduced a bill to abolish imprisonment for debt, and another to impose a tax on unproductive property. I supported a bill to abolish slavery. — Want more?

HAMILTON. I had no idea you were so full of noble motives.

JEFFERSON. As Virgil said, "the noblest motive is the public good," and I think Colonel Burr has just passed that test.

HAMILTON. Good old Virgil.

LENOX. Let's close on that classic note, but not before asking each whether you have any Do's, Don't or Bewares to recommend to us. — Mr. Vice President?

JEFFERSON. Well...(*Thinks.*)... to impress on minorities the duties of acquiescence in the will of the majority, and to impress on majorities a respect at all times for the rights of the minority. — Also to beware of too strong a military force, even of citizens. And never to place too much confidence in any one man.

BURR. Yourself included?

JEFFERSON. Myself included.

LENOX. General Hamilton?

HAMILTON. I'd say that in a government framed for durable liberty, as much regard must be paid to the authority to make and execute laws with vigor, as to guarding against the encroachment of rights.

LENOX. Colonel Burr?

BURR. The old Romans had a saying: "To enjoy life is to live twice." Therefore, I say *enjoy*! And I add this amendment: Never do today what you can put off till tomorrow.

HAMILTON. May I ask our philosopher why?

BURR. Because delay may give you a clearer light as to what is *best* to be done.

JEFFERSON (*laughing*). I must try that.

LENOX. Our time is up. — I thank you, gentlemen, in behalf of the Open View Society. And I wish thank our audience for coming out in this weather. I just hope the roads have not melted under the downpour while our esteemed guests have been raining down their opinions. Good night — and drive your carriages safely.

Applause.

The audience getting up and leaving. Over this:

NARRATOR. The speakers are still on the platform as the audience begins to leave. Messrs. Burr, Jefferson, Hamilton and Lenox are shaking hands with each other — (*Now surprised.*) — but no, Mr. Hamilton has *refused to shake hands* with Mr. Lenox! He turned his back when Lenox offered his hand and walked off. — Well! The General has apparently not forgiven the moderator for bringing up the matter of a woman with whom Mr. Hamilton had an affair. — Hmm — I must say *none* of the panelists tonight succeeded in suppressing what one may well suspect is a latent, if not active, acrimony toward each other. I think it is fair to say there was no love lost in this hall tonight.

Music: A brief punctuation — not a curtain — just a few chords to separate the scene from a postscript.

POSTSCRIPT. Nor was any love lost in the years that followed this imagined meeting. In 1800, there was a bitter contest between Jefferson and Burr for the presidency. They were tied in electoral votes, and it took thirty-six ballots in the House of Representatives running over six days, before Jefferson was elected President with Burr as Vice President. Four years later, Burr, still Vice President, killed Hamilton is a duel. And three years after that, Burr found himself tried for treason for allegedly scheming to split the American Southwest from the Union. He was acquitted of that charge, to the very great disappointment of still President Thomas Jefferson, who worked very hard for him to be convicted.

Although the meeting recounted in this program never actually took place, all opinions and advocacies of the panelists were actually as stated by them, often in their exact words. All incidents and events cited, are likewise historically true.

Music: Curtain.

CORWIN ON *NO LOVE LOST*

The *Los Angeles Times* of August 14, 1996 ran on page one of its Calendar Section an article by Judith Michaelson captioned "A Great Debate on the Great Issues of Past and Present," and subtitled "Before the election, Jefferson, Hamilton, and Burr will engage one another in an open forum courtesy of dramatist Norman Corwin's *No Love Lost*."

It was presented on May 7, 2011 by the California Artists Radio Theatre as *Together Tonight* at the Beverly Garland Holiday Inn Little Theatre.

FROM THE EDITOR

Peggy Webber produced and directed the above-mentioned performance of 2011, one of Corwin's final public appearances. The cast included Monte Markham (Jefferson), Phil Proctor (Burr), John R. Lee (Hamilton), Richard Herd (Lenox), Samantha Eggar (Narrator) and CART Announcer John Harlan.

This radio play was originally written and directed by Corwin for the stage as *Together Tonight! Jefferson, Hamilton, and Burr* and toured during the 1976 Bicentennial with Dana Andrews (Jefferson), Howard Duff (Hamilton), Monte Markham (Burr) and Alan Manson (Lenox).

THE WRITER WITH THE LAME LEFT HAND

The second in the series *More By Corwin*, this program was broadcast over NPR beginning in December 1996. Charles Durning starred as Miguel de Cervantes. The supporting cast included Samantha Eggar, Charles Shaughnessey, Janet Waldo, Shirley Mitchell, Elliott Reid, Ed Asner, Walt Beaver, Mala Powers, Michael Gough, Marvin Kaplan, Norman Lloyd, William Shatner, and Yuri Rasovsky.

Technical direction was by Marty Halperin and Warren Dewey. Music by Ken Stange.

Mary Beth Kirchner produced. The author directed.

Music: Establish and hold under:

NARRATOR. Until he was past fifty he was just another writer. Some thought him a hack. He turned out mediocre verse, tried plays, got nowhere. He was poor for most of his life, was captured by pirates — genuine, not storybook pirates — was sentenced to prison in his native Spain more than once, through no fault of his own, was generally considered a loser. Then, in his mid-fifties — late start — he wrote a story that became, and remains, the second most widely published and translated book in the world, surpassed only by the Bible.

This was Miguel de Cervantes Saavedra, born four hundred and fifty years ago this year.[1] The book? *Don Quixote*, of course.

We meet him at age sixty-eight, his kidneys in poor repair, but his spirit intact.

Music: Curtain going up. Cross-fade to:

Man at dinner.

CERVANTES (*age 68*). Sit down, sit down, Pablo. — My supper, such as it is. — Have some wine?
PABLO. No, thanks. I can't stay long. Just dropped by to see how you're doing.
CERVANTES. Doing? I'm just what you see. I have six teeth left, but since none of the uppers is in agreement with the lowers, I'm reduced to this. — Quite a spectacle at feeding time, am I not? With this crippled hand, to add to the bargain. I was denied the use of it a long time ago — in battle.
PABLO. Lepanto, wasn't it?
CERVANTES. Lepanto, yes. I always say I lost the use of my left hand to the greater glory of my right.[2] (*Chuckles.*) — How's your family?
PABLO. Very well, thanks. — I've been reading the adventures of your Don, and enjoying him immensely.
CERVANTES. Good. — Change your mind about the wine?
PABLO. Uh-uh.
CERVANTES. Yes, well, I affect this glove for the same reason a one-eyed man wears a patch over the crater of the missing one. Cosmetic. But even a covered claw bothers some people. Once I…I raised it to touch the face of a lovely girl, and she recoiled from me.

---

1. Cervantes was born in 1547 and died in 1616.
2. Wounded by gunfire during the Battle of Lepanto in 1571.

PABLO. Ah, well, some women —
CERVANTES. However, other ladies came forward from time to time. (*Laughs.*) But I was never a roustabout, you understand. I think most of the time I've been as good a Catholic as ever bent a knee. — Hah…well…hell…nourishment. Got to keep going (*Slurps some soup.*) Truth is…truth is, my friend, the sap has pretty much dried up in these bones. — I'm not complaining, just reporting.
PABLO. I sympathize. Myself, I —
CERVANTES. These legs, these shoulders, my good right arm, my lance, so to speak, they all had proper juices flowing through them…some fine old Castilian claret has bubbled under my skull, I can tell you.
VOICE OF ANDREA (*calling, off*). Miguel…
CERVANTES (*up*). Yes, Andrea? (*To Pablo.*) My good sisters watch over me.
ANDREA (*still off*). Need anything?
CERVANTES (*up*). No, I'm fine. (*Down.*) Pablo, good friend, what I've learned in this life is that nothing good comes easy. Sometimes it's been very bitter. But now and then, when I'm half asleep, I think I'm in the present and the past and the future all at once — always, of course, in the service of God and charity, and not doing too badly! (*Laughs.*) How is that for covering ground? (*Laughs again.*)
ANDREA (*still from the other room*). You want more soup, Miguel?
CERVANTES (*up*). No — let me be! I'm entertaining Don Pablo. (*Down.*) As I was saying — I had bumps — knocks. Try spending four years in…in slavery. I was captured by pirates. Yes. At sea. This was after the battle of Lepanto, where I lost my — but I already told you that. Sometimes I think I wander, but not often. Not like my Quixote, who was *always* wandering. (*Chuckles.*) I once put him inside a wooden cage.
PABLO. That's a *marvelous* episode!…I read it to my children.
CERVANTES. Myself, I've been in *iron* cages. — In Algiers, Seville, Valladolid. — I was once jailed and held for questioning about a *murder*. Somebody stabbed a man outside my house in Valladolid one night. Stupid magistrate kept me in prison while they investigated, then let me go.
PABLO. Valladolid's a place I wouldn't want to do time in.
CERVANTES. *Nowhere's* a place you want to do time in. But I assure you, prison was very special in Algiers.[3] Very. Those bastards were extremely reluctant to let me go. Ah, sunny Algiers! I must say they didn't want to release me for good reason! Because, you see, I as far from a model prisoner. A model prisoner doesn't try to escape — not four times, anyway. God, was Hassan Pasha mad after the last one!

---

3. Cervantes was captured by Barbary Pirates in 1575 and imprisoned in Algiers until 1580.

Music: Brief transition, Arabic in flavor, retreating quickly under:

HASSAN (*roaring*). Where is that dog? Where's Cervantes? — I'll drive a spike through his guts!

GUARD. Over there, sitting on his haunches, just getting up.

HASSAN. Aha! *You* again! Four times, eh? Weren't three tries enough? — Answer me! — Weren't three times enough?

CERVANTES. No, because they didn't succeed.

HASSAN. Oh, you succeeded all right! You succeeded in getting four of your fellow prisoners hanged — another three roasted at the stake — and three more dragged by horses through the streets until they were a blood pulp.

CERVANTES. I know all about it.

HASSAN. You know all about it, do you? — Well, how about adding *this* to what you know!

Whiplash.

HASSAN. Don't try insolence on me, Christian! — Why aren't you cringing? Why aren't you bent double at my feet?

CERVANTES. It's my hand, not my back, that's crippled.

HASSAN. Ah, bravo! Señor Snotty! You're one of those heroes who make fine speeches at the foot of the gallows, the way they behave in storybooks, is that what you're trying to do? — You know how to die, is that right?

CERVANTES. I'm not a hero, and I don't know how to die. Nor do I want to know. All I've wanted is to get back to Spain and my people.

HASSAN. Then why haven't the people you're so anxious to get back to, paid your ransom these four years, and saved you the trouble of trying to escape, hm?

CERVANTES. Because five hundred gold ducats is enough to ransom a prince-and-a-half. Maybe two princes.

HASSAN. Don't try arrogance! You're not talking to one of your simple priests. And don't try to deny you're a man of means. We found those letters on you.

CERVANTES. Man of means! I come from one of the poorest families in Spain.

HASSAN. Be that as it may. — You will now tell me who your latest accomplices were. You will name them. The planners. Every last one.

CERVANTES. There were no accomplices.

HASSAN. You lie! The priest Blanco de Paz, a better Catholic than you, informed us of the whole plot.

CERVANTES. Then he must have told you that not a single one of the other men was responsible for organizing the escape. Only I.

HASSAN. You *alone* are to blame, is that what you insist on?

CERVANTES. Yes, and if Blanco de Paz told you any differently, he hasn't earned whatever you paid him.

HASSAN. I paid him one round ducat and a jar of butter.

CERVANTES. A ducat, and a jar of butter? — He's not worth it.

HASSAN (*narrowly*). I'll tell you something. I've had all kinds of characters standing where you are now, and they've tried every kind of trick to get away with their lives. Yours is a common ploy, trying to win clemency by a show of courage. It's not original. I'm not fooled by it. In fact, I have contempt for it.

CERVANTES. Why contempt, when courage in the face of danger is a very Moorish trait? Very Algerian. I should think you'd have respect for a quality so native to yourself and your adopted people.

HASSAN. Flattery is even more loathsome to me than bravado...What do you mean, "adopted people"?

CERVANTES. Aren't you a renegade Christian? That's the word in the dungeon — that you're a convert.

HASSAN (*after a pause*). So I am. But I don't take kindly to being told that to my face. If you had any *glimmer* of a chance to survive after I came in here, you've managed to lose it. The only question now is how much and what kind of torture to put you to, on your way to being converted to a meal for dogs. — Guard, remove this turd!

CERVANTES. You spoke of originality. I see you have no real taste for it.

HASSAN. No? (*Laughs.*) I'll show you originality where it hurts.

CERVANTES. No matter what the variations, torture, and execution no longer are novelties. The results are so predictable.

HASSAN. Do you seriously think you're capable of talking your way out of this?

CERVANTES. Why not, since I talked my way into it?

HASSAN (*after a pause*). Try harder.

CERVANTES. I'm trying.

HASSAN (*amused now*). I'll give you two minutes.

CERVANTES. It strikes me that a man in your situation, wielding the power of life and death every day of the year, any hour of the day, must get bored. You have a godlike position — and godship, like all absolutes, carries with it the risk of monotony — endless obedience to your orders, endless supplications, endless doling out torments for the same old trespasses, repeating punishments with variations that can only in the end become tiresome.

HASSAN. One more minute.
CERVANTES. But if you're lucky you'll encounter, maybe once in ten thousand cases, a prisoner whose inclinations, whose talents, experience, and capacity to distract, can afford you infinitely more entertainment than the gallows and the stake, however absorbing those may be.
HASSAN. And you are that prisoner?
CERVANTES. Certainly. Why should I deny it? I've read widely, I've travelled, I've fought, I've wenched, I've killed, I've gone hungry, I've padded under the dome of Saint Peter, I've written poems, told stories, gotten drunk, shot at the enemy and been shot, been captured at sea, planned escape, been caught, escaped again, been caught again, and have confronted a high suzerain of the Crescent, to make a speech for my life against the clock. How many prisoners can say they've done all that?
HASSAN. Your time is up. — Guard! Chain this man. *Heavily.*

Leg and hand chains being attached, under:

HASSAN. But, I'll say this, dog: your cunning has earned you one thing. I'll give you your choice of how you die.
CERVANTES (*gravely*). My choice?
HASSAN. Yes.
CERVANTES (*not lightly*). In bed, at the age of eighty.
HASSAN (*as a slow chuckle builds to laughter*). You're an amusing case.
CERVANTES. I tried to tell you that.
HASSAN. I admit you're more worthy of sucking air into your lungs, than the priest who betrayed you. Maybe as a reward I should give you a hundred lashes.
CERVANTES. Make it one.
HASSAN. Rather none than one. My guards would think I've gone soft. — I'll tell you what. You're to be kept under far stricter imprisonment than before. — Guard, tell Mohammed I want him to double the watch on this fellow. — I think I'll want you around for a while, Cervantes. You're the kind of eccentric who's brought me good luck. — You'll be here a long time.
CERVANTES. Not if *I* have good luck. And a ransom to go with it.
HASSAN. Well, the price has just gone up.

Music: A transition that starts our Arabic, but after a few moments turns Hispanic, suggesting change of venue.

ANA FRANCA (*a woman in her early 30s*). Miguel, is that you?

CERVANTES (*calling, off*). Yes, I'm back...
ANA. Where have you been?
CERVANTES (*coming on*). Out for a walk. It's a beautiful day. The kind of day you want to take inside with you. I tell you, the whole world is like a garden out there!
ANA. Bully for the world.
CERVANTES. Get dressed, and let's go down to the Mentidero and sit under the trees.
ANA. What, and pass all that slop and refuse lying in the gutters? Those streets stink.
CERVANTES. Oh, just concentrate on the aromatic plants growing all around, and you won't notice the stench. When I look at a rose bush, I don't count the thorns.
ANA. Why do you insist on finding good in all the garbage of existence?
CERVANTES (*lightly*). Hell, when you can't do anything about it, it makes sense to accept life's limitations.
ANA. Well, I don't. I squawk; and when I do, it makes me feel I'm getting back at the fates just a little.
CERVANTES. Yes, I know what you mean. It's a kind of ventilation that helped me through some rough times. In fact it's helping me right now, when I don't know where the next month's rent is coming from.
ANA. It could come from me, if it weren't for your pride.
CERVANTES. Not pride, my lover, just respect for tradition.
ANA. What tradition?
CERVANTES. A tradition I don't want to follow...accepting help from women.
ANA (*suddenly on guard*). Ah? What women?
CERVANTES. My sisters, you wench! Besides, a playwright...even a struggling playwright...should never accept money from an actress.
ANA. Why not?
CERVANTES. Because until he pays her back, he can't criticize her performance, or shorten her role, or write a new play that doesn't have part for her. — Wait a second, what are you hiding under your gown?
ANA (*laughing, as she pulls away*). You know very well what I've got down there!
CERVANTES. That's my script! — Give it to me!
ANA (*still laughing*). Are any of the women in this twaddle based on me?
CERVANTES. In the first place, it's not twaddle. In the second place, I don't like your sneaking it out of the room and peeking in it. — It's not a diary, you know. It's just a pastoral novel.
ANA. Well, you left it in bed!

CERVANTES. I was *preoccupied* in bed...now let me have it!
ANA. Who wants to read a pastoral novel that starts by promising something — let me go — and delivers very little?
CERVANTES. I'll keep kissing you until you hand it over —
ANA. Here, then. Take it.
CERVANTES. The public *goes* for this kind of romance.
ANA. Well, I'm the public, and I don't go for it.
CERVANTES. Besides, it just might sell a few copies...that is, if my luck changes. If it will *ever* change.
ANA. You feel you're pursued by hard luck?
CERVANTES. Positively. Misfortune *delights* in pursuing men of genius.
ANA. Now, I *like* that! A good estimate of yourself! You should proclaim genius, instead of beating your breast over back luck. — Promise you'll stop writing junk. Swear to it.
CERVANTES. This is definitely not junk, my sweet, but I'll swear to anything just now.
ANA. No, a real oath.
CERVANTES. I swear by the kidney stones of Charlemagne, I swear by the soiled britches of the giant Fierabras, I swear by the two left feet of the bastard son of the illegitimate nephew of our laundrywoman, herself a princess in disguise, I swear by my Lady Ana Franca de Rojas, who is even now listening to me with her mouth open, I swear by all the entrances and exits of her body —

Music: A lively passage wipes out the scene, but diminishes quickly under:

MORQUECHO. Have a seat, Señor — uh — Sermentis.
CERVANTES. Thank you.
MORQUECHO. I'm sorry it's taken me so long to get to your application.
CERVANTES (*archly*). Yes, it has been long.
MORQUECHO. You're lucky to get to see me at all...I'm a man of some importance in the court, if I say so myself.
CERVANTES. Señor, when I asked for an audience with Don Juan of Austria, the victor of Lepanto in whose forces I fought —
MORQUECHO. You don't have to tell me who Don Juan was. He's dead now, sad to say. And that letter you have from him is just a scrap of paper. — Now about your application. You mention that you served His Majesty for twenty-two years —
CERVANTES. Campaigns on land and sea...Corfu, Tunis, Naples, Portugal...
MORQUECHO (*impatiently*). Yes, yes. You were paid for all that, I believe.

CERVANTES (*angrily*). Paid? What about my ransom? All my parents' property, and the dowry of two sisters, went into buying my release from that dungeon in Algiers! I'm still paying off debts. My sister Andrea had to give up her —

MORQUECHO. In this petition you ask for quite a lot. You ask for a post abroad, without any proof that you're nearly as well qualified as the younger, experienced, substantial men who've been around His Majesty's court for years, and who are fully acquainted with the workings of —

CERVANTES. I have never asked for a *favor*, and I don't ask one now. I applied a good while back to be considered for *announced vacancies* in the services abroad.

MORQUECHO. Those posts have all been filled.

CERVANTES. They weren't all filled when I inquired, repeatedly, over the past few months.

MORQUECHO. Well, they are now.

CERVANTES. Why wasn't I notified in all this time?

MORQUECHO. We have more important things to do than notify rejected candidates. Isn't there some work you can find here at home?

CERVANTES. Such as what?

MORQUECHO. Well, anything?

CERVANTES. A one-handed porter? Carpenter? Mason? Painter? Ditch digger?

MORQUECHO. You can't use the hand at all?

CERVANTES. Do you mean to tell me that in all of the great Spanish empire that stretches across half the world...in all the countries where we quarter governors and regiments, in all our thriving outposts in France, Italy, Hungary, Flanders, Peru, Mexico, the Indies...in all those possessions there is no service I can do? — Are you really saying that?

MORQUECHO. Let me point out something, Sermantes. You have no degree of any kind...your military rank stopped at lieutenant. Besides, you have no patron. That makes it very difficult.

CERVANTES. So I've noticed.

MORQUECHO. Have you tried the municipal office?

CERVANTES. Yes.

MORQUECHO. The office of commerce?

CERVANTES. Yes, and the office of the privy council and the office of the President of Castile, and the office of the war minister, and so on down the whole directory.

MORQUECHO. And they held out no encouragement?

CERVANTES. No more than you do.

MORQUECHO (*shrug*). Well, these are hard times.
CERVANTES. Not for the opportunists and charlatans who fill offices like this, while the competent ones —
MORQUECHO. Just a moment! How dare you insult me? This interview is over!
CERVANTES. It was over the minute I came in. I waited ten whole months to talk to you, and you can damn well keep your seat until I've finished saying what I have to say. The court seems to have no regard for time. The simplest business is dragged on for years. All you hear is, "I shall look into it…" "we shall deal with the matter…" "we're doing our best…" One has to doff his hat even to speak to a doorman, and if you don't tip and bribe all sorts of flunkies, you never get in to see *anybody*. I apparently tipped too little to get to see you sooner. Not that it would have mattered, I'm sure.
MORQUECHO (*rising*). Let me tell you something, Sermantes —
CERVANTES (*sharply*). Cervantes! — Miguel de Cervantes Saavedra! Goddam it, at least get my name right!
MORQUECHO. Look here, Cervantes: there are martyrs and heroes in every village. You can find Algerian and Greek and Turkish adventurers on street corners and in taverns, bragging about their exploits and cadging drinks from gullible listeners. Now you may be several cuts above them — maybe you're one of the "competents" as you put it — but unfortunately there is no place for you at this time, in any of the offices under the purview of this department. If you wish, I'll put your name down on the waiting list for possible openings of a clerical nature somewhere. But you should know that there are about two hundred names ahead of yours. Perhaps a year's worth.
CERVANTES. Thank you for nothing.

Music: Wipe out

Door opens; closes. A few footsteps.

CERVANTES (*calling*). Sister?
ANDREA (*from off*). I'm in here.

More steps as Cervantes enters her room.

ANDREA. Any luck on the rounds?
CERVANTES. None. — What are you reading?
ANDREA. Chivalry, for a changed. Just started it.

CERVANTES. I've read that one.

ANDREA. Any good?

CERVANTES. It's astounding.

ANDREA. In what way?

CERVANTES. It's so thoroughly, sublimely stupid.

ANDREA. Really? It seems fairly well-written so far.

CERVANTES. Sister, do you know that a knight-errant never does a day's work? Never! There is no recorded instance of a knight paying for lodgings at an inn, or for a meal at a tavern. In books of chivalry — and I've read damn near all of them — a knight never pays a tailor, or a barber, or a surgeon.

ANDREA. What about the armor-maker? The lance-maker?

CERVANTES. They never send bills. Everything's complimentary. It has not yet entered the head of any of these writers that a boot-maker has to earn a living making boots, and a farmer from tilling soil so he can grow the corn that feeds the cow that grows the beef that the knight swills in order to be strong and valiant so he can go around rescuing maidens and righting wrongs.

ANDREA. What kind of wrongs?

CERVANTES. Well for one thing, knights are very hard on giants. Merely to be a giant is an abominable wrong, a grievously conspicuous sign of evil. And giants must have magnificent names, which makes them even worse. Take for example Curaculiambro of Malindrania. There he is, minding his own business, staggering under the weight he carries, knocking his head on the lintels of doorways, having to feed his oversized gut. And then suddenly a knight-errant who has nothing to do except burn up energy stored from years of fantastic chastity, comes down on the giant with a meat cleaver.

ANDREA. Does a knight-errant ever get beaten, or are they invincible?

CERVANTES. Oh, some may be vincible, but only to other knights.

ANDREA. Do they have bowel movements, like the rest of us?

CERVANTES. No, no. Knights and princesses are not prone to either major or minor excretions.

ANDREA. They never fart?

CERVANTES. Not audibly, anyway. They never pass wind or water. They never sweat. They may bleed, you understand, but they have magic ointments that restore the head on the neck in a matter of minutes and the scar doesn't even show.

ANDREA. You know so much about them, why don't you write a book of chivalry yourself?

CERVANTES. The authors of that rubbish ought to be sent to the galleys.

ANDREA. How about your friend Lope de Vega?
CERVANTES. What about him?
ANDREA. Wouldn't you like to see him in irons, too?
CERVANTES. Why? Because he's so successful?
ANDREA. No, because he says nasty things about you behind your back.
CERVANTES. So he doesn't like my sonnets. That's no reason to hate him.
ANDREA. It's shocking the way he runs around with women.
CERVANTES. If it's a pleasant shock to the ladies, what harm?
ANDREA. He married a seventeen-year-old.
CERVANTES. What's the crime there?
ANDREA. None, strictly speaking, but he's carrying on all over the city at the same time.
CERVANTES. Really, Andrea, there are bigger problems. In fact, what you're reading is one of them.
ANDREA. In what way is it a problem?
CERVANTES. Because there's a kind of chivalry sickness in this country. Do you realize how many ignorant people are impressed by these absurdities? They create whole systems and attitudes. I sometimes think if I can ever get away from having to grub for a living, I might write something to lay all this nonsense to rest.
ANDREA. Before you come around to that, what don't you get married?
CERVANTES. *Married?* What for? To find out later what sort of man my wife would have preferred?
ANDREA. Oh, don't be so negative, so cynical.
CERVANTES. Marriage is a heavy thing.
ANDREA. But there are two to carry it.
CERVANTES. Sometimes three.
ANDREA. You need someone to take care of you.
CERVANTES. Are you suggesting I marry a nurse?
ANDREA. I know about a woman in Esquivias. I've met her. Considered a catch by every young buck in the region. I could arrange a meeting, so it wouldn't look planned.
CERVANTES. Hymen's little helper.
ANDREA. How about next Sunday after mass?
CERVANTES. What's her name?
ANDREA. Catalina de Salazar y Palacios Vozmedia.
CERVANTES (*after a pause*). Not Sunday. Maybe some time next month. Meanwhile I've got a lady who keeps me warm.

Music: Wipeout, segueing to an organ passage of Gregorian mode, which diminishes behind:

CERVANTES. Father, I have a train of confessions.
PRIEST. Begin.
CERVANTES. I've been pawning articles belonging to my family.
PRIEST. What kind of articles?
CERVANTES. Well, for example, five rolls of taffeta that were given to one of my sisters. — I needed the money.
PRIEST. Did you do it with the permission of your sister?
CERVANTES. Of course.
PRIEST. That's hardly a sin. Unless you used the money for some sinful purpose.
CERVANTES. I am using it for the support of a child.
PRIEST. An admirable use.
CERVANTES. The child is illegitimate.
PRIEST. Still an admirable use.
CERVANTES. The child is my own. A daughter.[4]
PRIEST. Oh. (*Pause.*) Who is the mother?
CERVANTES. An actress.
PRIEST. Are you planning to marry?
CERVANTES. Yes, but not the actress.
PRIEST. Who, then?
CERVANTES. A woman from the village of Esquivias.[5]
PRIEST. Is there anything you have to confess in relation to the woman from Esquivias?
CERVANTES. No, except that she's eighteen years younger than I.
PRIEST. There's nothing in the canons of the Church against that. What's going to happen to the mother of your child?
CERVANTES. She's marrying someone else.
PRIEST. Who will keep the little girl?
CERVANTES. I. My sisters and mother will take care of her.
PRIEST. With the consent of the child's mother?
CERVANTES. Yes.
PRIEST. Then it's nothing very serious. Say a hundred *Our Fathers*, attend mass faithfully, and keep your thoughts pure and your actions likewise. Deo gratias —
CERVANTES. I haven't finished.
PRIEST. Oh? Go on.
CERVANTES. I've had no luck with my writing, so for some time I've been looking for other work. Recently a job has been offered to me... District Collector for the Royal Treasury. It would mean going around

---

4. Isabel de Saavedra, Cervantes' daughter with Ana de Villafranca.
5. Cervantes married Catalina de Salazar y Palacios Vozmedia in 1584.

commandeering supplies and goods for the Armada.[6] I need the work desperately, but hard up as I am, I'm not sure I should take it.

PRIEST. Why not?

CERVANTES. Because I'll be required by the job to appropriate — to seize, if need be — grain, oil, wine, barely, cheese, bacon, and a lot of other supplies. In effect, I'll be raiding the pantries of poor and low-income people who already have enough worries, what with widespread unemployment. All my life I've felt close to humble people. So how can I turn around now and harass them?

PRIEST. My good man, we are both aware of the coming war, and of the needs of the King's Armada. Have you asked yourself, the coming war against *whom*? Against the mortal enemy of our country and the Holy Church! Against that Protestant monster, that desecrator of the throne of England, the unspeakable Queen Elizabeth! Against her pirates who constantly prey on our shipping! Now how can you hesitate for a *moment*, to do everything in your power to help the Armada cast its thunderbolts against the shameless apostates of that godless island?

CERVANTES. So you're saying, in effect, it *wouldn't* be a sin against my conscience if I took that job?

PRIEST. Haven't you been listening to a word I've said? Of *course* it wouldn't be a sin, neither against your conscience nor the Lord!

CERVANTES. But there's one thing I should mention: It will also be my duty to collect from churches as well as merchants and workers and farmers. (*A silence.*) From monasteries, too. (*More silence.*) The clergy are expected to contribute a share of their stores, like everybody else.

Another silence.

CERVANTES. Father?

PRIEST. Ah, yes. — Well, now, you must use discretion. There is an Armada of the spirit as well as the flesh. The battles of heaven are even more arduous than those fought on land or sea. You must be extremely discreet in maintaining a balance between the needs of the corporeal world, and the requirements of the soul. Because, after all, the soul of every one of us is accountable to the Maker of us all.

CERVANTES. I understand. Peasants and workers support the Armada with crops and taxes, the clergy will support it with prayers.

PRIEST. Exactly, my son. — Do you have anything else to confess?

CERVANTES. Not at this time.

PRIEST. Then do as I have said, and go in peace.

---

6. The Spanish Armada, which was defeated by the British Navy in 1588.

Music: Transition to open country, cross-fading to:

Country sounds; intermittent distant church bells. In the foreground, forty or fifty people.

CERVANTES *(addressing the crowd)*. My friends, I want to thank you for taking time out of the Lord's Day to meet me here in the plaza. I come with orders from the department of the treasury to collect six hundred fanegas of barley and thirty-five hundred arribas of oil from this district. (*Crowd murmur.*) Please don't think of it as taxes — it's more like a loan. Each of you will get a receipt. Please bear in mind that the supplies you give us are for your sons, for your brothers who are about to go off to fight in a holy war, for loved ones ready to give up their lives, if need be, for Spain and for the King, for you and for me.

    Believe me, good people, if I had strength in this maimed hand and less gray in this beard, I'd be in Lisbon right now with the Armada, getting ready to do my part once more, as I did at the great battle of Lepanto when most of you were children. I assure you that everybody is being taxed a fair share, including rich people, including hidalgos, including bishops and parish priests. Tell the truth, I had a hard time over in Écija last week because I had to confiscate grain the church was hoarding. Yes — yes, I had to order the arrest of that sacristan for refusing to comply.

Crowd reacts.

CERVANTES. Now I'm as good a Catholic as ever attended mass, but when it comes to violating the law, I have no choice. Believe me, I'm fully sympathetic to your problems. But if it were not myself doing this job, it would be someone else, perhaps harder on you than I am. After all, there are some people who like to give orders, if only to a herd of cattle. I always say every man is as Heaven made him, and sometimes a great deal worse.

Under the foregoing, the sound of a horse approaches at a moderate gallop.

CERVANTES. I see we're getting a visitor.

The horse is reined to a stop and the rider dismounts.

RIDER *(shouting)*. You up there, are you the purveyor Cervantes Saavedra?

CERVANTES. I am. Who are you?

RIDER. An Officer authorized by the Ecclesiastical Prelature of Córdoba to apprehend you for grievous and repeated offenses against the Holy Church, as stated in the venire facias from which I now read, before public witness: (*Crowd reaction.*) "It is ordained that Miguel de Cervantes Saavedra, by order of the Provincial Office of the Inquisition, be immediately and henceforward anathematized and excommunicated, his name to be posted in black for display in all the churches, pending trial by ecclesiastic authority on the date slated in the accompanying writ of monition, then and there to answer to the following charges: First, that on the fifth of this month, he — "

Music: Swallows up the scene.

Interior of a cavernous court. Echoes.

FIRST INQUISITOR. What do you say to the charges?

CERVANTES. Innocent by reason of duties laid upon me as a servant of the Royal Treasury.

SECOND INQUISITOR. What answer to the Ordinances of Purity?

CERVANTES. I am of legitimate birth, baptized, and without any trace of the blood of Moors, Jews, or converts.

FIRST INQUISITOR. You were accused by the priest Blanco de Paz, of having conducted yourself in an un-Christian manner whilst in captivity in Algiers.

CERVANTES. Algiers? How dare he! Not true! Moreover it's been fifteen years since I —

FIRST INQUISITOR. Were you or were you not accused?

CERVANTES (*angrily*). Yes! By the traitor Blanco de Paz! I did not then, nor do I now, consider that priest to have been other than —

SECOND INQUISITOR. Silence! We have in our possession the interrogatories involving that period.

CERVANTES. I am glad to hear that! I humbly ask you to read the conclusions!

SECOND INQUISITOR. That has been done. Under seal of the notary apostolic you were declared by two apprizers to be courageous and sympathetic in your conduct at Algiers.

CERVANTES. Then I stand vindicated! My innocence has been established!

FIRST INQUISITOR. Not so! — The account of Father de Paz has not been *disproven*, only challenged! And what you call your innocence has lately been blemished, publicly, by your exercise of bad judgment.

CERVANTES. What bad judgment?

SECOND INQUISITOR. You know very well. In the village of Écija. There, as *everywhere*, you should have respected the sanctity of the Church that nourished you, should you not? (*No answer. More severely.*) Should you not? — Answer!
CERVANTES (*it comes hard*). Yes.
FIRST INQUISITOR. You should have honored the cleric who remonstrated against you — should you not?
CERVANTES. Yes.
SECOND INQUISITOR. You should have quit your employment rather than cause a sacristan of the Church to be arrested — should you not?
CERVANTES. Yes.
FIRST INQUISITOR. Do you repent of your action? (*No answer.*) Do you repent of your —
CERVANTES. I do.
FIRST INQUISITOR. Do you solemnly swear to make restitution of the seized stores?
CERVANTES. So far as lies within my power.
FIRST INQUISITOR. Stand forward to receive sentence.
SECOND INQUISITOR. Your term of excommunication shall be extended for an additional sixty days, during which period you will be denied the grace of the Church. You will be closely observed. You are dismissed by the order and mercy of the Office of the Holy Inquisition. — Sanctus, Dominus Deus.

Music: As before. When it concludes:

Interior of a tavern. Background voices. Some laughter.

CERVANTES. God, Pablo, I feel filthy.
PABLO. You shouldn't. Drink up. — Look, it's mad to argue with the Inquisition. Not when they torture a man for not fasting on Friday, and execute another for befriending a Jew. — You did the right thing. You saved your neck.
CERVANTES. Well, I suppose there *are* good uses for cowardice and rashness. In Algiers, I was rash when cowardice would have killed me. Yesterday I was cowardly when rashness would have killed me.
PABLO. Exactly. (*Lowering his voice.*) Ha! Here comes the actor Emilio Bazan. He's told me several times he'd like to meet you.
CERVANTES. I just as soon not. A failed playwright isn't comfortable with actors.
PABLO. Well, just say hello. We don't have to ask him to join us.

BAZAN (*approaching*). Ah, Pablo! And Señor Cervantes, I recognize you! (*Ad lib introductions.*) I feel I know you, because I was in your play *Numantia*[7] years ago! I saw you at rehearsal once, but we were not introduced.

CERVANTES. Ah, yes. — Well…

BAZAN. *Numantia* was a wonderful play! Ahead of its time! It should be by all means revived.

CERVANTES (*brightening*). Oh? — Well, thank you.

BAZAN. I've long wanted to look you up, but never knew where to find you.

CERVANTES. Well, here I am. — Why don't you join us for a drink? Pull up a chair.

BAZAN. Thank you. (*Sound of handling chair.*) Are you still writing plays?

CERVANTES. No, I gave up on it. Besides, how can a play get put on these days if it's not written by Lope de Vega? He's got six companies performing around the country right this minute — in Seville…Burgos…Valencia…Madrid…Granada…Valladolid…

BAZAN. So what are you doing these days, if I may ask?

CERVANTES. Odds and ends. Composing odes. I wrote two on the Armada. First when it set sail, then when it went down. I even got off an ode to kidney disease. It celebrates both kidneys. (*Laughs.*) Lately, though, I've been toying with the notion of a batty knight-errant who goes wandering around looking for excuses to be chivalrous.

BAZAN. I hope you'll be getting back to plays.

PABLO. So do I.

CERVANTES. No, I've had quite enough of sour critics and empty seats.

BAZAN. Don't go by that. You've been slandered!

CERVANTES. Well, it's not unusual for creative people to be envied by hacks who delight in *pissing*, rather than passing, on the works of others…It's their favorite sport.

PABLO. Flea-hunters, all of them. They look for spots on the surface of the sun, or carefully count the number of times Homer nodded, never how much time he spent awake, how much light he shed, and how little shade.

BAZAN. Has there ever been a totally flawless writer?

CERVANTES. No writer past or present is without flaws. I have more than my share, I can tell you.

BAZAN. But maybe what you think is a flaw in your writing, is like one of those moles which add to the beauty of a face.

CERVANTES. Pablo, I should have this fellow around all the time. Really, Señor Bazan, you must come to see me. I live over by the Junk Market.

---

7. *The Siege of Numantia*, performed about 1586.

BAZAN. How is it out that way?

CERVANTES. Dull, except for an occasional uproar like one that took place last week. Outside my house, a man was stabbed. I heard sounds of a scuffle, then a loud cry, and footsteps running away. When I went out to see what happened, there, lying in the street, was a man bleeding to death. I carried him into the house, and sent for a surgeon and priest. The man died before they got there. The police showed up and closely questioned me, my sisters and a niece who's staying with us, and warned us that we all may be clapped in prison while the investigation goes on.

BAZAN. How can they get away with doing that?

PABLO. You don't know our police.

CERVANTES. It doesn't help that living next door to us is a venomous widow, a nosey old bitch who thinks we're running a whorehouse because three women and a man live there. — But listen, Bazan, you must come and visit me. And it you find nobody home, you'll know we're still in prison.

Music: Closes the scene.

CERVANTES (*with surprise*). Catalina!

CATALINA. I came as soon as I heard. — Why didn't you write?

CERVANTES. I didn't want you worrying.

CATALINA (*not scolding*). That's the prerogative of a wife. The story I got — is it true?

CERVANTES. Yes. Lunatic, but true. We could be arrested any minute. The four of us. My sisters, my niece, and myself.

CATALINA. But good heavens, Miguel, all you did was to help a dying man! How can they possibly —

CERVANTES. Instead of trying to track down the murderer, they're using all kinds of diversions. We happen to be a diversion.

CATALINA. I don't understand.

CERVANTES. It's simple. Somebody high up wants to protect the killer. It turns out the dead man had been carrying on an affair with the wife of a prominent notary. The victim had been warned several times. Threatened with death.

CATALINA. Then why haven't they arrested the notary? In all probability he hired the assassin.

CERVANTES. Oh, that's too quick and simple a solution.

CATALINA. You mean they haven't *thought* of it?

CERVANTES. Oh, they've thought of it, all right. But why disturb a magistrate, when you can harass a writer and his family?

CATALINA. If you go to prison, how long can they hold you?

CERVANTES. I don't know. Probably until their joke of an investigation is over.

CATALINA (*after a pause*). I'd like to stay with you this time. — May I?

CERVANTES. Of course you may.

CATALINA. I've often thought you didn't want to — to be with me.

CERVANTES. I know I've been a poor husband to you, Catalina. (*Silence.*) From the start.

CATALINA. No, you were kind and gentle. — I'm sure resistance from my family didn't help. Every time you came to visit, it was as though a leper had arrived among them.

CERVANTES. Everyone except you old uncle would be suddenly called to Toledo, or to a baptism, or a wedding, or to attend a sick cow. After all, you had married an old, maimed cradle-robber unfit for physical work, a struggling writer, a misfit. — I thought after a time, you *welcomed* my long absences on the road.

CATALINA (*after a slight hesitation*). I did.

CERVANTES. I blame you for nothing. — How is Esquivias?

CATALINA. Quiet, as usual. — How is your book coming?

CERVANTES. Slowly. My Quixote is in almost as much trouble as I am. (*Laughs.*) The furies work impartially against both of us. The main difference is that when Quixote is enchanted, he's simply out of his head, whereas when *I'm* enchanted, I'm just out of luck.

CATALINA. Where are your sisters and your niece?

CERVANTES. Attending mass. Probably to complain to the Virgin. I don't expect the Mother of God will help much. I think she must have a deaf side when it comes to struggling writers. After all, it was words, not miracles, that got her Son into trouble.

CATALINA (*gently*). Don't blaspheme, Miguel.

CERVANTES. I'm sorry — I apologize. You're pious, and I respect that.

CATALINA. You're disturbed. — You have every right to be.

CERVANTES. No, that was careless of me.

CATALINA (*after a pause*). Oh Miguel, are things ever going to be better?

CERVANTES. They've got to be. The worst was last year, when I had to borrow money to buy a suit. Dame Hard Luck has been pursuing me, but maybe she'll get tired of it. — Speaking of tired, you must be worn out from the journey. Let me draw a bath for you.

CATALINA. No, I'll just rest for a while. — Your sisters keep a neat house. I see you still have the chalice, after all these years.

CERVANTES. Ah, you remember it.

CATALINA. How could I forget it? It was part of your dowry — five vines, four pieces of furniture, forty-five hens, a chalice of polished onyx…

CERVANTES. And a bride of polished gold, Catalina Salazar y Palacios Vozmedia, whom I love very much in my poor, halting, inadequate way.

Music: Transition.

Interior of a prison. Some background noise; occasional indistinguishable voices, the sounds of iron doors, unobtrusive.

PRISONER. Welcome to the grand calaboose.
CERVANTES. My honor.
PRISONER. I thought I saw you come in with some ladies.
CERVANTES. My family. They're in the women's section.
PRISONER. Family, huh? Are you all thieves, like us?
CERVANTES. It happens we're not.
PRISONER. Myself, I work as a thief but I pimp on the side. That's what I'm in for this time. Pimping. — You've never stolen?
CERVANTES. I'm afraid not.
PRISONER. Well, it won't take you long to catch on. We have great teachers here in every branch of felony.
CERVANTES. Apparently the course on how to keep from getting caught hasn't been entirely successful.
PRISONER. You forget all those who *haven't* been caught! What we have is a kind of crime school. It may look like a flea farm and smell like a sewer, but you'll find among us the very best in the business — murderers, blackmailers, highwaymen, kidnappers, embezzlers. I warrant every one of us Christians is at the service of God, charity, and all good people.
CERVANTES. I never knew thieves to be at the service of God and charity. How does that work?
PRISONER. See, every honest criminal in the business gives money to buy oil for the Sacred Lamp here in the city. I swear by my mother's navel that, taken all in all, we're a pious bunch. Most of us never steal on Good Friday, or speak to any women named Mary on a Sunday.
CERVANTES. Do you go to confession?
PRISONER (*offended*). Of course not.
CERVANTES. Suppose you're excommunicated?
PRISONER. We don't hear of it.
CERVANTES. Why?
PRISONER. Because we're never in church when it's announced. The only time we go is on a feast day, when the cathedral is packed, and there are plenty of pockets to pick. — What are you in for?

CERVANTES. Samaritanism.
PRISONER. Is that like fornication or buggery?
CERVANTES. Neither. It's going to the help somebody in trouble. Have you never heard of the Good Samaritan?
PRISONER. Wasn't he the guy hanged for rape in Córdoba?
CERVANTES. No no no, the Good Samaritan is a character in the Bible.
PRISONER. The *Bible?* You mean you can *read?* That's marvelous! We don't see many of your kind here, except lawyers who work for those of us as can afford 'em. (*Struck by an idea.*) Do y'think you could defend me on the pimp charge?
CERVANTES. I doubt that very much.
PRISONER. Why not try? What's there to lose? — Suppose I'm a judge, and you're in court speaking up for me.
CERVANTES. No, no, I'm not an actor. Or a clown.
PRISONER. Oh come on, try. It'll help pass the time. Come on.
CERVANTES (*after some hesitation, deciding to play along*). Worthy Magistrates…(*Pause.*)…Worthy Magistrates…
PRISONER. You already said that.
CERVANTES. I submit that this gentleman does not rate being sent to the galleys for the act of pimping. A dreg he is, to be sure — a carbuncle on the posterior of Spain — a fistula in the very rectum of rectitude —
PRISONER (*complimented*). Am I really? All that?
CERVANTES. Oh, and more. — But Honorable Judges, the office of pimp is performed by purveyors of distinction, since their labors gratify not merely one, but three parties; to wit, the seeker of recreation; the willing collaborator who puts her person — the whole of it — into the engagement — and the broker, which is to say, the pimp. All three profit from the transaction — and of how many arrangements in the secular world can this be said?
PRISONER. You're doing great. Go on.
CERVANTES. Given the attrition that works against the average marriage, where the wife fills out like a blowfish, and the husband goes stale with familiarity, where a mistress is a continual running expense costing even when not in use, like a seaside cabin in winter — given all these things, do you not discern the merit of the pimp?

Your Honor, if we exalt priests, who are stewards of a dubious peace on earth, why should we not honor pimps, who are intermediaries of a peace in bed? Pimps are but prompters of the carnal dialogue which began in the Garden of Eden, and which has come down unadulterated to the present.

Weigh this, worthy judges, and out of your copious store of wisdom, I beseech you to augment and compound the sentence you have in mind for this odious debaucher, this mucilaginous reprobate, this unparalleled excrescence of humanity.

PRISONER. That was great! Just beautiful! You could be a big help to me and my buddies and lady workers when you get out of this place. — If you do get out, that is. I take it you're not in for life?

CERVANTES. I would like to believe that.

PRISONER. Friend — to show you how much I appreciate the way you defended me, I want you to have this little token. — No, go ahead, take it.

CERVANTES. Two ducats!

PRISONER. I picked your pocket.

CERVANTES. But I had three ducats.

PRISONER. One is for charity.

Music: Playoff.

Interior, with very light echo.

ROYAL LICENSER. "Notice of Royal Privilege: Inasmuch as we have been informed that Miguel de Cervantes Savaadra has composed a book entitled *The Ingenious Gentlemen of La Mancha*, which book has cost him much labor and is a very useful work; and inasmuch as he has petitioned us to grant him a license to have it printed; and inasmuch as the said book has been duly scrutinized by the proper authorities, it has been decided to grant him permission for the said purpose, which we right willingly do."

Music: Fanfare.

CERVANTES. Well, there! You see? It's been *published*, Catalina![8] On sale for two hundred ninety-and-a-half maravedis...a small price for so big an adventure. Overnight! Overnight, I tell you! Yesterday, a mediocre writer! Today, an ornament to Spain! Remarkable, how suddenly the country's taste has improved! Oh, the sweet savor of fame! Now if only I'll be paid what's due me.

CATALINA (*beaming*). In the market yesterday I heard a man say to another, "Have you read *Don Quixote*?" And the other said, "Of course! Do you think I'm illiterate?" (*Laughs.*)

---

8. *The Ingenious Gentlemen Don Quixote of La Mancha*, published in 1605.

CERVANTES. Editions in Barcelona, Lisbon, Antwerp, Paris, London! — Last night, Dr. Ortega said to me, "There's a rumor you wrote *Quixote* in prison." And I replied, "Why, because some of the sentences are very long?"

CATALINA. (*Laughs.*)

CERVANTES. A barmaid told me she was halfway through the book, and I told her that the best was not all behind her. Then I added, "What you *do* have behind you is quite pretty, I must say." (*Laughs.*)

CATALINA (*good-naturedly*). Shame on you. (*Change of tone.*) Have you heard from Lope de Vega?

CERVANTES. No. One of the side benefits of all this, is the certainty that Lope must be seething with jealousy. He can't stand not being cock-of-the-walk!

CATALINA. You still think he was behind the pirated edition?

CERVANTES. I do. It wouldn't surprise me if he made up the author's name. Who ever heard of "Alonso de Avellaneda"?[9]

CATALINA. Have you read the book?

CERVANTES. Yes. It's godawful. Vulgar. Shoddy.

CATALINA. The worse it is, the better for you, no?

CERVANTES. I'm going down to the bookshop today to see whether it's selling at all. The only thing is, I might run into Lope. He goes there a lot. Goes for two reasons: to see how his books are selling, and to keep an eye on the proprietress, with whom he's having an affair.

CATALINA. If you don't want to see Lope, then stay away.

CERVANTES. My dear, Lope de Vega is not going to dictate my coming and going.

CATALINA. Besides, you're not feeling well enough to upset yourself.

CERVANTES. It will make me feel a lot better to know that the Avellaneda piracy is not selling.

CATALINA (*resigned*). I wouldn't go if I were you.

Music: Another part of town.

LOPE. Don't move! Stand there with that duster poised just as you are. You look like a figure on a Greek vase. A young Athena cleaning her temple. A little overdressed, perhaps.

ALTISORA. I know you prefer your goddesses underdressed.

LOPE. I didn't expect to find you alone, minding the shop.

ALTISORA. My husband is down with a bad back.

LOPE. If he strained it in your service, it's worth the pain.

---

9. Alonso Fernández Avellaneda's true identify is still a literary mystery.

ALTISORA. You should know. — Have you been busy?
LOPE. Writing.
ALTISORA. Is that all?
LOPE. That's never all. How many of the Avellaneda *Quixote* have you sold?
ALTISORA. Two or three.
LOPE. That few? — Well, it'll take some time to catch on. Personally, I prefer the Avellaneda to the Cervantes. It's more lifelike. — Does old Miguel ever come in?
ALTISORA. Now and then. He looks poorly. I shouldn't be surprised if he's got an affliction of the urine. That's how it is with men when they get old.
LOPE. I've heard that can happen.
ALTISORA. I must say I enjoyed his book. I laughed a lot and cried a little.
LOPE. Yes, there are some nice things in it.
ATLISORA. Some wisdom, too.
LOPE. If you want to call it that. Miguel used to show up at the theater, but his plays were such dismal failures, I suppose it's painful for him to return to the scene of his crimes. Have you read any of his poetry?
ALTISORA. Some.
LOPE. Embarrassing.
ALTISORA (*surprised*). You think so?
LOPE. Most of it is like badly scrambled eggs. He once had the effrontery to write a sonnet making a joke at my expense.
ALTISORA. Are you sure it was you he meant?
LOPE. No question of it.
ALTISORA. I know at least three writers who think *they* were meant.
LOPE. All right, forget the sonnet. Take his *Quixote*. It's full of veiled references to me and my work. Didn't you recognize them?
ALTISORA. I wasn't looking for them.
LOPE. Of course, I don't pay it the slightest heed, nor does it bother me.
ALTISORA. So I gather.
LOPE (*defensively*). Wasn't I one of the judges who awarded him a prize for a poem he entered in a competition at the beatification of Saint Teresa?
ALTISORA. Then it must have been a good poem.
LOPE. Not really. I took pity on the old curmudgeon, and voted for him. He's tried so hard, and he's so full of the envy and malice that are the comfort of the mediocre. Ever since Lepanto, he's made a big thing of that hand he lost. You'd think he was the only man ever wounded in battle.
ALTISORA. But if that comforts him, let him enjoy it.

LOPE. The trouble is, he enjoys nothing. Whereas I, on the other hand, enjoy everything. My rod and my staff, they comfort me.
ALTISORA. Kindly take your hands off my chest, Lope.
LOPE. Just to make sure...
ALTISORA. Are you satisfied they're still there?
LOPE. I'm reassured, but not yet satisfied.
ALTISORA. Let me go. I have work to do. — I believe you're jealous of Cervantes.
LOPE. Jealous? That's funny enough to be in one of my comedies.
ALTISORA. Especially about his novel.
LOPE. Oh well, as I said, there *are* some good things in it. But as someone remarked at dinner last night, most of it is merely good for wrapping grocery or, better still, to be used in a privy. And speaking of privy-goers, here's the great man himself crossing the street. God, he looks in a bad way.

Door opens, closes.

LOPE. Cervantes! How good to see you!
CERVANTES. Lope de Vega! What a pleasant surprise! It's been a long time.
LOPE. Yes...not since the poetry competition at the beatification.
CERVANTES. For which I have you to thank, in part.
LOPE. It was a privilege to reward a distinguished and gifted fellow artist.
CERVANTES. Thank you again. — You look the pinnacle of prosperity. I only wish I could be half as prolific as you. Just the other day I was wondering how many plays you have done.
LOPE. Oh, I've lost count.
CERVANTES. There's a rumor you've written over two thousand.
LOPE. Give or take a few hundred.[10]
CERVANTES. And every one a gem. To say nothing of your lyrics, and the epic poems. No wonder they call you King of the Theater and the Phoenix of Spain.
LOPE (*dryly*). As well as the Monster of Nature.
CERVANTES (*laughs a little hollowly*). Ah yes, I did allude to you that way in *Quixote*, but it was in an admiring context, intended in good fun.
LOPE. And that is exactly how I understood it. I hope you are feeling as well as you look, Cervantes.
CERVANTES. I hope I look better than *that*, but thank you, nevertheless. And yourself? And the Señora?

---

10. Lope de Vega is credited with about 1,800 plays.

LOPE. Very well, thank you. But she will be vexed with me for being late. — Well, how good to run into you, my old friend.
CERVANTES. And I the same.
LOPE. God go with you.
CERVANTES. And may He continue to smile on you.

Door opens, closes.

CERVANTES. My dear Altisora, have you ever seen such a display of mutual hypocrisy? The man detests me. He defames me at every turn. He simply can't stand another peak in the Alps.
ALTISORA. You really think so?
CERVANTES. Here is proof positive, right in your own merchandise. — This book.

Handling of book; turning a few pages.

CERVANTES (*reading aloud*). "Second volume of *The Ingenious Knight, Don Quixote of La Mancha*...written by Alonzo de Avellaneda, native of the town of Tordesillas."
ALTISORA. We've sold only three copies to date.
CERVANTES. Now I ask you, who could resent me so much that he'd want to pirate my invention, to steal outright my Quixote and Sancho Panza? They're as much a part of me as my two arms. What am I to assume, when the preface attacks me in the almost the same words that Lope has been saying about me right along? — Here, read this out loud.
ALTISORA. "Because of his age, Cervantes dislikes everybody and everything, and as a result has so few friends that no one will demean himself by speaking his name. Let us excuse the faults of his *Quixote* on the ground that it was written in prison, so it could not fail to emerge with a prison taint, or be anything but vindictive and choleric..." That's terrible.
CERVANTES. He ridicules me for being old and one-handed, as though it were in my power to make time stand still; as though I'd lost my hand in some tavern brawl.
ALTISORA. What does he have against you?
CERVANTES. Envy! It's true I took some nips at him in *Quixote*, but I didn't abuse him or attack his genius, a genius I freely acknowledge and admire.
ALTISORA. It's a pity that two such important writers as you and he —

CERVANTES. One good thing this plagiarism *has* done for me is to set me writing *Quixote Part* II.[11] I suppose I have Lope to thank for spurring me to a sequel while I'm still able to put words on paper.

ALTISORA. I'm glad you're doing it.

CERVANTES. I leave you with one additional proof. Do you know Lope's book called *Jerusalem Conquered?*

ALTISORA. No.

CERVANTES. Well, in it he mentions the name of every writer of merit in Spain. My name does not appear. I cannot, for the blood of me, understand that degree of hostility.

ALTISORA (*sadly*). Neither can I.

CERVANTES. Forgive me outburst. My greetings to your husband.

ALTISORA. I'll tell him. He'll be sorry to have missed you.

CERVANTES. Next time, if Lope is here, put a small black flag in your window. In which case I'll just walk past. — Goodbye.

Music: Punctuation.

Tinkling of glass and metal objects, as on a medical tray.

DOCTOR (*low voice*). If he is in pain, Señora, give him this, it will help him sleep.

CATALINA (*also quietly*). Is there any chance he'll improve?

DOCTOR. I'm sorry…

CATALINA. I think he heard us. His eyes are open.

DOCTOR. You're doing all you can. Bear up. — Goodbye, Señora.

CERVANTES (*weakly*). Catalina…a student met me on the street and asked after my health. "I'm crumbling of old age," I said, and he said to me, "Ah, but you're not that old." I answered, "Trust me to know how weathered I am. I'm telling you, boy, old age is an incurable disease." "But, Señor Cervantes," he came back, "when you disparage old age, aren't you speaking ill of something everybody in the world eagerly wants to *reach?*" "Not everybody," I told him.

CATALINA (*gently*). Would you return to youth, if you could?

CERVANTES. No, Catalina. Only a crazy man, worn out after a long and tiring journey, would want to begin his trip over again. There's nothing more welcome to the weary traveler than to arrive at the Inn. A man would have to be *senseless* to love, above everything else, the thing he's lost.

CATALINA. The doctor left these powders for you.

---

11. *Don Quixote Part II* was published in 1615.

CERVANTES. Ah, so many things unwritten! So much I would like to put down! Perhaps if I had longer to go, I might pick up the broken thread and say all that I've still left unsaid. But there's not much sun left on the top of the wall...

CATALINA. Are you thirsty?

CERVANTES. I am the only old man who ever gave birth to an old man.

CATALINA. A most wonderful old man.

CERVANTES. At first there were rooms to let inside his head, but they've all been filled. He's no longer a solemn clown. — Don Quixote de la Mancha! May I forfeit my interest in heaven if you're not quite a man!

CATALINA. Yes. Rest now, Miguel...

CERVANTES (*after a pause*). When they get home from mass, please be sure to tell my sisters, tell my daughter, my niece, tell Pablo and his family, tell them I said goodbye — tell them for me much love, and many many thanks... — Dear, dearest Catalina, goodbye...

CATALINA (*softly*). Miguel —

CERVANTES. My wish is that I may see you all again, happy, in the life to come.

Music: Curtain.

CORWIN ON *THE WRITER WITH THE LAME LEFT HAND*

I was disappointed that *no habla Espagnole* country paid the slightest attention to the existence of the [original stage] play, in contrast to my expectations. The play was not performed elsewhere, but I thought sure it would succeed in Mexico. Nobody paid the slightest attention to it, and it is down in my books as a complete failure. Its star was Richard Kiley.

Nobody was impressed by the writing except Daniel Selznick, son of David O., who read the play not long after it was written, and got a full sense of its distinctiveness. Or so he wrote me in 2010, long after it was written.

FROM THE EDITOR

Corwin left no doubt at his disappointment of this project. The original stage play was titled *Cervantes* and starred Richard Kiley (Broadway star of *Man of La Mancha*) in the title role. Its 1973 run was brief and critics were not impressed. However, Corwin was proud of this work despite the lack of attention it received. He retitled the play and adapted it for the 1996 radio production starring Charles Durning.

THE CURSE OF 589

The third in the series *More By Corwin*, this program was broadcast over NPR in March 1997. William Shatner starred as Dr. Ted Bigelow along with Samantha Eggar as Fairy Number 589 and Carl Reiner as General Duffus, Dr. Grosskopf and the Security Chief. The show was recorded before a live audience at the Museum of Television and Radio in Beverly Hills.

Technical direction by Marty Halperin and Warren Dewey. Music by Ken Stange.

Mary Beth Kirchner produced. The author directed.

Music: Introduction. Hold briefly under:

Ringing telephone. Receiver off the hook.

TED. Hello? — Benny! — Yes, it has been busy. — Friends have been calling and dropping in all evening to congratulate me on the award. — No, you didn't awaken me. Matter of fact, I'm in the kitchen making myself a snack before hitting the sack. — Yup. — Yup. — Well, thanks, Ben. — Thanks a lot. Coming from you it means a great deal to me, you know that. Right. — See you at the lab when you get back from your trip. — Take care.

Receiver back on the hook. Light kitchen noises for a few moments.

Then: door chimes. Footsteps as Ted crosses and opens the door. Sound of rain.

FAIRY (*over the last of the sound pattern*). Are you Dr. T. Emerson Bigelow, otherwise known as Ted Bigelow?
TED. Yes.
FAIRY. Winner of the Nobel Award for the strombilization of energy?
TED. Not Nobel. Galaxy Award.
FAIRY. Doesn't matter. Scientific award.
TED. What are you doing at this back door?
FAIRY. There was no answer at the front. May I come in out of the rain?

She pushes her way past him. Door closes. Rain out.

TED. Isn't it pretty late, and wet, to come here just to congratulate me?
FAIRY. Congratulate you? I came to tell you what a horror you are, and to wish you bad success!
TED. Who are you?
FAIRY. Who am I?
TED. That was the question.
FAIRY. Oh, well…credentials. Here's my card.
TED (*reading the card*). "Fairy No. 589."
FAIRY. That's me.
TED (*continuing*). "…North American Division of the Leprechaun International"…see here, this is a damn late hour for a prank.
FAIRY. This is no prank. I am here to place a curse upon all science!
TED. Look — I'm afraid you've mistaken me for a crack party somewhere down the block. Now if you'll excuse me —

FAIRY. I certainly will not. And while you're recovering from you misapprehension, the least you might do is invite me to stay until the rain lets up.
TED. It may not let up for days!
FAIRY. At the same time, you might offer me something to eat, on a basis of common hospitality.

Footsteps, as she crosses the kitchen.

TED. Do you mind staying away from my refrigerator?

Refrigerator door opens. Trays and other objects are moved under the following:

FAIRY. Well, well, a tray of wilted vegetables. — How long had *this* been here?
TED. Just put that back, if you please.
FAIRY. Take it away and dump it.
TED. You have some *nerve* to come barging into —
FAIRY. This bread is moldy. — Are you making penicillin?
TED. Do you realize you're trespassing, and that I could call the police?
FAIRY. What a household! — Have you any canned goods?
TED. No. And what's more, I have no intention of taking inventory.
FAIRY. Why do you dissemble? I *know* you have cans. I can smell them: chicken noodle and mulligatawney. I'll have you know a fairy's sense of smell can penetrate up to an eighth-of-an-inch of tin.
TED. That's some talent.
FAIRY. Let's see what's in this cabinet…

Cabinet doors opened. Tins are moved.

FAIRY. Just as I thought. Chicken noodle…Here, will you open this, like a gentleman?
TED. If you were a lady, you wouldn't be —
FAIRY. I am *not* a lady!! I'm a *fairy*, which seems hard for you to get through your head.
TED (*trying another tack*). Madam — let's get something straight. I'd be glad to take you to a blue plate special down the street, but this —
FAIRY. If that motorized can-opener is working, will you do the honors?
TED. Oh, very well…but only because you do look a little hungry.
FAIRY. That I am. I could do with a steak…

Can opener turns.

TED. Level with me — who put you up to this?
FAIRY. Kindly pour the contents of the can into the pot.

Soup poured into pot.

TED. I don't mind a little crude aggression in its place, but —
FAIRY. Now add a can of water.
TED (*as he pours the water*). You're lucky I was born with a sense of chivalry. I've never struck a woman, but this is the closest I've come to kicking one out.
FAIRY. I'm not interested in your memoirs. — Stir it.
TED (*stirring*). Can't you think of anything less feeble, in the corny style of the novelty shop, than handing out a card describing yourself as a fairy?
FAIRY. Watch what you're doing! Your cuff will be in the soup.
TED. Here's your pot. — And there's your stove.
FAIRY. I don't need a stove. — Stand back.
TED. What are you going to do, heat it with your briefcase?
FAIRY. No, but with something I have tucked away *in* it.

A zipper being pulled as the briefcase is opened.

TED. What do you hope to do with that chopstick?
FAIRY. Never you mind.
TED. What do you hope to do by *waving* it?
FAIRY. I hereby pronounce this soup ready to serve!

Soup boiling in pot.

TED (*astonished*). It's *boiling*! How the blazes did you do that?
FAIRY. No, don't reach. It's not polite to grab. (*Inhaling the soup.*) And please don't hover over me while I'm eating. (*Another slurp.*) Do you have any rolls?
TED (*still agog*). What *is* this thing?
FAIRY. Wand, we call it.
TED. Very interesting. Let me see it.
FAIRY. I should say not!

She slaps his hand away.

TED. You didn't have to slap my hand!
FAIRY. A scientist may not touch any part of a fairy's equipment!
TED. You got a battery in there?
FAIRY. You *don't believe* I'm a fairy, do you?
TED (*with a chuckle*). Well, I've never put much stock in Fairies. Where did you *get* that thing?
FAIRY (*between draughts of soup*). Wouldn't you like to know...
TED. May I just feel the weight of it?
FAIRY. No.
TED. Could you tell me if it uses ultra-high-frequency?
FAIRY. I warn you against abusing me with technical terms. — It's quite light, if you must know, and its energy is inexhaustible, unlike my own.
TED (*after a pause; with amused curiosity*). I'll say this much for you, you're original. I'm beginning to like your line. What college are you working your way through?
FAIRY. Sir?
TED. Mab, would you like to do something sensible?
FAIRY. My name is not Mab; not even *Miss* Mab. I'm called Fairy 589!
TED. Relax. Now, do you want to make some money?
FAIRY. Hm? — What did you say?
TED. Money. Dinero. Moola.
FAIRY (*after a pause*). Nothing shady, now.
TED. Not shady — scientific.
FAIRY (*drawing back*). Scientific! I should have known!

She knocks over a chair.

TED. Please refrain from knocking over your chair.
FAIRY. We *loathe* science! It's displaced thousands of us! Put us on the dole! Destroyed our morale! You are monsters! — Why, when I think of what you've done to us!
TED. Like what?
FAIRY. Take one little thing! Just one! We used to make sounds come from afar, over hill and dale and out of the cowslip's bell and across seas and mountains. And then some Italian garage mechanic named Macaroni or something had to invent the wireless, with its singing commercials...
TED. Yes, go on.
FAIRY. We used to radiate magical flickerings, and all kinds of tweedy halos, all wonderfully unstable, so that the eye of man was confounded by them, and couldn't tell whether the image was deceiving him or not. And now it's all déclassé, thanks to TV!

TED. Don't stop there.
FAIRY. Take my own dear mother. Her proudest accomplishment was an enchanted carpet — a superb thing made out of raw materials from Persia —
TED. Now Iran.
FAIRY. Yes! And it was soft and downy and smelled like pomegranate blossoms. It was lovely, quite lovely, and it flew at a cruising speed of forty miles an hour, which at that time was considered astonishingly fast. And then some inventors — countrymen of yours, I believe — made the airplane. I say you scientists are *swine*! You poke your snouts into everything that's lovely; you study it so that you can make it artificially; even the pearls that are cast before you!
TED. Where did you pick up all this moonshine?
FAIRY (*after a pregnant pause*). Dr. Bigelow — would you, as a form of penance for your part in science, make a contribution to the Fund for Indigent Leprechauns?
TED. No.
FAIRY. Well, then, since I have delivered my curse, which is what I came for, I must be going.
TED. That is not altogether bad news.
FAIRY. Heavens! Is that clock right? Three-ten a.m.!
TED. Is it really?
FAIRY. And, sir, in view of the lateness of the hour, and the unpleasantness of the weather, I think it would be advisable for me to spend the night here.
TED (*startled*). Well now, I'm not so sure about that!
FAIRY. Do you have a guest room?
TED. No!
FAIRY. Then whatever you *do* have will be fine. (*Going off.*) I take it the bedroom is down this hall.

She marches down the hall.

TED (*following her*). Just a second! Hold on! (*Shouting after her.*) Even Cinderella went home at midnight!
FAIRY. Slippers and a robe will be appreciated. And no other attentions.
TED. Your aggressiveness is exceeded only by your repartee.
FAIRY. I hate coarse flattery.
TED. Here are robe and slippers, both much too large for you.
FAIRY. Thank you.
TED. Since you won't let go of that chopstick, do you mind my sitting on the edge of the bed with you to have a close look at it?

FAIRY. I can't stop you from sitting, but keep your distance from my corpus.
TED. You know, seen in a certain light, you are not exactly unattractive.
FAIRY. I think I know the light you mean, and I warn you not only to keep your distance, but increase it. In other words, *get off my bed*!
TED. *Your* bed?
FAIRY. Must I inflict the power of this wand on you?
TED. Now, Mab — as your host I simply want to point out some of the features of this room, like for example, the electric blanket. If you should get cold during the night — why are you pointing that at me?
FAIRY. You asked for it. *I pronounce you should have a Charlie Horse.*
TED (*chuckling*). Why, you little fake.
FAIRY. Try getting up.
TED. Put that silly thing down.
FAIRY. Go ahead, try getting up.
TED. Very well. (*He gets up. Suddenly stricken, he howls, groans and moans. Finally he can stand it no longer.*) All right already! Call it off!
FAIRY. I'll hold my fire so long as you mind your manners.
TED. That's a *weapon*, that's what that is! You're *dangerous*!
FAIRY. Not when treated respectfully. — You may now retire in good order.
TED. More than *ever*, I am interested in that wand!
FAIRY. I warn you, scientist, my vexation threshold is very low.
TED (*giving up*). Very well, I will not cross your little threshold. — Anything else you want besides my bed?
FAIRY. Yes. Sleep and privacy.
TED. Well then, good night.
FAIRY. One thing more: I think you should know that fairies are magically protected against sleepwalkers.
TED. Are sleepwalkers protected against fairies?
FAIRY. Irrelevant. In any case, good night to you.
TED. Good night. — Wait a minute — are you seriously proposing to put on my slippers? You'll get *lost* in them.
FAIRY. I'll fix that. — Stand back while I flourish my wand. — I pronounce these slippers size three!
TED (*stunned*). My God! They *shrank*! How did you — ? Let me have that wand!
FAIRY. Good *night*, Dr. Bigelow!
TED. Hey! Just a minute! How does that thing work? Let me see it, will you?
FAIRY (*defiantly*). Are you looking for chronic neuro-arthritis?
TED. No. But I am looking for something else. And you may be able to help me *find* it, with that divining rod of yours.

FAIRY. Thank you, but no thanks. We've been fighting scientists for centuries, and we don't intend to stop now. We *hate* Science!
TED. Maybe if you stopped hating it and made friends with it, you could regain some of your old power, and you wouldn't have to worry about where your next meal is coming from.
FAIRY. Make friends with it?
TED. Certainly.
FAIRY. Impossible! — How?
TED. By exchanging information.
FAIRY. What good will that do *us*?
TED. If it's done you harm, as you claim, maybe it could also be made to do you good.
FAIRY. Exchanging information, eh? (*Considering.*) Are there scientific ways of predicting the outcome of a hand of poker?
TED. Certainly, by deductive analysis.
FAIRY (*considering further*). Hmmm...I'll see if exchange is covered in the code.
TED. What code?
FAIRY (*opening her briefcase*). F.E.P.C. — Fairy Employment Practices Code. I've got the manual right here in my briefcase.
TED. Good! Then look it up!
FAIRY. Okay. Now let's see...Don't crowd me. I can read without your help. (*She riffles through it.*) Here we are: "Information — Exchange of. Strictly forbidden." (*She snaps the book shut.*) That settles that.
TED. I never thought fairies would be so stodgy.
FAIRY. Rules are rules.
TED. Can't you get around them?
FAIRY. I have many times.
TED. Then why don't you now? Here's all you have to do: let me search for the source of power in your stick.
FAIRY. How very curious! As a scientist, I should think you'd be more interested in our Code, in the origins of our species, than in our wand.
TED. As a scientist, I'm not interested in kooks or how they came to kookhood. But I *am* concerned with physical phenomenon.
FAIRY. What's a kook?
TED. Well...let's say a non-conformist.
FAIRY. That, I'm proud to be. I once read Thoreau.
TED (*surprised*). *You* read Henry Thoreau?
FAIRY. With difficulty, of course.
TED. Well, good for you. — Now if you'll just let me test your, uh — your instrument in a laboratory...

FAIRY. *Can't be done.*
TED. Is there anything in the Code Book about it?
FAIRY. Doesn't matter if there is or isn't.
TED *(continuing)*. Well, *is* there? — Let me look it up.
FAIRY. Give that back to me! — I'll look it up!
TED. Be my guest.
FAIRY. I already am. — Here it is…(*Reading from the book.*) "Wand — Care of; Renewal of; Use of; Wrist motions in manipulation of…"
TED. Nothing about "Searching for the source of power of"?
FAIRY. No.
TED. Well, there you are.
FAIRY. What would you do if you found "the source of power of"?
TED. Control it in such a way as to benefit both humanity and — (*As a concession to her.*) — fairies.
FAIRY. Hmmmm. Amplify that.
TED. Well, you see, there's need for new types of energy.
FAIRY (*bristling*). People have too much energy as it is! They attack each other to get rid of it!
TED. No, no, no, I mean *power*…new kinds of it…we're going to run *out* of gas and oil and coal someday — even uranium, eventually —
FAIRY. Good. Can't happen too soon to suit me.
TED. If you sneer at all forms of energy, what about your wand? Don't you consider that constructive and useful? Maybe its principle could be applied to all kinds of peaceful uses of energy — objects the size of a fountain pen, under easy control, without having to build bulky, dangerous reactors. Don't you see, Mab? This gismo of yours may hold the key, the secret, to a cosmic force —
FAIRY. So it's a *secret* you're after?
TED. Yes.
FAIRY. And if you *find* the secret, would you use it just to make money out of it?
TED. Certainly not!
FAIRY. Well, at least I'm glad to see you're not venal and grasping.
TED. That, I believe I can say, I am *not*.
FAIRY. Good! — Now what is there in it for me?
TED (*taken aback*). Well — what would you like?
FAIRY. I'm going to be very straight about this. My losses at poker have been ugly of late.
TED. But with all this magic at your disposal, can't you control a simple deck of cards?

FAIRY. Listen to him! — Can't you get it through your head that numbers are mathematical, and cards are numbered? When I play cards I do so at my own risk. Now as I was saying, I should like something fairly substantial by way of emolument.
TED. Well, if it's not too big, maybe I could underwrite a little advance.
FAIRY. In scientific terms, what would you define as "a little advance"?
TED. Oh, say five hundred dollars?
FAIRY (*after some thought*). Seven-fifty.
TED. I can try.
FAIRY. Cash, of course.
TED. Naturally. — Now here's my plan: I have a little private laboratory in a cottage up at Pinecrest.
FAIRY. Where's that?
TED. Near Lake Ossowottopassymaquoddyquom.
FAIRY. The Welsh made me sick with their long names. Never catch the Irish doing that! When *we* name a place, it's short and snappy. Cork! Shannon! Dublin! Eire!
TED. The name happens to be Indian.
FAIRY. That doesn't excuse it. — When do you want to start at the laboratory?
TED. Yesterday.
FAIRY. I take it that means soon.
TED. Yes. Now if you'll just let me borrow the wand —
FAIRY. Oh, no! I never let it out of my sight. I have to accompany the wand.
TED. Well…all right…but I warn you it's very rustic up there.
FAIRY. I come from a rustic race. Leprechauns are woodsy. What do you aim to do in your laboratory?
TED. Identify the source of energy. If I discover that, then I can move up the heavy artillery — I'll take it to Operation Galaxy, which is a big hush-hush government project. And there I can test it for capacity and versatility and applicability and so on.
FAIRY. By the way, did I tell you I find your nose attractive?
TED. That's nice.
FAIRY. I rather like your eyes, too.
TED (*dismissing it*). And I like yours. — We'll leave in the morning, okay? It's about three hours by car.
FAIRY. It's a deal.

Music: Wipes out the scene.

Crickets and night sounds.

FAIRY (*in a tone of loud reverie*). Moonlight on pine woods makes such a pretty combination.

A grandfather's clock strikes twice.

FAIRY. I thought you were going to oil that grandfather's clock of yours. It struck twice, and it's 10 p.m. Who did you say your grandfather was?
TED. Charlie Bulova.
FAIRY. Well, he wouldn't like the way you neglect his clock. — Are you going to work at that bench all night? We've been here two weeks now, and all you do is twiddle with hardware and make sparks are write down things and scratch your head.

The clock unaccountably delivers another bong.

FAIRY. Stupid clock! — My, that is *such* a very lovely moon up there! My mother once taught me a song about the moon (*Sings.*):

> Slowly, silently, now the moon
> Walks the night in her silver shoon.[1] (*Stops singing.*)

Whoever wrote that must have meant sheen, not shoon…And yet you don't walk in sheen, do you? Maybe he meant shoes. But shoes don't rhyme with moon, so I suppose he had to say shoon. Which is cheating, of course. Yet what else could he do?

> Listen: "Slowly, silently, now the *moos*
> Walks the night in her silver shoes?"

That's terrible!

(She is silent for a moment.)

You're lucky to have a cottage up here in the woods. It's so tranquil one can almost hear the — the pulsation of the stars. In fact, I can sometimes hear the pulsation of your heart, clear across the room.

(Affectionately.) It's a nice sound.

(Silence.)

---

1. The opening lines of the poem *Silver* by Walter de la Mare.

It was on a night like this that my mother met my father — he was an inspector of nectar bottling.

(Again she is silent.)

See how the stars glow — like fairy dust sprinkled on blue velvet... What are stars made of, Dr. Bigelow?

TED. Gas.

FAIRY. That's a vulgar answer, if you don't mind my saying so! A typical scientific answer! As though the holy stars in heaven are made up of that smelly stuff you cook eggs with! *(Laughs.)*
As though the Great Dipper up there has anything in common with what a human has on his stomach when he gets indigestion! Really now! The arrogance of science! All kids of stuffy equations — and no room for the lovely dark superstitions, the beautiful ignorances that make magic such a joy to perform. Science is *nosey* and *prying*, and I'm proud of my fairy forefathers for having long ago ruled it out of bounds!
Believe me, if it weren't for you idealism, you could never get me to spend ten seconds in this wicked room.
— What accounts for your rampant silence?

TED *(suddenly excited).* Mab! I think I've got the *answer!* *This wand is catalytically suffused with gravitrodes!*

FAIRY. You don't say.

TED. And it shoots off fast astriomatic fermions! The spontaneous interaction of a five-stranded polynucleoride chain! *Proof* of the quantum genesis hypothesis!

FAIRY. Lovely. You seem very happy about your discovery.

TED. I am! By God, I am!

FAIRY. Well, happiness seems to go with your posture, which I consider one of your best features.

TED. Mab! You're not listening. I'm ready! I mean *we're* ready. You've got to come with me to Operation Galaxy so I can convince General Duffus!

FAIRY. Why must I go with you?

TED. Because you won't let this wand out of your sight. Without it, I have nothing to go on.

FAIRY. Well...I don't know as I can do it, under the F.E.P.C.

TED. Look it up!

FAIRY. Some things I don't *have* to look up! Such as provisions of the code I consider worth violating. There is in me a touch of scofflaw, you know — a streak of civil disobedience. Me and Thoreau.

TED. Does that mean you will come?

FAIRY. Don't rush me. I'm considering...(*Low and to herself.*) On the one hand, I'd be helping a scientist, which would give aid and comfort to them and theirs. On the other hand, I'd be helping myself, which would give aid and comfort to me and mine. But as me and mine are more important than him and his, and need more help, it's obvious that an even exchange would benefit us most. (*Returning to Ted.*) Yes, I might as well come!

Music: A change of venue.

TED. Well, here we are. — Look, Mab, here's the way we handle it: I'll go in and prepare the ground. You wait here in the hall until I come out and fetch you.
FAIRY. Good. I loathe preliminaries.
TED. Also, there's the matter of security. Until you're cleared —
FAIRY. Spare me all this exposition. Just go in, see the General, get down to business, then come out and get me.
TED. Okay. I'll make it as fast as I can.

Music: Punctuation.

DUFFUS. Get to the point, Ted. So far you've been explaining to me that you're going to explain something to me. Suppose you begin.
TED. Ah — uh — first I want to settle a few things. — Would it be possible for me to make use of certain equipment?
DUFFUS. Like what?
TED. Heptagrid with capacitance of two billion adfarads — duodial discriminator — and the MRA trigatron.
DUFFUS. Well, possibly.
TED. Also the klavitrode inhibitor, the self-correcting inverter, and the momentum-defining thermocalutron.
DUFFUS. What do you want all *that* for? Every bit of that stuff is busy.
TED. I know, but you must realize I'm onto possibly the greatest thing that has happened to science in a thousand years!
DUFFUS. What are you *saying*?
TED. Just that. — Benny, we've known each other a long time, right?
DUFFUS. Right.
TED. We've shared confidences, and always trusted each other with personal and professional intelligence?
DUFFUS. Routine, classified and top secret.
TED. You know me for a man who has never gone off on a wild tangent.

DUFFUS. Roger.

TED. I want you to believe me *now*.

DUFFUS (*impatiently*). Well, shoot, man, let me have it.

TED. All right, Benny — here it is: I have access to a revolutionary device that sublimates energy into the most subtle and variegated forms conceivable. It's no bigger that a baton — light as meringue — nonmetallic — has no discrete source of power — may well be inexhaustible.

DUFFUS (*rocked*). *You* have developed a thing like *that*?

TED. I didn't *say* that. I just happened to stumble across it. It was brought to me by its owner.

DUFFUS. Who's that?

TED. Don't ask me to answer.

DUFFUS. I don't understand you. Here you are reminding me of how many confidences we've shared, and how trustworthy —

TED. It's just that it would get awfully complicated. You see, she insists on being present when her device is tested.

DUFFUS. *She?*

TED. Yes.

DUFFUS. A physicist?

TED. No.

DUFFUS. A layman, so to speak? A laywoman?

TED. Not that either.

DUFFUS. Don't tell me it's Shirley MacLaine channeling with Madame Curie!

TED. It's nobody that you ever heard of. And she wants nothing to do with scientists.

DUFFUS. Well, but Ted — this doesn't make any sense. If this mystery woman invented anything like what you've described, she must *be* a scientist!

TED. Don't ask questions, Benny — just authorize my use of the equipment at hours when it's not booked.

DUFFUS. In the first place, you know it's forbidden for any outsider to come in. Secondly, if we did let her in, we'd have to know everything about her. In the third place, if you're hoping for me to turn over the resources of Operation Galaxy, you *owe* it to me to spell out what the hell you're asking me to believe is the mystery of the age.

TED. It is, by George, it is!

DUFFUS. Will you cut the yak and tell me *what* it is?

TED (*after a pause; bracing himself*). Benny — Benny — when I described the nature of this device, you half rose out of your chair. When I tell you about this woman, you'll rise *all* the way.

DUFFUS. With that much notice, I'll manage to keep seated.

TED. All right. — Listen, Benny (*Very firmly.*) There *are* such things as fairies.

DUFFUS. I *know*, damn it. They're a problem in all government agencies from time to time.

TED. No, Ben…Leprechaun-type fairies. Creatures. (*Even more firmly.*) This woman is a fairy. A she-fairy. (*Big pause as Duffus starts to get up from him chair.*) You said you'd keep your seat. (*With increasing force.*) And she carries a wand. — Why are you getting up? The wand, in fact, is exactly what I'm talking about. — Don't keep backing away from me!

DUFFUS. I'm — I'm tired of sitting…

TED. React as much as you like, but there is no getting around the palpable, tangible, empirically sound, categorically demonstrable *performance* of the device.

DUFFUS. Well — uh —

TED. Before my very eyes, not once but several times, I saw this thing transmit energy under extraordinary conditions of control. You won't believe what it can do. It boils soups instantly — and no scorching. Percolates coffee. Changes the size of shoes to predetermined dimensions. It even induces spasms in members of the body — and then relieves them — all in the flick of a wrist.

DUFFUS (*at last finding his voice, but a little shakily*). I don't quite get the picture of the shoes.

TED. Neither do I, but there was instantaneous shrinkage. Yet the shoes were on her feet at the time, and she seemed not affected. The wand was held no closer than this — and was directed at a pair of bedroom slippers — my own.

DUFFUS (*trying to mask his apprehension*). I see. — Did you, uh — examine this — uh — this wand?

TED. She wouldn't let me, at first; but then —

DUFFUS. You didn't happen to bring this device *with* you, by any chance?

TED. She doesn't let it out of her sight.

DUFFUS (*guardedly*). Oh. Too bad.

TED. I'm not surprised by your doubts, Benny, but what I've come across is an occluded front between fantasy and reality — where, as in weather, when a warm front and a cold front impinge on each other, something happens — precipitation. Only *this* precipitation is beyond anything in our ken. In a sense it's a link between two worlds, the hyphen between cyclotron and leprechaun.

DUFFUS. The hyphen.

TED. Yes, such is the phenomenon of this wand, and the fairy attached to it! — However, I don't ask or expect you to take my word. The proof is in the pudding, and the pudding happens to be outside. In the hall.

DUFFUS. You mean — you mean the lady is here with you?
TED. Yes, and she has the instrument. — Come outside with me and meet her.
DUFFUS. By all means.

Two pairs of footsteps as they go out to meet the fairy.

TED. You'll find her inclined to be blunt, but she's reasonable, once she gets to know you.
DUFFUS. You say she's right outside?
TED. Yes. — If she throws you any fast ones, better let me handle her.

The footsteps stop. Door opens.

DUFFUS. Well, where's your fairy?
TED. I left her here.
DUFFUS. Of course you did.
TED. Damn it to hell. She promised she wouldn't leave!
DUFFUS. Does your — er — fairy by any chance have the power of invisibility?
TED. ...Don't be ridiculous! I tell you, she was here a minute ago!
DUFFUS. Well, let's wait. — I'm sure she'll be right back.
TED. I tell you, I left her right *here*! Now you've got to *believe* me, Benny!
DUFFUS (*going off*). Tell you what — why don't you look for her, while I take care of a little business in my office. Then bring her in when she returns.
TED (*calling out with increasing frustration and loudness*). Fairy! — Mab! — Where are you? HALLO! MAB! 589! COME BACK HERE!

Music: Big quandary. It continues briefly under:

Knock on a door. Repeated, more heavily.

TED. Come in, whoever you are.

Door opens.

CHIEF. Dr. Bigelow?
TED. Who the hell are you?
CHIEF. We're from Security.
TED. How'd you get in my house?
CHIEF. The door was unlocked.

TED. What do you want?
CHIEF. We understand you haven't been feeling well.
TED. I'm fine.
CHIEF. Wouldn't you like to come in for a check-up? At government expense? A little rest, maybe, in nice surroundings?
TED. No, I'm fine where I am, thank you.
CHIEF. Be much easier, doctor, if you'd just let us take you to see your friend General Duffus.
TED. I'll not come voluntarily. You'll have to carry me out of here sitting in my chair.
CHIEF. Okay, sir, if that's the way you want it. — All right, men, get both arms of the chair and I'll lift from the bottom.

Music: Punctuation.

TED (*into a phone*). Well, at last. — Why should it take so long to reach my lawyer on the phone? — Well, I pressed 1, and then I pressed 2, and then pressed the star key, and then 3, and then the pound key, and then waited ten minutes for you to come on. — I'm calling from the Irongate Sanitarium, *that's* where. — I'm being held here under great secrecy. — Why? — Because the Pentagon and Operation Galaxy don't want it to get out that their top scientist, heading up the biggest project in space exploration, has gone off his rocker. — I've been here a week, and this is the first they've let me call out. — No, it's a kind of isolation. I see only medics and shrinks. — No visitors except men in white who buzz my door every fifteen minutes to bring me this pill and that capsule and meals that my cat would turn up her nose at. — Well, you better get over here…

Door buzzer.

TED. There's the damn buzzer again. I'll hang up. Make it soon.

Phone hangs up. The door buzzer sounds again.

TED. Come in, come in, come in.

Door opens.

FAIRY. Greetings.
TED. You! — How did you get in here?

FAIRY. Paved my way with the wand. Gave 'em a shot of it all the way up and down the line. — I've come to say goodbye to you.

TED. Why did you run out on me when we went to see Duffus?

FAIRY. You didn't tell me about the high-tension lines around there. I got so dizzy I had to flee. — How did you make out with the general?

TED. Well, he thinks I'm completely mad. So does everybody else.

FAIRY. Excuse me while I peel this Chiclet. Do you approve of fairies chewing gum?

TED. I couldn't be more neutral.

FAIRY. Care for one? Spearmint?

TED. You don't take my troubles very seriously, do you?

FAIRY. Dr. Bigelow: You ask me to take your troubles seriously. — I have troubles enough of my own, thank you, and I prefer to lavish my seriousness on *them*. Aren't you going to invite me to sit down?

TED. By all means — pull up a stool.

FAIRY. I'm afraid I can't stay long.

TED. That's all right.

FAIRY. How are things going?

TED. Beautifully, as you can see. I'm being examined by psychiatrists.

FAIRY. I wouldn't sit still for an analyst, if you I were you.

TED. What do you know about such things?

FAIRY. Most every mortal we deal with winds up on a couch. But buck up, there are worse things. Take me, for example — the mess I'm in.

TED. You lost at poker?

FAIRY. Worse. It's an offense for a fairy to occupy the premises of a scientist — and I was seen by a spongehead of a leprechaun spy, entering and leaving your laboratory. So I got a summons. I was tried in the Leprechaun Circuit Court and disciplined, that's all.

TED. And are you here under the terms of your punishment?

FAIRY (*with forced cheer*). No, not at all. But I may be laying by my wand indefinitely. One can get tired of carrying it up one's sleeve. It itches when not used enough, and its protons champ at the bit. — I learned that from you. About the protons, I mean.

TED. I learned some things from you, too. — Why *are* you here?

FAIRY. Because I'm — well, I'm interested in you, so to speak. And I'd like to help you. I don't relish the idea of you being kept indeterminately in the booby preserve.

TED (*patiently*). Mab, there will be some difficulty explaining to my colleagues why the winner of the Galaxy Award has neglected space research and missile development, to investigate the wand of a fairy. I can't explain to them that fairies are fickle and that I can't rely on my sole fairy contact always being around...I can't explain that, because they'd never let me get that far. — But I'd try to persuade mountains of granite about you, if only you didn't abandon me at strategic moments.

FAIRY. You're being very hard on me.

TED. In short, you're wonderful but untrustworthy. You're the very essence and distillation of mischief. Once before, in a moment of pique, I wanted to throw you out. But right now, coolly, with no sense of recrimination — in fact with the friendliest esteem and envy of your powers, I ask you to go and let me be. Just let me be, dear Mab.

FAIRY. You are not yourself, Dr. Bigelow. — I beg you to ask for a boon. You have it coming to you.

TED. No, thank you. Goodbye, Mab.

FAIRY. Please! Please ask for *something*!

TED (*not unkindly*). Don't you understand? The most you can do for me is to stay away.

FAIRY. Please! Don't say that! Ask the boon of being released — of being judged entirely compos mentis in the eyes of your cockeyed society. — Do as I say.

TED. Go away, Mab.

FAIRY. Then I've come here in vain?

TED. You were good to come. You're really enchanting in a kind of perverse way, which just happens to be bad medicine for me. But thanks just the same.

FAIRY (*sadly*). You're most welcome. — Goodbye, then.

TED. Just as a point of idle curiosity — where do you go from here?

FAIRY. To expire.

TED. To what?

FAIRY (*going off*). Expire...as an act of purification in release of the mundane.

TED. Well...ask a silly question, get a silly answer.

Music: Punctuation.

DR. GROSSKOPF. Now, Dr. Bigelow, you mentioned to General Duffus, I believe it was, an idea you had concerning an "occluded front" between reality and fantasy. Would you care to elaborate on that?

TED. Not particularly.

DR. GROSSKOPF. Why?

TED. I don't think you'd understand it.

DR. GROSSKOPF. Why don't you think so?

TED. Because nobody else seems to.

DR. GROSSKOPF. Why do you suppose that is?
TED. Because it's beyond their capacity to assimilate.
DR. GROSSKOPF. Why is that?
TED. Dr. Grosskopf — does your technique consist only of the adverb WHY?
DR. GROSSKOPF. Why do you ask?
TED. Because it's getting to be a bore.
DR. GROSSKOPF. My purpose is to help you. — Why do you feel hostile?
TED. I'm not hostile in the slightest. And *since* I'm not hostile, there can be no hostility for me to mask, hence no need to be polite.
DR. GROSSKOPF. Why do you say "no hostility to mask?" (*Ted does not answer.*) You said that, didn't you?
TED. Yes, that's what I said.
DR. GROSSKOPF. Why?
TED. Why *what*?
DR. GROSSKOPF. Why did you *say* that?
TED. Why did I say "Why what?" or why did I ask why you keep asking why?
DR. GROSSKOPF (*after a pause*). Let's begin again. — Perhaps you'd explain to me about this — uh — fairy you met, whose wand I understand you are investigating.
TED. Let's not beat about the bush. You are using this approach to find whether I can distinguish between what you conveniently call the real and the unreal. You are convinced that I'm suffering from cathexis — an enchantment developing into obsession.
DR. GROSSKOPF. Why do you think I'm convinced of that?
TED. Dr. Grosskopf, are you at all times certain where the ponderable leaves off and the imponderable begins? Where today's fancy and tomorrow's fact overlap?
DR. GROSSKOPF (*indulgently*). Perhaps you will teach me. I'd like to share in your involvement.
TED. Now you're trying participation therapy. But it will never work.
DR. GROSSKOPF. Why not?
TED. Because you have an inflexible code, and you are not aware of meanings outside of it.
DR. GROSSKOPF. What do you mean by "meanings outside of it?"
TED. I mean the meaning of meaning.
DR. GROSSKOPF. What is your meaning of the meaning of meaning?
TED. Let me help you, doctor. Have you ever read Karl Abel's monograph[2] in which he points out that in the language of ancient Egypt

---

2. Published circa 1884.

there were a number of words with double meaning, each the exact contrary and *mate* of the other? Thus the word for light also meant dark; old also meant young; near meant far; outside, inside; united, divided. These twins, though forming contrasts, gave rise to very clear concepts. — And the Egyptians had no trouble understanding each other. Do you follow me?

DR. GROSSKOPF. Just a moment…want to make a note of that…Karl Abel, you say?

TED. Yes. — But we don't have to go back to Egypt. All *our* concepts arise through contrasts, too. Freud said that if it were always light, we'd never distinguish between light and darkness, and accordingly we'd have neither the *concept* of light nor the word that describes it. Everything, my dear Grosskopf, is relative; everything has independent existence only insofar as it stands in relation to, and differs from, other objects. Thus every concept is the twin of its opposite. So the Egyptians were really on the beam.

DR. GROSSKOPF. Go on.

TED. All right then, follow me further: negative and positive are contrasts, yet together, electrically, they turn motors and light cities. Male and female are contrasts; together they create new life. In the same way reality and fantasy are contrasts; when *they* keep house together they create Fairy Number 589.

DR. GROSSKOPF. Ah, yes — now *about* this fairy, Dr. Bigelow —

TED. Of course you acknowledge that reality is not equally real to all persons?

DR. GROSSKOPF. Well, that goes without saying.

TED. Now in childhood, reality is fresh, it's invested with wonder and curiosity and a delightful strangeness.

DR. GROSSKOPF. Correct.

TED. To the extent that it's invested with wonder and curiosity and strangeness, it is fantasy. Later, as we grow older, the balance shifts. What we commonly accept as the dawning of sense of reality, is actually only our stopping at the standard focus of our society, a pre-set focus on the sequence of microscopic slides that we call our lives… Do you mind if I walk around?

DR. GROSSKOPF. No.

TED. We are entranced and enslaved by details on the slides, and we hardly ever look up from them. Perhaps now and then a moment of sublime music catches our ear, and we lift our heads long enough to listen, and have a limited séance with unreality. But as soon as the music ends, back we go to the slides.

Now, you take children. By degrees, they abandon, because they're taught to, that superbly fantasized view of reality that can make their art sometimes equal to that of the masters. And masters *are* masters, let me add, only because they fight their way *back* to the great staging ground — that marginal area between light and dark where events of cosmic bearing, such as new days, or the *Victory of Samothrace*,[3] are conceived.

Love, too, has the genius to take us back to that Egyptian twin-contrary of reality. Or to that patch of magical friction between male and female, whence springs such a mighty power of creation as to make every man and woman half a god. And when that bright image fades, the honeymoon is over.

DR. GROSSKOPF (*a sudden uncontrollable outburst*). God, Bigelow, I have the damndest wife! You'd never believe the kind of creeping ivy she is — *poison* ivy! And my mother-in-law! Cut out of the same rib! (*He catches himself with a start, shocked by his position vis a vis his patient.*) Forgive me. (*Recovering his dignity under forced draft.*) Go on. — I'm all right now. Quite all right. — You were talking about the suppression of fantasy.

TED. Well, it adds up to the existence of zones of occlusion between reality and its contrasting mate. — Zones in which quasi-beings like the fairy of my acquaintance, are hatched.

DR. GROSSKOPF. Yes, now — to get back to these fairies —

TED. Why do you insist on getting back to these fairies?

DR. GROSSKOPF. Because I'm an investigator. I must find *out* about them.

TED. Not about *them*, but about *me*.

DR. GROSSKOPF. That's right.

TED. But that was a slip.

DR. GROSSKOPF. Why do you think it was a slip?

TED. Because you acknowledge me as reality, and dismiss "them" as fantasy. That's the whole point of our being here, isn't it?

DR. GROSSKOPF. Ah, well — it's a question of — uh — perception. My! — Good heavens! It's later than I thought. I have another appointment. — Uh, well now, Dr. Bigelow — I'm afraid our time is up. — That will be all for today.

Music: Punctuation, continues briefly under:

TED. Ah, General B.J. Duffus himself!

---

3. Ancient Greek sculpture also known as the *Nike of Samothrace*, displayed at the Louvre Museum since 1883.

DUFFUS. Well, Ted, I'm not a mountain, and you're not Mohammed, but I've come to you because you're not answering your phone.

TED. In person comes the General without even a bodyguard, to the home of psychotic Dr. Bigelow, after the doctor is released from an asylum for lunatic scientists, whither he had been sent by order of this same General. Sources close to both believe the General must either have mellowed, or gone off his own rocker.

DUFFUS. Oh cut it out, Ted. I was just trying to protect you.

TED. Over my head and behind my back.

DUFFUS. That was before I read the transcript of your meetings with Grosskopf. Fact is, I felt guilty even *before* then, because as an old friend, I should have tried to know more about what looked to me like a breakdown. — Will you accept this visit as an apology?

TED (*after a moment*). You're a decent man, Ben. I guess if the tables were reversed, and you told me *you'd* been zapped by a fairy, I'd have done as you did.

DUFFUS. I'm relieved to hear you say that. — So what now? What about the — so to speak — spook?

TED. From the beginning, I took the wrong approach. I was more interested in knowing what made her *wand* tick than what made *her* tick. I came to realize she's a poor sassy wanderer, a bit of flotsam from the wreck of romanticism. A waif of the space age.

DUFFUS. Yuh. A waif. A cyberwaif.

TED. So when I got back home, I set out to find all there is to know about leprechaunology. I read McGonigle's great work on Fairies, published in 1792 — have you heard of it?

DUFFUS. Can't say I have.

TED. And the *Variorum Fairiorum*. Famous compendium.

DUFFUS. Don't know that either.

TED. I ransacked bookstores and libraries trying to find clues that might lead to the whereabouts of Mab. And finally I came across an old, crumbling copy if a Finkelstein.

DUFFUS. What's a Finkelstein?

TED. *Orlando* Finkelstein! Dean of Leprechaunologists! He *taught* McGonigle! Well, I poured over this thing…its pages could hardly be touched, they were so brittle. And I found something that electrified me. I copied it down. Here…read this…

DUFFUS (*reading*). "The worst crime of which a she-fairy can be accused, is the falling in love with a mortal who is given to the mathematical arts. If found guilty of this offense she is condensed — "

TED (*correcting*). Condemned.

DUFFUS. Can't read your writing…"she is condemned to give up her existence…to expire in an act of purification in release of the mundane. It hath not been established whether she dieth outright or passeth into the body of a warm-blooded inferior animal. Further, it is posing strange that —"

TED. *Passing* strange…

DUFFUS. "Passing strange that the guilty one must expire in a haunt where she hath imbibed the poisonous elixirs of her love." Well, Ted, I must say —

TED. No, turn it over. There's more on the other side.

DUFFUS. Oh yes. (*Reads again*.) "In the process of transubstantiation to an inferior warm-blooded creature, all dress of the expirer is discarded."— Hey, how about that? (*Back to reading*.) "Thus the offender, to survive, must keep on as much clothing as possible, alike to the keeping awake of one who hath swallowed poison. But whether this assureth survival, no one knoweth, all postulates thereunto being of rank suppository."

TED. Rank *supposition*.

DUFFUS. Very complicated stuff. And vindictive, too.

TED. Chauvinist pig leprechaun lawmakers!

DUFFUS. So what are you going to do?

TED. Find her. I've got to find her.

DUFFUS. If Finkelstein is right, and she's condemned to expire in a place where she committed the crime of falling in love with a mortal, where would that be?

TED. Could be my kitchen — or my bedroom —

DUFFUS. Or your lab at Pinecrest!

TED. Right! Right you are! And that's where I'm going as fast as I can get there!

Music: Transport to Ossowottopassymaquoddyquom.

Key in a lock. A knob turns. A door opens.

TED (*to himself*). Can never find the light switch…Ah, here we are…

Light switch.

TED. Well…nobody home…If ever a place was cold and barren, it's this damn lab…And dusty, too — (*He sneezes*.)

FAIRY (*muffled*). Gezundheit, for God's sake.

TED (*electrified*). MAB! Is that you?

FAIRY (*muffled*). Who else?

Rapid steps to closet. Door opens.

TED. What are you doing in that closet? — I've been looking all over hell for you!
FAIRY. Now — of all times — I ask you to guard your language.
TED. What are you doing, hunched up like that?
FAIRY. I'm meditating about what's befallen me.
TED. Come on, get up off the floor.
FAIRY. Let me be.
TED. I've got *plans* for you! I'm going to teach you how to win at poker! I'm going to buy you filet mignon and caviar — for breakfast! I'm going to —
FAIRY. I'll thank you not to rub salt in fatal wounds. Look at your clock.
TED. Ten minutes to twelve. — What of it?
FAIRY. At midnight I shall be no more. I've been sentenced to die in the unholiest place in all the earth — a laboratory!
TED. I won't even listen to such folderol.
FAIRY. Good. Then leave me alone to meditate in silence.
TED. Don't go back to that closet! Listen — We're going to *do* things together! You're going to *help* me!
FAIRY. It was helping you that brought me to *this* pass.
TED. My dear, sweet Mab...
FAIRY. Don't "dear sweet Mab" me. I did what I did knowing what would happen if I were caught. It wasn't your fault.
TED. But it *was*! I coaxed you into working with me against your will. I disbelieved you — I accused you!
FAIRY. Please, no confessions. It's hard enough to expire without having a scene made over it. I'm through. And obviously nothing can be done for somebody who's done for. — Stop following me around.
TED. If you'll just give me a chance to get a word in, I'll *convince* you that you're being very silly! You *can't* expire!
FAIRY. Oh, why did I *do* it? I was so happy!
TED. Happy? Always on the prowl for a free meal? Belonging to a powerless minority? — Don't unbutton that blouse!
FAIRY. I'll ask you to be more respectful of our powers. It's not *our* fault that magic got tangled up in your so-called "progress." We had the most marvelously complex rituals —
TED. Sure. All technique and no heart. You don't know what to do with your own tricks.

FAIRY. Is that so? Well, the same goes for your kind! So full of know-how and getting jobs done on time. Everything is rush, rush, rush — it's obscene! Instant coffee! Minute steaks! — Imagine! — Even a Minute Waltz! Tell me one good thing you do!

TED. We build engines to the stars.

FAIRY. Engines. Big deal. A fish has better engines than those of the *Queen Elizabeth*.

TED (*commandingly*). Don't you undress here!

FAIRY. What's the matter? Afraid you'll see wings?

TED. I know why you're undressing! I've read Orlando Finkelstein.

FAIRY. Keep your hands off my person, you fresh thing! Don't try to keep me dressed!

TED. Besides, I don't want you to catch cold. It's freezing in here.

FAIRY. I haven't *time* to catch cold. More than that, my kind never catches cold even when there *is* time. That's one of the advantages of being a fairy.

TED. Another advantage, I suppose, is being so *lonely*.

FAIRY (*defiantly*). Who said I was lonely?

TED. Well — aren't you?

FAIRY (*after a pause*). Sure I am! All my life I've been on the inside of a dream looking out on a world full of facts.

TED. But 589! — See how wrong you are — here let me button you up.

FAIRY. No.

TED. Don't you know that dreams and facts are translatable into each other, and chase each other in circles? Fact: The world is round. Dream: Columbus. Fact: Reproduction. Dream: Love.

FAIRY. Hah! What do scientists know about love?

TED. Oh, stop harping on scientists. We've done a lot less harm in the world than —

FAIRY. *Less* harm? You've cheapened mystery and left nothing to guesswork! You make x-ray machines that look right inside people, so there's not even any *privacy* left! You have a horrid instrument that detects such lovely, soft, fluttering things as white lies. And all the time there seems to be *more* suffering, not less. Everybody suffering from something.

TED. Don't you think scientists ever suffer?

FAIRY (*brightening*). They — they do?

TED. Yes, but you mustn't smile. There have been good ones, people you would have liked.

FAIRY. Pooh! Name two!

TED. See that picture of Einstein on the wall? There's one of the greatest men who ever lived. Does *he* look like a scoundrel?

FAIRY (*against her will*). No, he looks sweet. He looks a little like my great-grandfather MacMarrachu.

TED. Well, there you are. If you had known men like him, you'd have liked them. They advanced knowledge. Even at the risk of persecution; at the risk of their lives, sometimes. They helped us to understand all sorts of wonderful things. Like how to conquer disease and pain, which I don't think even you approve of.

FAIRY (*after a pause*). No, I don't, and that's a fact.

TED. So you see science *can* be useful. And it doesn't have the limitations of magic. Why think of the ordinary telephone. It makes ventriloquists out of every one of us. We throw our voice and it comes out anywhere we like, even half a world away.

FAIRY. Why shouldn't it, for the money it costs? Twelve thousand leprechaun pounds for the first three minutes to call Ireland!

TED. Think of the wonders we have come to understand…the mysteries of birth; the movements of the stars…

FAIRY. Which are made of *gas*! What knowledge to have! I tell you, your whole profession is *destructive*!

TED. It isn't we who are destructive, it's what is —

FAIRY. I know what you're going to say. — It's what is *done* with your gismos that gets you into trouble.

TED. Will you stop putting words in my mouth and *listen* to me?

FAIRY. No! When I first heard of science, as a mere fairykin — I thought it was cute. I thought it was a kind of servant to you mortals, so you could have more time to play poker and write poems and figure out ways of staying out of trouble. But when I grew up, I saw that far from being your butler and handyman, it was your executioner. You invent the wheel — CRUNCH! — people get run over; you discover electricity? BZZT! The electric chair! You split atoms? BOOM! Cities wiped out! See what I mean?

TED. Yes. — But the scientist has to mature like everyone else. He has to do more than create — he has to help bring up what he creates — rear it — like a child — and not run away from it. He has to see that it grows up to be a good citizen and not a criminal. *That's* his goal, *that's* the knowledge we're after in the end — to link what IS with what SHOULD BE.

FAIRY. By the snakes, *must* you torture me in my last *seconds*, with all this palaver about what should be?

TED (*with a burst of enthusiasm*). Listen, Mab! — I'm going to finish my work! I'm going back to Duffus with a new bundle of dreams and facts — and, by God, you're coming with me! — Put those fluffies back on!

FAIRY (*defiantly*). I took them off for a *reason*!

TED. I happen to know the reason. — "Act of purification in release of the mundane." — And I'm *not* going to let you *do* it.

FAIRY. I kicked them off in order to *dance*, before the hour strikes.

TED. You're not dancing on a cold floor. You're keeping those fluffies on, and you're going to —

FAIRY (*listening to something*). Shh!

TED. What is it?

FAIRY. Don't you hear?

Music: Faint, spiritual harp music seems to be coming out of the walls.

TED. Yes. Where's it coming from? What is it?

FAIRY. My Swan Song. Look at the clock. I've got just a few seconds… and every expiring fairy is permitted one last request. — I've always wanted to dance because it's so dreamy, and I've never had time to do it. I'm taking what time is left to me.

The clock begins to strike twelve: first bong.

TED. Mab!

FAIRY. But before I go, Dr. Bigelow…(*Bong.*)…before I pass out of this sphere which contains my beloved Ireland…(*Bong.*)…I must tell you that I — I — (*Bong.*) — I am as fond of you as a fairy may possibly become…(*Bong.*)…

TED. My dear, wonderful, magical Mab — (*Bong.*)

FAIRY. No — don't touch me! (*Bong.*) I begin to expire…

TED. Mab! Mab! Listen to me! (*Bong.*) You can't *do* such a preposterous thing! (*Bong.*)

FAIRY (*her voice fading*). I leave you sadly, Dr. Bigleow…(*Bong.*)…So fare thee well…fare thee well…(*Bong.*)

Music: Fades as mysteriously as it began. There is a moment of silence before:

FAIRY (*weakening*). I'm going limp…I've lost my breath…

TED. Put your lips to mine — I'll breathe into you — mouth-to-mouth resuscitation…

A few moments of heavy breathing. Just heavy breathing.

FAIRY. I — I suddenly feel very — warm-blooded…

TED. It's working…it's working!
FAIRY. I do believe that — nary am I — anymore — a fairy! I suspect I have — expired — as such —
TED. Welcome to my inferior species!
FAIRY. I must say, in all candor — that I like having your arms around me.
TED. And so do I. And so do I.

Music: A warm-blooded curtain.

CORWIN ON
THE CURSE OF 589

This one owes its life to several prior productions: principally to *Mary and the Fairy*, whence cometh the Fairy, except that she was now Leprechaun No. 589, a member of the North American Division of the Leprechaun International, a worldwide organization now dedicated to a program of hostility against anything scientific.

It is her express mission to mortify a prominent scientist named Dr. Ted Bigelow, who has just been honored by space scientists by conferring upon him the title of Winner of the Galaxy Award.

It is my thesis that any vehicle which can exceed 45 mph, is flying too fast. Also that scientists must be servitors of mankind, and not the enemies thereof. I call upon science as servitor of mankind, not its enemy.

FROM THE EDITOR

This script began as a stage play written for especially the University of Utah in 1966 to inaugurate their new campus theater. The play, then called *The Hyphen*, starred William Shatner immediately prior to his work on the television series *Star Trek*. In 1971 Corwin adapted the play for his television series, *Norman Corwin Presents*. The show was retitled *The Discovery* and again starred William Shatner. Thirty-one years later, Shatner again returned to the role of Dr. Ted Bigelow for this radio production.

OUR LADY OF THE FREEDOMS AND SOME OF HER FRIENDS

The fourth in the series *More By Corwin*, this program was broadcast over NPR in July 1997. The script began as an essay commemorating the centennial of the Statue of Liberty in 1986. It was then recorded and released as a record album narrated by Norman Corwin.

This broadcast starred Charles Kuralt as the Narrator (recorded just prior to his death on July 4, 1997). Others in the cast were: Alice Backes, Jeff Corey, Steve Franken, Bonnie Grice, Louis Nye, Monte Markham, Mala Powers, Phil Proctor, and Elliott Reid.

Technical direction by Marty Halperin and Warren Dewey. Music by Ken Stange.

Mary Beth Kirchner produced. The author directed.

Interior airport atmosphere. Over this:

LOUDSPEAKER. Flight 797 for Paris is now boarding at Gate 26…Flight 797 for Paris is now boarding at Gate 26.

Fade airport ambiance under:

NARRATOR. There is no question about which Paris that flight is bound for. But there happen to be fourteen other Parises. One is in Canada, and the rest —
VOICE ONE. Paris, Arkansas.
VOICE TWO. Paris, Idaho.
VOICE THREE. Paris, Illinois.
VOICE FOUR. Paris Crossing, Indiana.
VOICE ONE. Paris, Kentucky.
VOICE TWO. Paris, Maine.
VOICE THREE. Paris, Mississippi.
VOICE FOUR. Paris, Missouri.
VOICE ONE. Paris, New York.
VOICE TWO. Paris, Ohio.
VOICE THREE. Paris, Tennessee.
VOICE FOUR. Paris, Texas.
VOICE ONE. Paris, Virginia.
NARRATOR. But it's the Paris in *France*, the one Oliver Wendell Holmes thought all good Americans want to go to when they die, that all good Americans now alive and listening may go to right *now* simply by staying tuned. — To meet some friends of a great lady we all know and love, and the Lady herself.

Music: Gallic, garnished with a sprinkling of "Hail Columbia," dissolving into:

Interior of a jet plane, sustained under:

NARRATOR. Ah, there she is — Paree — brilliant from the air, the Champs, the Arch, the skeletal Eiffel, the holy cluster of the Sacré Coeur, the pale Seine wearing her bridges like bracelets, the Boulevards, the Place de la Concorde, Notre Dame, the Panthéon, the Opera, Les Invalides. And out there half way to the horizon, in a working class district, is the Rue de Chazelles, the street on which, one-and-a-quarter centuries ago, our Statue of Liberty was born and raised, before she was taken down and sent abroad. — But all that comes later.

Fade jet background under continuing narration, of which there has been no pause.

NARRATOR. First, let it be said that, thanks largely to the influence of that very Statue as a symbol of hospitality, we are the only country in the world in which honor and respect are shown people and nations far from one's own borders, in all directions. A glorious proof of that uniqueness is the roster of places we have named after foreign parts and populations, for there is nothing like our tally in either Europe, Asia, Africa, the rest of our hemisphere, or the Antipodes.

VOICE ONE. Bagdad, Arizona.
VOICE TWO. Albuquerque, New Mexico.
VOICE THREE. Manila, Utah.
VOICE FOUR. Madrid, Kentucky.
VOICE ONE. Waterloo, Iowa.
VOICE TWO. Bombay, New York.
VOICE THREE. Trafalgar, Indiana.
VOICE FOUR. Amazonia, Missouri.
VOICE ONE. Syria, Virginia.
VOICE TWO. Five Toledos.
VOICE THREE. Athens in Georgia and fourteen other states.
VOICE FOUR. Havanas in Kansas and four other states.
VOICE ONE. Twelve Genevas.
VOICE TWO. Panama City, Florida.
VOICE THREE. Seven Bethlehems.
VOICE FOUR. Jerusalems in Ohio and three other states.
VOICE ONE. Two Jerichos.
VOICE TWO. Four Nazareths.
VOICE THREE. Ten Hebrons.
VOICE FOUR. Eight Cubas.

As the Voices continue, they drop behind the Narrator and serve as background, slowly fading toward the end of the list.

VOICE ONE. Granada, Minnesota.
VOICE TWO. Two dozen Oxfords.
VOICE THREE. Five Belgrades.
VOICE FOUR. Five Corinths.

VOICE ONE. Two Johannesburgs.
VOICE TWO. Three Egypts.
VOICE THREE. Nine Viennas.
VOICE FOUR. Four Smyrnas.
VOICE ONE. Twelve Alexandrias.
VOICE TWO. Seven Memphises.
NARRATOR. It never occurred to us to change the names of towns and cities because we happened to fall out with, or go to war against, the governments of those countries. We kept all nine of our Berlins, nine Hamburgs, five Dresdens, two Potsdams, and two Weimars. Nor did we think it ironic that even when the people of those cities whose names we borrowed, were arrayed against us, we kept two Tokios here at home, and seven Romes, and seven Naples, and eleven Genoas. And all through a long Cold War, no one introduced a bill, or even a *notion*, to rename Moscow in Idaho, or any of the other nine Moscows around the country. Nor did anybody object to our having two Kemlins, one in Montana, the other in Oklahoma.

So, to get down to it, we were certainly the first, and still may claim to be the *only* international country — easily the most pluralized; a society so idea-driven from the start, that the very names we gave our communities derive from ideals that may seem quaint today, but which are worth recalling when we celebrate, as we do every summer, our evolution from the revolution of 1776.

Music: Twenty bars for thirteen states.

NARRATOR. By now we're reasonably safe in calling her an enduring phenomenon — a four hundred and fifty thousand pound lady who occupies a very small island off the shores of our greatest city. At first she wasn't even called the Statue of Liberty, but by a longer and less graceful name...*Liberty Enlightening the World*. She was never intended to represent Liberty casting off chains or anything like that — although there *are* broken chains at her feet — but instead she was given the role of a dispenser of Enlightenment. Which meant that her work was cut out for her, since God knows enlightenment is something the need for which will never end.

But as for the Lady herself — ah! Well! Think of her! To begin with, she's beautiful. Not like a Venus, or a starlet, or an anchorwoman, or a dreamgirl on the cover of a magazine, but closer to everyone's notion of how a goddess should look — strong and serene, imperturbable, with majestic grace — awesome, yet benign — Luminous.

Unsmiling, but not solemn — with a downward gaze, which is understandable, because she's taller than anything around her. And big. Very big. Her index finger measures eight feet, her nose four feet. Her eyes, each two-and-a-half feet wide, look down on the waters of the Atlantic at her feet.

And radiating from her crown are seven huge spikes, symbolic of the rays of the sun that light her each morning before anything else surrounding her. — Her right arm is held high above her head, and her massive hand clutches a torch. She stands taller than a fifteen-story building.

Our Lady of the Freedoms, she might be called. Mother of Exiles, she *has* been called. The torch, from which sculptured flames billow, is not incendiary, not intended to set a fire, but to glow as a beacon against storm and darkness.

Cradled in her massive left arm is a tablet on whose three hundred square foot surface one might expect to find some inscription in Greek or Latin, or an elegant passage from the Bible or Shakespeare — but there is only a date:

VOICE THREE. July 4, 1776.

NARRATOR. For Americans, that's elegant enough.

But wait. — This is ahead of our story. We know where our goddess was born on the Rue de Chazelles — but where was she conceived and by whom?

B.G. of a small dinner party, and sustain behind:

NARRATOR. It happened one evening in 1865, in a château near Versailles at the home of a prominent French jurist, Édouard René Lefebvre de Laboulaye, a liberal who liked everything he knew about America — and he knew a lot. Among his guests that night was a thirty-four year old sculptor named Frédéric Auguste Bartholdi. They got to talking about amity between nations, of which there was as little then as there is now.

LABOULAYE. Think of it, Bartholdi — on this whole swarming globe, there are only two countries that can truly be called friends.

BARTHOLDI. Possibly because they're the only two republics.

LABOULAYE. No. That helps, of course, but it's not enough to explain the attachment. I think our relationship with America runs deeper than parallels of government — it's a kinship of *spirit* — a shared love of freedom. — I'm not being sentimental.

BARTHOLDI. No, I agree with you.

LABOULAYE. Then — then, my dear Bartholdi — I have a proposition for you! The States have a very big birthday coming up in just a few years. In '76 they'll be a hundred years old.

BARTHOLDI. Their Centennial!

LABOULAYE. Yes, and I've been thinking how great it would be if France, to show the world and ourselves that we've recovered from the humiliation of losing that damn stupid war with Prussia — to show that our love of liberty is undiminished, and to signal our return to moral vigor — if we were to make a GIFT — a *birthday present* — to the people we helped win freedom from our old nemesis across the Channel —

BARTHOLDI. What kind of gift?

LABOULAYE. Ah! — That's where you come in. — I understand you lean toward monumental sculpture — that you were inspired by the great works of Egypt — the pyramids, the Sphinx, the colossi —

BARTHOLDI. Who *wouldn't* be inspired by them?

LABOULAYE. Well, here's a chance to do some inspiring *yourself!* — By sculpting a mammoth statue, one that would rival the Seven Wonders of the World! The figure of a female — as godly as Mother Earth herself. I'd call her *Liberty Enlightening the World*, or something like that. Do you know what I'm saying?

BARTHOLDI. Yes, yes — I hardly know how to comment…(*After a pause.*) I — I'd be more than honored — I'd be *thrilled* to take on such a commission, especially since my feelings about America are like your own. — But how on earth could such a thing be *funded*? I'm not talking about my fee, though I do like to eat, drink and wear clothes. I mean the enormous expense of planning, designing, fabricating, constructing, transporting, and setting in place a huge statue! — Also there might be some question as to whether a colossus made in France would be *accepted* by Americans — or, if accepted, whether it would be given a decent location and a pedestal to stand on.

LABOULAYE. Yes, yes, yes, but all that would be managed in good time. *Certainly* it will take tremendous organization — committees and sub-committees on both sides of the water — private and public funding — contributions — lobbying — ingenuities and prodigies of hard work. But, my dear fellow, no great good comes easy, and this would be both great and good!

BARTHOLDI (*still puzzled*). But where would America choose to *place* a colossus, if she takes her in? She shouldn't be stuck away in some outback, or where she'd be hard to get to, like those ancient relics in remote deserts or jungles. Also, a statue as titanic as this would demand a pedestal, and no trifling one either. Something dignified and durable. A goddess created to stand tall for centuries, perhaps millennia, can't be simply set down on the ground like a totem pole. Who in America would decide on that? The President? Congress? A state? A city? How would we begin to —

LABOULAYE. Look, Bartholdi — these matters will be carefully studied and worked out. The important question right now is whether you'll accept the challenge and take on the task. You'd have all the help you need. — Now, I don't expect you to go home tonight and start sketching the eighth wonder of the world. I simply want to know whether, from where you stand right now, you think it's possible to do what we're talking about.

BARTHOLDI. Well…(*After some thought.*) I think it *is* possible.

LABOULAYE. Good!

BARTHOLDI. Moreover, I'd give my life to do it.

LABOULAYE. Ah! Bravo! Bravo! Now you're talking! — Let's drink to it!

Music: A Franco-American toast.

NARRATOR. Agendas. Conferences. Opinions. Decisions. What will it take to get started? What more to carry it off? Important — lose no time lining up Ferdinand de Lesseps, who built the Suez Canal — and Gustave Eiffel, who later will build the Eiffel Tower — to forge the guts of the statue, to design an inner structure strong enough to withstand wind, storm, extremes of weather, long range wear and tear. But first — first you must go to the States and travel around it, and make friends — yes, you, Bartholdi — you have the prestige, the charisma, to persuade. — Laboulaye will give you letters of introduction to important Americans — artists, scholars, editors, opinion-makers, office holders. Take as long as you need to break ground, so you can proceed with confidence.

BARTHOLDI. Yes. All right. By God, I'll do it. I'll go.

NARRATOR. And Bartholdi went.[1] In those days it took two weeks by sea. Even before his ship docked, as it was steaming into New York harbor, he spotted the site where he'd like to see his Lady domiciled — a small island, so small that *seventy* of them could fit into New York's Central Park. With room left over.

When Bartholdi reached port, he asked about that island. It took a while to find somebody who knew:

NEW YORKER. Oh, *that*. It was first owned by Indians. They called it Kilksh.

---

1. The year was 1871.

BARTHOLDI. *Kilksh?*
NEW YORKER. Means gull. Seagull. Then the Dutch got hold of it and used it for oyster fishing. And then it was bought by a man named Isaac Bedloe, who sold it to the federal government to use as a quarantine station. There's even a small graveyard for some people who died there. And then it became an ammunition dump, and then a fort. — Ever hear of General William Tecumseh Sherman?
BARTHOLDI. The Sherman of the march through Georgia?
NEW YORKER. The same. Well, it was he who inspected the island and approved it as a fort.
BARTHOLDI. And the government still owns it?
NEW YORKER. Far as I know.
BARTHOLDI. And it's called?
NEW YORKER. Bedloe's Island.
BARTHOLDI. Thank you very much.

Music: First of a series of brief interludes between vignettes, each dipping under the scene which follows it:

NARRATOR. One of Bartholdi's many letters of introduction took him to Cambridge, Massachusetts, where he was invited to dinner at the home of Henry Wadsworth Longfellow, then America's most famous poet.

Dinner background.

LONGFELLOW. *Audaciously* beautiful! A great vision! I'm especially drawn to the conceit of the torch serving as a beacon for ships at sea. That would make her the tallest lighthouse in the world, by a wide margin.
BARTHOLDI. It's use as a lighthouse is by no means a certainty. It would depend on the wishes of your government — assuming the statue is accepted in the first place.
LONGFELLOW. Oh, there can be no doubt about that. — By the way, I take as a good augury, as well as a coincidence, that in a poem I once wrote about Florence Nightingale,[2] that saintly nurse known as "the Lady with the Lamp" because she haunted hospital wards at night tending wounded soldiers, there is a verse that in a way fits your Lady of Liberty. Just a few short lines. Would you care to hear them?
BARTHOLDI. Please.

2. *Santa Filomena* published in 1857.

LONGFELLOW. "A lady with a Lamp shall stand
   In the great history of the land,
   A noble type of good
   Heroic womanhood."
BARTHOLDI. Most apt. That would please her...
LONGFELLOW. Well now, sir — what can I do to help your mission?
BARTHOLDI. Raise your voice, Mr. Longfellow. Spread the word. If the statue is accepted, we hope your government will respond by giving it a worthy setting, and will at the same time assume the responsibility and cost of building a pedestal for it.
LONGFELLOW. Do you actually believe there is any *question* of that happening?
BARTHOLDI. Well, sir, I've already been told there may be all kinds of hesitations — that your country is recovering from a depression; that people are preoccupied settling the West; are absorbed in developing new industries; are coping with urban problems. Hence they may not be keen about accepting a gift that will cost them a lot of money to put in place.
LONGFELLOW. Still, it's hard for me to imagine either the government or the public turning you down. — In your campaign, who are you planning to see?
BARTHOLDI. Among others, I have appointments with the President of Harvard College, and your Senator Charles Sumner, and on to Washington to meet with President Grant.
LONGFELLOW. Aha! Ulysses S. Grant! That should do it! — And the cities you intend to visit?
BARTHOLDI. Let's see if I remember them: Philadelphia, Pittsburgh, Cincinnati, St. Louis, Chicago, Denver, Salt Lake City, Cheyenne, Stockton, San Francisco.
LONGFELLOW. To meet with?
BARTHOLDI. Financiers, office holders, artists, industrialists, philanthropists, journalists, and — I trust — ordinary citizens.
LONGFELLOW. Good! Good! I warrant you'll see more of America than ever I have or will. You'll see a lot of raw half-built boom towns, and may even run into herds of buffalo en route. I certainly wish you well in your travels, and in the success of your project. A noble project if there ever was one!

Music: Another quick cue.

NARRATOR. Washington. The White House. President Ulysses S. Grant.
GRANT. Sounds good to me. It would definitely make a nice gift, which I know my countrymen will appreciate.

BARTHOLDI. May it be assumed, Mr. President, that the government will provide a site for the Statue on Bedloe's Island?
GRANT. Ah — well now — that would have to be taken up with Congress. While I personally might be inclined to be in favor of it, I don't have the authority to dispose of government property.
BARTHOLDI. Do you anticipate any problem in getting the support of Congress?
GRANT. Who knows? Generally Congress is more interested in statutes than statues.
BARTHOLDI. Wouldn't your advocacy help?
GRANT. There's no guarantee of that.
BARTHOLDI (*disappointed*). Oh.
GRANT. The facts of life in Washington. — Will you have a cigar, Mr. Bartholdi?
BARTHOLDI. No, thank you. I'm afraid cigars are too strong for me.
GRANT. I smoke twenty of them every day.
BARTHOLDI. Really? Twenty? Every day?
GRANT. At least that many. — Mind if I light up?
BARTHOLDI. Not at all.

Music: Another interstice. Before it fades:

NARRATOR. Footnote: President Grant died of throat cancer.

Music: Concludes.

NARRATOR. In Salt Lake City, Bartholdi was invited to model a bust of the Mormon leader and first territorial governor of Utah, Brigham Young. Several appointments were made for sittings, but each was postponed. After several days...
WOMAN. I'm very sorry, Mr. Bartholdi, but Governor Young has again been detained, and will be unable to meet with you until sometime next week.
BARTHOLDI. I'm sorry, too, because I'm afraid I can wait no longer.
WOMAN. He's been terribly busy. In addition to matters of state, family concerns have intervened. The Governor has fifty-six children, you see.
BARTHOLDI. I understand. Please convey my many respects to Mr. Young.

Music: Once more unto the breach.

NARRATOR. For five months Bartholdi toured, covering seventeen of the thirty-seven states that then made up the Union. Although many people supported his project, public officials seemed indifferent. So Bartholdi went back to France — not to sulk, but to work. The trip had by no means been wasted. He had met, charmed, and persuaded many people who would later help his cause, and he had found the place where he hoped his lady would be settled — just a mile-and-a-half off the tip of Manhattan.

In Paris, no one associated with the project lost any zeal. It would take more than official coolness to discourage Laboulaye...

LABOULAYE. A passion for liberty is not turned off by a few rejections, or by a lack of imagination in certain people along the way.

NARRATOR. For the next three years, off and on, without any assurance that his statue, which he now called "my American," would ever make it to Bedloe's acres, Bartholdi kept experimenting with sketches and models — and then the undertaking got a big boost: an international committee was formed, the Union Franco-Américaine, whose goal was — come what may — to present the Statue to America on July 4, 1876, the hundredth anniversary of the Declaration of Independence.

Bartholdi went back to the drawing board with renewed energy...

Naturally there were detractors — just about everything worthwhile tends to attract detractors. But after a while French newspapers began running appeals for funds to finish the work. And there were special occasions — Without any pause in the narration, sneak in background of a crowd in a large banquet hall, and sustain under:

NARRATOR. — such as a grand banquet at the Grand Hôtel du Louvre, a fund-raiser, the centerpiece of which was a painting of how the Statue would look at night when in residence in New York. The banqueters included men of the arts well known today — Jacques Offenbach, composer; Alexandre Dumas fils, novelist; the art dealer Goupil who had advised Vincent Van Gogh that he painted too fast, and was in return advised by Vincent that he, Goupil, *looked* too fast. Everybody who was anybody in Paris showed up.

Music: Without interrupting narration, cross-fade to brief reprise of Gounod cantata under:

NARRATOR. Next there was a gala at the Paris Opera, at which the Gounod[3] cantata was performed, and at which Laboulaye made a speech in which he prophesied:

---

3. Refers to French composer Charles-François Gounod.

LABOULAYE. A little over a century from now, in 1976, America, with an enormous population, will celebrate her *second* Centennial. By then she will have forgotten us in this palace of music, but I'm confident she will not have forgotten either Washington or Lafayette. For the Statue of Liberty, created in a common effort, will preserve among future generations, the eternal friendship of the United States and France.

NARRATOR. Footnote to that prediction: In the United States today there are twenty-five Washingtons, including the chief one in the District of Columbus — and the *state* Washington. — As for forgetting Lafayette...

VOICE ONE. Lafayette, Alabama.
VOICE TWO. Lafayette, California.
VOICE THREE. Lafayette, Colorado.
VOICE FOUR. Lafayette, Georgia.
VOICE ONE. Lafayette, Illinois.
VOICE TWO. Lafayette, Indiana.
VOICE THREE. Lafayette, Kentucky.
VOICE FOUR. Lafayette, Louisiana.
VOICE ONE. Lafayette, Minnesota.
VOICE TWO. Lafayetteville, North Carolina.
VOICE THREE. Lafayette, New Jersey.
VOICE FOUR. Lafayette, New York.
VOICE ONE. Lafayette Hill, Pennsylvania.

NARRATOR. Ah, but again — again — we're ahead of the story. — Notwithstanding a succession of fund-raising events, there remained sticky money problems, and it would be some time before anybody came up with a solution. Still, that didn't stay Bartholdi's hand. His goddess grew, not from the ground up, the way a house is built, but piecemeal, to be assembled later. And when it became clear that the sculpture couldn't possibly be finished, sent across the Atlantic, and lifted onto a pedestal — any pedestal — by the target date of the centennial, July 4, 1876, Bartholdi and Laboulaye decided to dispatch, for preview, at least *part* of the statue. So the right forearm and hand holding the torch were shipped to America in twenty-one crates, *years* before the rest of the body would follow.

The limb, which by itself stood thirty feet high, was for display at the Philadelphia Centennial Exposition; and when that fair ended, the segment was hauled to New York and set up in the open at Fifth Avenue and Twenty-Third Street, where visitors, at fifty cents a head, could climb a ladder to a balcony encircling the torch.

Also, years before the Statue was completed, Bartholdi, on one of his many trips to America, decided to patent his creation. He went to the Copyright Office in Washington and registered his work until the title of *Design for a Statue of American Independence*. It was entered in the patent books as Number 11,023.

BARTHOLDI. "To all whom it may concern: Be it known that I, August Bartholdi of Paris, in the Republic of France, have originated and produced a Design of a Monumental Statue being a commemorative monument of the independence of the United States; and I hereby declare the following to be a full, clear, and exact description of the same...The statue is that of a female figure standing erect upon a pedestal, (*Start fading under the following lines.*) the body being thrown slightly over to the left leg so as to gravitate upon the left leg, the whole figure being thus in equilibrium, and symmetrically arranged with respect to..."

COPYRIGHT OFFICIAL. Term of patent for Design Number 11,023 — fourteen years.

NARRATOR. Meanwhile in France, torrents of publicity, intense fund-raising, and donations from forty thousand men, women and children — produced enough francs for the heavy going to start. Bartholdi and a team of helpers took over the workshop of Gaget & Gauthier, a company that had just installed a new dome on the Paris Opera House.

Pattern of hammering on metals and the roar of forges fading slowly behind:

NARRATOR. The job required as much industry as it did art. It took thirty men working ten hours a day — carpenters for the scaffolding; engineers; metalworkers; a supervisor of copper plating; welders for the skeleton. The statue was made up of three hundred sections, each involving complex mathematical calculations to accommodate weight, stress, gravity, and wind resistance — and yet all of these had to come together to serve Bartholdi's vision:

BARTHOLDI. I have a horror of frippery of detail in sculpture. Forms and effects should be broad, massive, simple. I'm not wasting the force of the work on frivolous details...As for attitude, I want something of the serenity of the Egyptian colossi — a figure that will stress prudence and legality.

NARRATOR. But as work progressed, there were lingering worries about American reluctance to offer up Bedloe's Island or any other site, and an even more conspicuous hesitation to underwrite a pedestal. Grumblers grumbled, and so did some of the press:

FIRST GRUMBLER. Look — I'm a farmer in Ohio, trying to make ends meet, and I don't see why I should spend hard-earned money for something that's just going to make New York look good. That's a rich city they got there, lousy with banks and trusts and millionaires running all over the place, and gamblers getting fat from the stock market, so I say to hell with 'em, let 'em buy their own big dolls.

SECOND GRUMBLER. Yeah, well, it's nice that the Frenchies are giving us a present, but I tell you, as a soldier who fought for the Union and got roughed up — see these scars? — I wasn't too happy about the way France played nice with the South during our Civil War. Sure, I know France helped us win our Revolution, but that was long ago, wasn't it?

NARRATOR. The *New York Times*, in an editorial:

THE TIMES. No true patriot can support large expenditures for a bronze female in the present state of our finances.

NARRATOR. The *New York Herald* thought the idea of the Statue was too big, too abstract, too far out.

THE HERALD. Why not just present a simple life-sized statue of General Lafayette, who is after all well-known and well liked in this country? We don't need a giant.

NARRATOR. But there were also avid supporters of the Statue, and some were angry enough with the opposition, to organized fresh subscription drives for the pedestal. They also tried to get New York's legislature to authorize New York City to make a gift of fifty thousand dollars, but Grover Cleveland, then Governor of the state, vetoed the bill.

CLEVELAND. This is no time to be spending money on statuary.

NARRATOR. So response to the new fund drives was slow and meager. After weeks, the amount collected wouldn't have paid for a knuckle on one of the statue's toes. And then Congress finally got around to voting on a bill for an appropriation of one hundred thousand dollars. It was bluntly rejected.

The granting of a patent to Bartholdi having no way advanced prospects for acceptance in New York, he thought maybe he should offer it to other cities. And so he did. To his happy surprise, Philadelphia was interested. And so were Boston, Baltimore, Chicago, Cleveland, St. Louis and Minneapolis. A newspaper in Baltimore went so far as to proclaim:

BALTIMORE. New York doesn't *deserve* a Statue of Liberty! Baltimore alone, without asking help from Congress or anybody else, will build a pedestal in Chesapeake Bay!

NARRATOR. Closer to New York, Boston was especially receptive, and *that* so shocked the *New York Times* that it completely reversed itself:

THE TIMES. The Statue is *dear* to us, and no third-rate town is going to step in and take it from us. Let Boston be warned that she can't have our Liberty! We have more than a million people in this city who are resolved that that great statue shall be smashed into minute fragments before it shall be stuck up in Boston harbor. If we are to lose the statue it shall go to some worthier and more modest place — Painted Post,[4] for example, or Glover, Vermont.

NARRATOR. Notwithstanding the *Times'* somersault, there was no great rush to climb on Bartholdi's bandwagon. It was not until a Jewish immigrant from Hungary who had settled in St. Louis twenty years earlier, and had worked his way up in journalism to the point where he was able to buy the *New York World*, that the campaign to bring the Statue to America began to look promising. Pulitzer treated the Statue as a personal and passionate crusade, keeping up a steady barrage of editorials and rallying the public to compensate for the indifference of the affluent who, he complained, could underwrite the pedestal in no more time than it takes to sign a half dozen checks.

PULITZER. The noble gift of the statue is ready for us. And here, in the commercial metropolis of the Western world, where hundreds of our citizens reckon their wealth by millions, where our merchants and bankers and brokers are spoken of as "princes," we stand haggling and begging in order to raise money to procure a pedestal…New York ought to blush at this humiliating spectacle. Only a quarter of a million dollars needed for the work, and subscriptions crawling along at a snail's pace! As the rich citizens have shown such apathy in the matter, let the poorer classes move. The *New York World* offers to receive all sums of one dollar and up that may be sent in its care. Let's see if the people have more respect for their Statue of Liberty and the reputation of their city, than the millionaires and merchant princes!

NARRATOR. Contributions started coming in, slowly at first, then with gathering momentum, not only from New York but from as far away as Minnesota and Texas — a dollar here and a dollar there, mostly less than a dollar — from workers, farmers, factory hands, country doctors, clerks, salesmen, widows, children. Donations that were touching in their smallness were frequently accompanied by moving letters, like the one from a boy who wrote:

BOY. Enclosed find ten cents, my pocket piece.

NARRATOR. And another from three kids who pooled their resources, explaining:

---

4. Painted Post, NY.

SECOND BOY. We send you one dollar, the money we saved to go to the circus with.

NARRATOR. A nine-year-old girl offered a pair of pets.

LITTLE GIRL. I have two pet bantams, and I love them a lot, but I will send them to you to sell and give the money to the Statue.

NARRATOR. At last, at what can fairly be called long last, the goal was reached. All those sous, centimes and francs donated by the French, all the pennies, nickels, dimes, quarters, and dollars chipped in by humble Americans, added to the monies accrued from benefits and balcony admissions, were enough to put the drive over. One hundred twenty thousand people had responded to Pulitzer's appeals by sending in one hundred and two thousand dollars — an average of eighty-five cents per contributor. And now it was time to move.

The statue, which for years had towered above the rooftops of Rue de Chazelles, was now disassembled. All segments were labeled and numbered, packed in 214 crates, loaded onto seventeen railroad cars headed for the port of Rouen, and there lowered into the holds of the steamship *Isere*, bound for the New World.

Music: Over the boundless main. After enough, cross-fade to:

Saluting cannon where indicated in the following:

NARRATOR. Almost as though to atone for having dragged its feet, New York went out of its way to celebrate what was, and remains, the greatest single import in American history. France dispatched her entire North American naval force to meet the *Isere* in the outer harbor and escort her past the saluting guns of forts along the way. Our own ships joined in the welcome, blasting whistles and sirens and firing whatever would make a loud noise. On land, there were ceremonies — a parade, concerts by orchestras and choral societies, an official reception at City Hall.

Meanwhile the *Isere's* cargo was unloaded on Bedloe's Island, and everything was set to begin reassembling. But now there were new problems. Bartholdi and his supporters learned that the success of Pulitzer's campaign was only temporary — the costs estimates of the pedestal had gone up. So all those crates containing pieces of the goddess, lay unopened for almost a year while donations straggled in.

Finally — *finally* — there was enough in the coffers to finish the job. Immediately workers swarmed over the island, a hundred of them bunking on it full time. They excavated a pit deep enough to contain the greatest tonnage of concrete ever poured into a single block, then for four months unpacked and rejoined the dismembered parts. After which the skeleton was bolted to iron beams encased in the foundation of the pedestal. A construction engineer summed it up:

ENGINEER. One thing for sure — she'll never fall down. She couldn't be overturned without overturning the island.

Riveting, sometimes multiple, at intervals behind:

NARRATOR. The first two plates to be riveted to the inner structure were dedicated to — and bear the names of — Auguste Bartholdi and Joseph Pulitzer. For months on end, the statue was the biggest and busiest construction site in America.

A solo rivet, clear and loud.

NARRATOR. In October 1886, the last section was riveted to the sole of the right foot, and the goddess was ready to be dedicated. It was ten years and four months too late for the Centennial — but who cared about that now? Bartholdi was happy, and so were the French and American committees that had worked so hard, and so were the artists who had given benefit concerts and performances, and so were the thousands of French citizens who had raised a quarter of a million dollars, and so were thousands of Americans who had paid for the pedestal, and so was Grover Cleveland, now President of the United States and no longer in a veto mood. Happiest of all perhaps would have been Laboulaye, whose idealism had started the whole adventure. But he had died three years earlier.

The hour of consecration had come. The day so long delayed, dawned raw and overcast, but already the big city was astir, primed to add to its allurement a new wonder of the world, the first colossus in history assigned to proclaim liberty.

A cacophony of cheering crowds, and the music of several brass bands. These occur at intervals behind:

NARRATOR. The inauguration itself was glorious in every way but the weather. It rained on the parade that started at Fifth Avenue and Fifty-Seventh Street and sloshed four miles down to the Battery at the foot of Manhattan. It rained on the twenty thousand marchers, and on the cheering crowds who lined the route. It rained on the

President, on Secretaries of his Cabinet, on state and city officials, on members of the clergy, on the brass bands that played the *Marseillaise* and the *Star Spangled Banner* alternately and repeatedly as the procession advanced downtown. It rained on the three hundred ships of all sizes lined up to pass in review before the President, now standing on the poop deck of the SS *Despatch*. It rained impartially on Bedloe's Island, on the officials and orators gathered there, on the shrouded Statue itself, and on everything else for hundreds of miles around. It rained all afternoon; but in the measureless domain of the American spirit, there had never been a sunnier day.

A tri-colored drape big as a mainsail covered the face of Our Lady. Three hundred feet up, inside the crown, Bartholdi had ensconced himself in order to be able to unveil the head on a signal from below, by loosening a cord at the moment when the President of the American Committee, William Evarts, finished speaking.

First to address the scene was a minister whose invocation nobody heard because there was so much noise from the throng at the base of the Statue that his words were swallowed up; and then Evarts got up and tried in vain to outshout the din; and when he paused for a moment to rest his voice, the lookout whose job it was to cue Bartholdi, assumed Evarts had finished, and flashed the signal minutes too soon...Down came the veil!

Pandemonium.

NARRATOR. The clamor of the ages! Cheering such as old New York harbor had never heard before and would never hear again.

The tumult diminishes under:

NARRATOR. When the noise subsided, the ceremony resumed. President Cleveland thanked France and accepted the Statue in the name of the United States; then the French Consul General Lefaivre responded, then there was another speech, which went on too long, followed by a closing benediction, after which celebrants left the island, many of them to party into the night.

Alone at last, Bartholdi's Patent Number 11,023 stood where she was destined to stand, and held aloft the torch that would catch the first rays of the sun when it rose, clear and dazzling, the next morning.

Music: Deliverance.

NARRATOR. Yes, the Goddess of copper and iron now stood securely in place. But before long, a question was raised by friends and cynics alike — what did she stand *for*? If the inscription on the tablet was any clue, she stood for Independence; there it was, plain as could be:

INSCRIPTION. July 4, 1776.

NARRATOR. A noble concept, to be sure, but was independence from Great Britain *all* she stood for? Many countries had been more or less "enlightened," but very few were able to hold on to their liberties if they ever had any in the first place.

The speakers at the inauguration hailed the Statue as a monument to peace and international friendship, both of which are fine genteel abstractions. Laboulaye, at the very onset, defined her in equally abstract terms:

LABOULAYE. The Statue tells us at one and the same time, that Liberty lives only through Truth and Justice, Light and Law.

NARRATOR. But neither Laboulaye nor anybody else at the time, spoke about the statue symbolizing a new life for the unfortunates of the world; about America as a haven for persecuted and homeless peoples; about the lately preserved Union opening wide a Golden Door to millions of immigrants. Nothing of that sort had entered the calculations or expectations of Bartholdi, Pulitzer, Grover Cleveland, or William Evarts. None anticipated that the Lady with the Lamp betokened any of that. But it *had* occurred to a thirty-two-year-old New York woman, a minor poet named Emma Lazarus. In just thirty-six words set down at the end of a sonnet written on request, she struck a chord that reverberates to this day and will likely resound for as long as our nation exists.

Here's what happened: Three years before the inauguration of the statue, the same hardworking William Evarts who would later speak — or try to speak — at the unveiling, approached Emma, as he had already done other writers.

EVARTS. Miss Lazarus, I'm here to ask you to compose a poem on the subject of the Statue of Liberty, for a literary auction to raise money for the pedestal.

EMMA. I'm honored to be asked, Mr. Evarts, but I must be frank with you. I don't like writing to order.

EVARTS. You'd be in good company. We've got manuscripts by Walt Whitman, Bret Harte, and Mark Twain, among others.

EMMA. Then you don't need me.

EVARTS. We need the participation of as many writers as I can persuade. I hope you'll change your mind. No date has yet been set for the auction, but we'd like it to be soon. Will you keep an open mind about it?

NARRATOR. Emma overcame her reluctance, wrote a poem and sent it to Evarts, who caused it to be published together with other pieces written for the auction. Nobody paid much attention to any of this, except for a writer far better known than Emma — James Russell Lowell, who wrote her:

LOWELL. I liked your sonnet about the Statue much better than the Statue itself. It gives its subject *raison d'être* which it wanted before quite as much as it wanted a pedestal.

NARRATOR. When the statue was unveiled, Emma was in Europe. Four months later she returned to New York, very ill, and got her first glimpse of the statue from the deck of her ship. Her illness worsened; in a few weeks she was dead. For the next seventeen years, she was not even a footnote in anything said or written about the Statue; and then one day someone discovered a poem inscribed on a small plaque fastened to an inner wall of the pedestal. The first part of the poem described the statue, but the rest, those thirty-six words, gave it a mission:

EMMA. Give me your tired, your poor
   Your huddled masses yearning to breathe free,
   The wretched refuse of your teeming shore.
   Send these, the homeless, tempest-tost to me.
   I lift my lamp beside the golden door![5]

NARRATOR. There had been no ceremony for the placing of the plaque, no reporters, no announcement of any kind. But the poem, so modestly tendered and quietly posted, bound the name of Emma Lazarus to Bartholdi's masterpiece as surely as if it were graven in steel.

Music: Act curtain.

NARRATOR. A question to ask at the edge of a new millennium: What other nation, before or since, has ever called out, "Give me your tired, your poor, your huddled masses yearning to breathe free?"
   But Emma Lazarus was not the first American to assign to liberty the requirement of humaneness. That very quality was in the thinking of some of the most eminent of our founders. Édouard de Laboulaye's idol, George Washington, had petitioned to a higher Magistrate than himself:

WASHINGTON. I humbly beseech God to render this country, more and more, a propitious asylum for the unfortunate of other countries...

---

5. *The New Colossus* by Emma Lazarus, published in 1883.

NARRATOR. And Thomas Paine, as fiery as Washington was cool, declared in his pamphlet *Common Sense* — published in the very year of our Independence:
PAINE. Every spot of the Old World is overrun with oppression. Freedom hath been hunted round the globe!...O receive the fugitive, and prepare in time an asylum for mankind!
NARRATOR. Thomas Jefferson, for his hilltop, under the dome of Monticello, asked two questions of his countrymen:
JEFFERSON. Shall we refuse to the fugitives from distress, that hospitality which the savages of the wilderness extended to our fathers arriving in this land? — Shall oppressed humanity find no asylum on this globe?
NARRATOR. All three had invoked the word *asylum*. So too, in essence, had Emma Lazarus.

Music: In and behind:

NARRATOR. The sonnet was as good as its word, and its offer stood. The huddled masses came on — a blur of faces and a blear of names. The roll of immigrants was like a directory of realms and races — self-exiled peoples who left blighted countries, cruel societies, vicious systems, taking with them only their dreams, hopes, and apprehensions. They uprooted everything that was familiar to them, and set out for far places, some of the places not yet named or tamed or taken from the wilderness.

They plodded their way across whatever had to be crossed; and when they reached the land that offered what no other did — freedom of opportunity, freedom to think and say what they thought, freedom to worship their own Gods in their own way, they rolled up their sleeves and went to work.

And there was a directness in what they called their towns and villages, a no-nonsense category of place names, in number and variety unlike anything found in any other country. If a place yielded a valuable crop or metal or mineral, its founders named it after the product:
VOICE ONE. Cucumber, West Virginia — Strawberry, Arizona.
VOICE TWO. Cherry, Illinois.
VOICE THREE. Apple Valley, Pearblossom, Orange County, Lemon Grove, California.
VOICE FOUR. Alabaster, Alabama.
VOICE ONE. Bromide, Oklahoma.
VOICE TWO. Hematite, Missouri.

VOICE THREE. Boron, California.
VOICE FOUR. Agate, Colorado.
VOICE ONE. Iron, Minnesota.
VOICE TWO. Copperopolis, California.
VOICE THREE. Petroleum, Indiana.
VOICE FOUR. Oil City, Pennsylvania.
VOICE ONE. Oil Trough, Arizona; Two Oiltons, two Oil Cities elsewhere.
VOICE TWO. Coalville, Coal City, Coal Center, Coalinga, Coalmont, Coal Valley, Coal Run, Coalburg.
VOICE THREE. Topaz, California.
VOICE FOUR. Vanadium, New Mexico.
VOICE ONE. Quartzite, Arizona.
VOICE TWO. Platinum, Arkansas.
VOICE THREE. Cinebar, Washington.
VOICE FOUR. Calcium, New York.
VOICE ONE. Nine states with towns named Sulphur or Sulphur Springs or Sulphur Bluff.
VOICE TWO. Sandstone, Minnesota.
VOICE THREE. Leadville, Colorado.
VOICE FOUR. Gypsums in three states.
VOICE ONE. Granite, Chloride, Onyx, Pyrite, seven Galenas, four Carbons, Basalt, Dolomite, Marble, Mica, Crystal, Emerald, Sapphire, Silver, Gold Bar...

Music: And so on. Pause. Then a darker mood, behind:

NARRATOR. Of course it was not all relish, achievement, and prosperity. No land since Eden has been without blemish, and no people either. Among the hordes, among the millions who passed through Ellis Island, there were dreamers who thought they would find streets paved with silver, and kindness everywhere, and a bottomless soup-kettle of democracy. But the mirage faded on approach; the sun was not warm in the sweatshop, the water was cold in the cold-water flat; there were no rubies lying in the gutters. Children toiled twelve hours a day in factories. At times wages were thrown to workers like scraps to a scrawny dog that had run from a drunken master. As well as good times and peace and progress, there were wars, depressions, antagonisms, meanness and violence.

No, it was not Eden, but in spite of everything, it lay closer to the Garden than any land before it in all history. During and since the great floods of immigration that carried the fathers and mothers of us all, every generation has found — that American perfection, or close to it as any of us will ever come — lies in the seeking of our imperfections, and the tending to them.

Music: Stately-folksy, like the Supreme Court trying out a slow quadrille. It sustains for a while behind:

NARRATOR. The soaring symbol of our liberty is a Woman, and rightly so. Most greatnesses of substance, whether material, intellectual or fanciful, are designated feminine — great ships, fire-breathing locomotives, the mother lodes of mining, mother tongues, the mother church, Mother Earth, Mother Nature.

And the Muses — all nine of them — not brothers or uncles, but sisters! Goddesses, every one. Thus the sovereign logo of our Liberty could not be other than a woman. No one quarrels with that. Were we to rescue the voice of President Cleveland from the din of New York harbor at the inaugural, this is what he said by way of welcoming the gender of the Statue:

CLEVELAND. We are not here today to bow before the representative force of a fierce and warlike god filled with wrath and vengeance, but instead we contemplate our own peaceful deity…instead of grasping in her hand the thunderbolts of terror and of death, she holds aloft the light that illuminates the way to man's enfranchisement…

NARRATOR. And the enfranchisement of women, too, although Our Lady of Bedloe had to wait thirty-four years before her sex was given the right to vote. That freedom, too, had advocates in Washington's time — among them Abigail Adams, wife of John Adams, to whom she wrote during the first session of the Continental Congress:

ABIGAIL. In the new code of laws which I suppose it will be necessary for you to make, I desire you would remember the ladies, and be more gracious and favorable to them than your ancestors…If particular care and attention is not paid the ladies, we are determined to foment a rebellion, and will not hold ourselves bound by any laws in which we have no voice or representation.

NARRATOR. The care and attention Mrs. Adams demanded were long in coming, but still America was from the start, happily aware of her ladies, a consciousness reflected in the names given communities throughout the land. No other country in the world has named so many places for the distaff sex — not for saints or princesses or heroines, but mostly for girls next door:

VOICE ONE. Ruby, Alicia, Edna, Alma, Elaine, Elizabeth, Ida, Eudora, Marcella — and ten other women, in Arkansas alone.

VOICE TWO. Anna Maria, Eloise, Lulu, Mary, Esther, Kathleen — and four others, all in Florida.

VOICE THREE. Bonnie, Clare, Laura, Lena, Nora, Shirley — and eight more, all in Illinois.

VOICE FOUR. Charlotte, Helena, Beverly, Katy, Ruth, Peggy, Sharon, Rebecca, Ava, Eva, Adelaide, Donna, Elsie, Peggy, Leonia, Kim…

NARRATOR. Dozens more, *lots* more. Evidence that male America loves and honors its females. And there is ample evidence, too, that most of us love and revere Our Lady of the Freedoms. But note, fellow Americans, that Freedoms is plural. There are many to be treasured, beyond those staked out in our Bill of Rights, freedoms including the famous Four of FDR — freedom of speech and worship, freedom from want and fear.[6] And still more freedoms were promulgated in a Universal Declaration of Human Rights signed by the United States half a century ago.[7] They include, among other rights:

VOICE ONE. The right to work.

VOICE TWO. The right to equal pay for equal work.

VOICE THREE. The right to rest and leisure, including periodic holidays with pay.

VOICE FOUR. The right to education.

VOICE ONE. The right to participate freely in the cultural life of the community, to enjoy the arts.

Music: Out.

NARRATOR. Idealistic? Impossible goals? Were it not for our having steered course by a compass of ideals, there would likely be no Independence Day to celebrate, and Our Lady in the harbor might mean as little to our national ethos as a showpiece in Las Vegas. Instead of a treasure-filled America, there would lie before us a desert of diminished expectations in which we pursue not the happiness hoped for in Jefferson's Declaration, but a humdrum complacency, comfortable with mediocrity, inspired mainly by the ambition to get along by going along.

In the engaging realm of Names, there is a category that deals squarely with ideals, and it brings this to mind: Unlike any other country, we were, in our youth, so respectful of ideals that we advertised

---

6. Refers to Roosevelt's *Four Freedoms* speech to Congress on January 6, 1941. For the four-network celebration of FDR's birthday, broadcast on January 30, 1943, Corwin wrote and directed a six-minute piece titled *A Moment of the Nation's Time* based on the Four Freedoms.

7. Refers to *Document A/777: International Declaration of Human Rights* (1948).

them and posted them proudly; we named towns and sometimes even children after them. Whereas around the world there are many thousands of communities, there are only *three* outside of the United States, that are named Liberty or Freedom. One is in Canada; the other two — Libertad — are in Peru and Venezuela. But in this country alone there are *forty-three*!

There is also a Fair Play in each of five states, and a Fairchance in a sixth; a town named Amity in Arkansas, a Fidelity in Illinois, a Concord in New Hampshire and thirteen other states — a Felicity in Ohio, a Tranquility in Georgia, a Reliance, Wyoming…

VOICE ONE. Faith, South Dakota.
VOICE TWO. Hope, Kansas.
VOICE THREE. Charity, Missouri.
VOICE FOUR. Grace, North Carolina.
VOICE ONE. Inspiration in Arizona.
VOICE TWO. Accord, New York.
VOICE THREE. Six states with towns named Unity, and a seventh called Pleasant Unity.
VOICE FOUR. Serenity, Colorado.
VOICE ONE. Triumph, Illinois.
VOICE TWO. Honor, Michigan.
VOICE THREE. Towns named Friendship in eight states.
VOICE FOUR. Three named Prosperity.
VOICE ONE. A Happy and a Busy in Kentucky.
VOICE TWO. Blessing, Texas.
VOICE THREE. Temperance, Michigan.
VOICE FOUR. Endeavor and Effort in Pennsylvania.
VOICE ONE. Loving, New Mexico.
VOICE TWO. Loving, Texas.
VOICE THREE. Romance, West Virginia — also Arkansas.
VOICE FOUR. Equality, Alabama.
VOICE ONE. Excel, Alaska.
NARRATOR. And then that gem in the atlas, the euphonious name of Philadelphia, which translates from the Greek, to Brotherly Love.

So there you have it. The people who built America did more than clear woods and build cabins. They named many of the places they lived in for their dreams and ideals, for qualities they admired and sought, concepts that are still around us, still with us, like a ghostly inspiriting inheritance.

A certain man in Avon — there are twelve Avons in America, by the way — once wrote about Special Days:

SHAKESPEARE. What hath this day deserved? What hath it done,
That it in golden letters should be set
Among the high tides in the calendar?[8]

NARRATOR. It hath done much, Mr. S. For starters, it gave us our national birthday; gave us our liberties, gave us our Statue. And since birthdays induce greetings, here are several that are borne in on a high tide:

VOICE ONE. Greetings, Bartholdi! You were a favorite on these shores in your own time, with an Inn and a hotel named for you; yes, and there was a *Bartholdi Day* observed; and right now, at this very hour, in Jersey City, not far from your American Lady, traffic is flowing as usual along Bartholdi Avenue.

VOICE TWO. Greetings, Édouard Laboulaye, in whose learned head this whole grand enterprise began. Also, apologies that you're not nearly as well remembered and honored by us as you deserve to be. But that flaw is easy to remedy: all it takes is a Board of Aldermen, or a City Council somewhere, simply to change their Chestnut street, or Oak, or Maple, to Laboulaye. — Or to rename a quiet byway in the French Quarter of New Orleans. Or better yet, since you've been overlooked, to substitute your name for what is now Overlook Avenue in Washington, D.C., Zip Code 20032.

VOICE THREE. Greetings, Henry Wadsworth Longfellow! It's our pleasure to inform you, not in mournful numbers but in boastful ones, that the Lady sculptured by the man who came to dinner at your house in Cambridge, receives four-and-a-quarter million visitors a year.

VOICE FOUR. Greetings, Joseph Pulitzer, co-dedicatee with August Bartholdi, of the Statue! If the Pulitzer Prize that you established in 1917 had been current in 1886, you'd have won it yourself, hands down, for Meritorious Public Service!

VOICE ONE. And greetings, you kids who chipped in allowance money for marbles, and dolls, and ice cream cones, and thus helped make it possible for your great-great-grandchildren to take a ferry to Liberty Island — no longer called Bedloe's Island — to visit the Lady. Overwhelmingly they count her a rich return on your investment.

WOMAN. And greetings, Emma Lazarus! Greetings, along with our abiding sorrow that you died too soon to know the effect, and the worldwide fame, of your sonnet. You should know that the original manuscript of that poem, written in your hand, rests in the Library of the American Jewish Historical Society, where, be assured, it's cherished and well cared for.

8. *King John*, Act III, Sc i. (1596)

NARRATOR. And greetings, immigrant multitudes who were bid good morrows and good fortune by the Statue — the millions who came, saw, toiled and begat, who created as descent a society as ever this venerable world has known. Naturally it has not been all harmony and innocence. Our purple mountain majesties are rocked at times by temblors, our fruited plains devastated by drought or flood. We have indeed, like all great nations, our knaves and petty tyrants, bullies and exploiters, madmen and murderers. But we are peace-loving and good at removing tarnish by the polishing agents of law and justice and the ballot box.

Hell's bells and the harps of Heaven, what a lady is Our Lady! There are no jewels in her crown, no commercials on her tablets, no commands recorded on a sound track. She is neither an overbearing landlady nor Policewoman to the World, but instead, and in short, the Conscience of the United States of America.

Hail, then, Mighty Woman whose flame Emma Lazarus called "the imprisoned lightning!" Hail, Mother of Exiles! Hail, thou gift of the Gods — in collaboration with good friends in France!

Live always, Our Lady of the Freedoms! Live forever!

Music: Curtain.

CORWIN ON
OUR LADY OF THE FREEDOMS AND SOME OF HER FRIENDS

The Statue of Liberty was devised over the dinner table at a banquet to raise funds for a gift to the then new democracy called the United States of America. It was a gemitlich meeting of Jack Delson and Ellis Backes out of which the concept was born for a program about the origin of the idea for that gift.

There was a dinner party in Paris, France, to raise funds for a gift to America from the oldest republic in the world, which was then the revolutionary republic in the world; to furnish a platform on which to raise a statue of liberty, which was to stand at some designated spot in America where it could welcome visitors to the newest republic of them all. A Frenchman named Bartholdi, nominated himself as the sculptor of the new project: a female robed in a flowing gown and holding a torch high over her head which would light the path to the city. Thus was the concept of a giant statue born. The only questions to be considered were where to put it, and who would pay for it.

Bartholdi volunteered to tour America looking for a city that wanted the statue. The trip began in the east, where President Grant was approached. Grant approved of the idea, but offered no financial support for its construction. So Bartholdi was forced to appeal for funds which took him to the door of Henry Wadsworth Longfellow, a poet and writer of the legendary *Hiawatha*. Longfellow agreed to support the campaign to establish the statue somewhere in America that cared about freedom enough to support building a pedestal, the site of which was offered and turned down by Detroit. Bartholdi then moved west, crossing the country with important stops in Denver, where he waited for days to see Mayor Rogers, and Salt Lake City to see Brigham Young, Governor of Utah, who was too busy to see Bartholdi. The sculptor hung around for days, trying to set an appointment to see the Governor and gave up trying after days of neglect, and reluctantly moved on.

Meanwhile, in New York, a Jewish publisher named Pulitzer was seized by ambition to nominate one of the many islands of New York City to welcome the pedestal Bertholdi was seeking, and nominated a barren island to receive it. Thus, New York was selected as the site of the pedestal and Pulitzer arranged for the funding of it by voluntary contributions of the public. Work on the pedestal began, funded by Pulitzer's campaign, and the pedestal arose higher than anything around it. When it was finished, the statue of the head appeared, and was appropriately displayed in Union Square, downtown where it was shown on Broadway. The rest of the body followed, and the statue was raised. The torch in the upraised left hand was lit, and the statue was in business.

A verse was composed by a Jewish poetess named Emma Lazarus, who arrived in New York after the statue was raised. She would have been pleased that her poem was inscribed inside the statue.

FROM THE EDITOR

Our Lady of the Freedoms was originally recorded and released on audiocassette and record by Anaheim-based Mark 56 Records in 1986. George Garabedian produced and Corwin read the essay. In a *Los Angeles Times* article titled "Norman Corwin, the sage of Los Angles, carries a torch for the Statue of Liberty," published May 19, 1986, columnist Jack Smith praised the piece, writing, "Corwin's tape…should be played in every classroom."

THE SECRETARIAT

The fifth in the series *More By Corwin*, this program was recorded before a live audience at the Museum of Television and Radio in New York on the evening of November 6, 1997 and broadcast over NPR on Thanksgiving weekend 1997. Starring William Shatner (as Bob), Hume Cronyn (the Chief) and Tandy Cronyn (as Joan). Others in the cast were Walt Beaver, Melanie Chartoff, Steve Franken, Elizabeth O'Reilly, Melinda Peterson, Elliott Reid, Phil Proctor, Yuri Rasovsky, and Zack Walker.

Technical direction was by Warren Dewey. Music by Steve Zuckerman.

Mary Beth Kirchner produced. The author directed.

Music: Introduction.

BOB. Joan, are you awake?
JOAN (*sleepily*). I am now.
BOB. Sorry. Go back to sleep.
JOAN. No, what is it?
BOB. Terry asked me a lot of questions today.
JOAN. About the usual?
BOB. No, he already knows more about that than I did at his age. He was asking about prayer.
JOAN (*surprised*). Prayer? What did he want to know?
BOB. He wondered how, with five billion people in the world — and increasing by hundreds of thousands everyday — God keeps track of all their prayers.
JOAN. What did you tell him?
BOB. That God must have a lot of secretaries.
JOAN. Not a great answer, but it'll do for tonight. — Go to sleep, dear, it's late.
BOB. I've wondered about it myself. We assume God is absolutely omniscient, but that doesn't mean he's a bookkeeper. Terry has a right to wonder. Because to handle half the prayers that come swarming in by the millions every single minute of every day — it would take a Secretariat the size of the Pentagon to sort them out, to digest them, and recommend to God's attention whatever merits a response.
JOAN. A *what* the size of the Pentagon?
BOB. A secretariat. A heavenly secretariat.
JOAN. Oh, boy. — Honey, go to sleep and dream about the way heaven is run, so when you wake up you'll have some answers. — Okay?
BOB. Yeah. Okay. G'night.

Music: Eine kleine celestial passage. Sustain faint shimmering for a few moments under:

CHIEF. Welcome. We were expecting you.
BOB. Thank you.
CHIEF. And what were *you* expecting?
BOB. I?
CHIEF. Pearly gates? Grandiosity? White-robed, harp-playing creatures?
BOB. No, not quite, but —
CHIEF. Those are caricatures of Heaven. — I see from your dossier, that you're from a small bubble of a solar system.
BOB. Third planet out from a sun. — In the Milky Way.

CHIEF. Ah, yes. The one you call Earth.

BOB. Correct.

CHIEF. I must tell you that among the very many worlds to which we administer, yours has a certain fame here.

BOB. For what?

CHIEF. For being restless, volatile, ingenious, stupid, artful, violent, noble, debased, inspiring and dismaying, all at once.

BOB. Sorry about that.

CHIEF. I gather from your application, that you're interested in the communication and processing of prayer.

BOB. Yes.

CHIEF. Why the interest?

BOB. My little boy was asking.

CHIEF. Ah! That's a good enough reason. The Maker encourages curiosity and the quest of knowledge.

BOB. The Maker?

CHIEF. God. The Creator. The Supreme. The Infinite. The Absolute. The Omniscient. The Merciful. The Eternal.

BOB. Does he personally — or she — does the Maker, whom I assume is occupied with creating new worlds —

CHIEF. Always, never ending.

BOB. Does the Maker, in spite of being profoundly busy —

CHIEF. Perpetually attending the birth and death of stars, monitoring elements and species, inventing or discontinuing dinosaurs, whales, ants, bacteria, glaciers, dandelions, mountains, the shifting of continental plates, seeding new populations in hitherto unoccupied infinities —

BOB. Does the Maker himself, or herself, weigh, pass on, accept or reject, or in an way respond to all the prayers that pour in — couched, as they must be, in all kinds of codes and languages, every one of them, I imagine, seeking help or favors of some kind?

CHIEF. Are you a lawyer?

BOB. Yes. Why?

CHIEF. The way you asked, "Does the Maker weigh, pass on, accept or reject, or in any way respond"…but continue with your question.

BOB. Specifically, if I may ask, how does the Maker *deal* with prayers from my planet?

CHIEF. With the help of a Secretariat.

BOB (*thrilled*). A *Secretariat*! Aha! Aha! I was *right*! That's what I *figured*! Wait till I tell my wife!

CHIEF. And I am Chief of that Secretariat.

BOB. You are? I am honored beyond expression, to be talking to you.

CHIEF. You should be.

BOB. May I make bold to request — to pray, if you will, that I be enlightened as to just how the system works?

CHIEF. Since your request is humble, and you are not asking forgiveness for a trespass, which would mean sending you to another department, you will be admitted, as a credentialed visitor, to the Temple of the Secretariat. — Follow me.

Music: By shuttle to the Temple. Establish and fade behind:

A slightly cavernous atmosphere. Sound of faint whirring.

BOB (*awed*). Oh my! Enormous! Enormous and beautiful!

CHIEF. And this is only the Prayer Storage and Retrieval Wing for a single minor planet — your own — yet these files go back for millennia, back even to the prayers of nameless primitives.

BOB. But all these tremendous computers and monitors! They look superior to the ones we have on Earth. I had no idea there would be *technology* in the heavens!

CHIEF (*laughing*). Where do you think science and technology *came from*? Who invented the inventors? Your great makers were, and continue to be, made by the Greatest of the Makers.

BOB. Of course. I should have assumed that.

CHIEF. Incidentally, we were interested when a voyager, a cosmonaut, first man to orbit your earth,[1] addressed this very subject. He announced, "Some people believe there is a God out there, but in my travels around the earth, I saw no God or angels. No God helped build our rocket. The rocket was made by our *people*."

BOB. How was that received up here?

CHIEF. It was referred to the Maker, who said, "It is perfectly true that I had no hand in building the rocket. It was not the rocket I made, only the people."

BOB. Very good comment.

CHIEF. But to the point: You wish to know how the prayer system operates. It works this way: We can at any time call up any prayer ever made.

BOB. *Ever* made?

CHIEF. Ever made, by any member of your species; and the prayer will be delivered on command, pre-translated to the language of the inquirer, and identified by region, subject, and petitioner. I will show you how it functions. Make a choice.

1. The Soviet Union's Yuri Gagarin orbited the Earth on April 12, 1961.

BOB. You mentioned primitives. Could you bring up a prayer from one?

CHIEF. No problem, as your jargon puts it. But I should caution you before we get started, that you are within a dream, and when you awaken — now listen carefully — you will find that every one of the prayers you request will actually have been chanted, or spoken, or written — in any case, passed down, so that all place names, as well as the names of the local god or gods to whom the prayers were addressed — for forwarding, you understand — are authentic. None will have been made up for your benefit. You might want to make note of that.

BOB. Thank you, I will.

CHIEF. And now to demonstrate. Attend. I press a combination of command keys — watch.

Action of Computer keys. (This same effect will precede each subsequent retrieved prayer.)

CHIEF. And forthwith you will hear the voice of a primitive in what has, very long since, become Zulu territory:

SHAMAN. When have we ever forgotten to make sacrifices to you? Why are you so miserly? If you don't improve, we will let your name fall into oblivion; we will *forget* you. What's the good of praising you? You bring us neither harvests nor abundant herds. You show no gratitude at all for the trouble we take. However, we don't want to cut you off altogether. We'll tell other tribes about you, and you will suffer for it. We're warning you. We are angry with you.

BOB *(astonished)*. There are really *scolding* prayers?

CHIEF. Oh yes. Also contradictory prayers, like this pair of ancient ones from two regions that are not far from each other:

Computer keys.

WOMAN. Mbamba, you have denied us rain. Grant us rain so that we may not die. Deliver us from death by starvation. For thou art our father and we are your children. Thou hast created us. Why, then, dost thou wish us to die? Give us maize, bananas, and beans. Thou hast given us feet to walk with, and sons. Grant us also rain that we may harvest.

BOB. Sad...

CHIEF. But at the same time, just across a mountain range from where that woman lived, there was an opposite need. Listen to this:

Computer keys.

OLD PYGMY. Epilipili, Epilipili, stop the rain. The rains come, the rains fall, the rains burden us with misery. Our sons are in the forest. Let the rain be slow, let the rain be slow.

BOB. Equally sad...

CHIEF. And there are also some very fierce prayers, too. Here's one from Thailand, when it was still known as Siam. It boasts of integrity.

Computer keys.

SIAMESE. May I be torn in pieces by preternaturally endowed lions, or devoured by alligators, or fatally stricken with cholera, after which may I be precipitated into hell, there to go through innumerable stages of torture, if I pervert the truth so as to lead the judgment of others astray!

BOB. That's a pretty vehement vow. Was it ever broken?

CHIEF. Yes.

BOB. Did punishment follow?

CHIEF. We don't bother the Maker with cases of that sort unless harm is done to others. We let the local authority handle it. — Of course the vast preponderance of prayers seek protection against, or relief from, sickness, poverty, bad luck, accidents, earthquakes, fire, flood, storm, drought, and various other negatives of existence.

BOB. Is every last prayer given consideration?

CHIEF. Heavens no. Let me give you examples of ones that don't. Here's a prayer from a merchant in India:

Computer keys.

MERCHANT. With my prayers I sing this divine song, that I may gain a hundredfold in profits. May my purchases and sales be successful for me. May what I get in barter, render me a gainer. May the accruing of profit be auspicious! May I acquire ever increasing wealth through wealth!

CHIEF. And this one, in an opposite mode:

Computer keys.

OSAGE INDIAN. Wakanda, have pity on me, because I am poor. Give me what I need. Let me win against my enemies. Help me, so I may steal many horses.

BOB. At least he leveled with God.

CHIEF. Always a good thing to do.

BOB. I dare say much as been made, in legend and drama, about fierce and warlike American Indians, but Your Honor, they were greatly outnumbered by peaceable, gentle, and friendly tribes. Do you have any prayers from those people?

CHIEF. A great many, some of them sublime. One, I remember, is an ancient hymn to the Great Sun Power, a prayer still spoken or sung by Indians living here and there in what I believe you call the Great Plains. Would you like for me to bring it up?

BOB. Please.

Computer keys.

GREAT PLAINS INDIAN. I pray for my people, that they may be happy in the summer and endure the cold of winter. Many are sick and in want. Pity them and let them live. May there be rain to water the prairies, so the grass may grow tall and there will be an abundance of berries. Give us peace, Great Spirit, and refreshing sleep. May our pathways and trails lie straight and level before us. Let us live to an old age. We are all your children and ask these things of you with good heart.

BOB. Nice. No crabbing, no bandying. I suppose you get a lot of the bargaining kind.

CHIEF. Naturally. Here's a Sioux warrior of old, offering goods in return for a granted prayer:

Computer keys.

SIOUX WARRIOR. O Wakanda, I promise thee a calico shirt and dress, and I will also give you a blanket, if you grant that I will return whole and well after having killed a Pawnee.

BOB. I can't help wondering if it's any more grotesque to pray for success in killing a Pawnee, one to one, than for nations to pray for divine help in annihilating millions of their enemies?

CHIEF. Yes, that is commonly done in time of war, and it always puts a strain on Heaven, because praying to kill under any circumstances is like using holy water to flush a toilet. But in this connection, I'm going to call up a sly fragment for you, which I think you'll recognize. In only seven words it combines military and religious objectives:

Computer keys.

CHAPLAIN. Praise the Lord and pass the ammunition.

BOB. Made in America.

CHIEF. Said by a chaplain,[2] I believe, in one of those wars that your world calls by number.

BOB. World War II. I must say, Your Eminence —

CHIEF. No honorifics, please.

BOB. I find it strange to be discussing wars in Heaven; but then war fills many pages of the most sacred of our writings.

CHIEF. To say nothing of a great war in Heaven itself. Have you read *Paradise Lost*, by one of your writers named Milton?

BOB. Not yet, but I've always meant to.

CHIEF. Noble, but long. Came to us right off the press. — Are you interested in matters military?

BOB. As they apply to prayer. I know that chaplains of all faiths are attached to armies, but do Generals ever pray? I mean publicly?

CHIEF. Now and then. Their prayers are usually terse, like battle orders. A General named Astley, in one of those English Civil Wars, fired off just such a prayer:

Computer keys.

ASTLEY. O Lord, thou knowest how busy I must be this day. If I forget Thee, do not Thou forget me.[3]

CHIEF. And here is one Admiral Nelson offering thanks in advance, to The Great Disposer:

Computer keys.

NELSON. Men, we trust in The Great Disposer of all events, and in the justice of our cause. I thank God for this opportunity of doing our duty.[4]

BOB. The Admiral had a thing about duty. I read somewhere that just before the battle of Trafalgar, he signaled to his fleet, "England expects every man to do his duty."

CHIEF. That was a declaration of intent, and since it was not in the form of a prayer, we have no record of it. — Who won that battle, by the way?

BOB. Nelson, but he lost his life doing it. They say his last words were, "Thank God I have done my duty." — By the way, are there duties in Heaven?

---

2. Chaplain Howell Forgy, aboard the USS *New Orleans* during the Japanese attack on Pearl Harbor.
3. Jacob Astley before the Battle of Edgehill in 1642.
4. Horatio Nelson before the Battle of Trafalgar in 1805.

CHIEF. Not in the sense of something performed grudgingly and then bragged about afterward.
BOB. A last question on the subject, if you don't mind. Did you ever hear from any General whose request for divine help was — uh — well, I suppose you could say more *general* than a plea for support in armed conflict?
CHIEF. While the Secretariat does not specialize in military history, I believe we do have something along that line. But from an *ex*-General. Someone I think you'll recognize:

Computer keys.

WASHINGTON. Almighty God, we make our earnest prayer that Thou will keep the United States in Thy holy protection; that Thou will incline the hearts of the citizens to cultivate a spirit of subordination and obedience to the government; to entertain a brotherly affection and love for one another and for their fellow citizens at large.
BOB. Why, that has to be George Washington! — Either his Farewell Speech to the Army, or his inauguration as first President.
CHIEF. The latter. — But shouldn't we be getting back to your boy's wonderment about prayer?
BOB. Yes. Thank you. — Uh — how do you deal with *children's* prayers? Are they taken seriously?
CHIEF. It depends. Of course the fears and tears of children tend to be of small scale — on matters not unimportant to them, certainly — but when a prayer asks for the repair of a broken doll, or for a new pet, or for protection against a rumored goblin — it should properly be addressed to the child's parents, and not to the author of the universe…You see, the sheer magnitude of staff needed to sift through, sort out and respond to the prayers of children in all the widely scattered worlds including your own — plus the heavy prayer traffic of their elders throughout the infinite systems — the obvious angel-power necessary for such monitoring, would be far beyond the capacity of —
BOB. I understand.
CHIEF. You interrupted.
BOB. I'm sorry.
CHIEF. In this realm, interruption is construed as a misdemeanor.
BOB. Oh. Gosh.
CHIEF. The word "gosh," I should inform you, is an alteration of the word God.

BOB. I never knew that.
CHIEF. So is "golly."
BOB. I'll be more careful.
CHIEF. Now, notwithstanding the limitations that I've mentioned concerning the appeals of children, I must add that of all prayers reaching the Secretariat, those of children are the most direct and specific, tending to be even more terse than those of Generals. You see, children don't wheedle, or flatter, or try to make deals with the Maker; they don't resort to praise or repetition or circumlocution. — Would you like examples of what I'm telling you?
BOB. Very much so.
CHIEF. Then let's go to the Children's Division.
BOB. You even have a Children's Division? Wow, are you organized!
CHIEF. We'll be accompanied, in transit, by children's music. You see, we have instant access to a complete repertoire of music from all the worlds — some of it, I'm sure, rather strange by your standards.
BOB. Oh, we have abundant strange music of our own; but by and large —
CHIEF. Do you have any favorite children's music?
BOB. Well — (*Thinks.*) — um — how about *Golliwog's Cakewalk*?
CHIEF. By Claude Debussy.
BOB (*surprised*). Yes! You even know *that*?
CHIEF. Nothing is remote to us.

Music: Golliwog's Cakewalk, as requested. When it concludes:

BOB. Wonder upon wonder, just looking around this facility! It's more like a palace! Whole grandiosities of equipment!
CHIEF. We wouldn't use that term, but we'll accept it.
BOB. Are all these devices dedicated to receive the prayers only of children?
CHIEF. Exclusively. — And bear in mind, the prayers you'll hear, whether of petition, or of thanks, or to question, or to seek reassurance, all were actually voiced by children. — To begin with, do you have any source in mind? National or geographical?
BOB. Well, being American, suppose we start out with —
CHIEF. Simple. Here is one from Mary Thomas, then age six:

Computer keys (different pitch from those heard previously).

MARY (*age 6*). Lord, we thank you for making so many wonderful animals and insects. — Especially butterflies.
CHIEF. And Harry Biddlescome, age eight:

Computer keys.

HARRY (*age 8*). BANG! Fireworks make a really loud noise! BING BANG HISS CRACKLE ZOOM! I wish I could fly in the sky with all those *colors*! Thank you, God, for all the fireworks!
CHIEF. And from South Africa — Rupeah Data, age seven:

Computer keys.

RUPEAH (*age 7*). Dear Father, thank you for the trees that give us fruit, and the plants that grow underground, like peanuts. Amen.
CHIEF. Here's one on a darker note, from Anne Campbell:

Computer keys.

ANNE (*age 9*). Dear Lord, it's really horrible seeing my friend Polly sick in bed. I pray that you'll hurry up and make her better so we can play together again.
CHIEF. And we also have on record a brief scene in a little boy's bedroom, when his mother instructed him to kneel by the side of his bed and pray:

Computer keys.

MOTHER. Are you praying?
BOY. Yes.
MOTHER. I can't hear you.
BOY. I wasn't talking to you.
CHIEF. And then there was a deeply concerned seven-year-old named Rick Madden:

Computer keys.

RICK (*age 7*). Lord, God, I'm worried about the future because I think the sun will hit us one day. (*Pause.*) — Will it?
BOB. I'm forty-two, and I ask the same question.
CHIEF. The Secretariat is not authorized to speculate on astronomical disorders, nor are we privy to cosmic programming. We deal solely with the reception, distribution and archiving of incoming prayers. — Have you any further questions about children's prayers?
BOB. Yes. What about the prayers of *older* children?

CHIEF. How old?
BOB. Say, around the age of confirmation. Do you process those?
CHIEF. All the time. Not long ago we received a challenging discourse from a young lady named Johanna Ring Jacobson, who, at her Bat Mitzvah, put some questions to her elders:

Computer keys.

JOHANNA (*age 13*). God has all these phenomenal powers, so it's easy for Him to keep His part of any bargain, while we have to pray constantly, and fast on occasion, and that's not so easy if you don't have phenomenal powers. And if we're all supposed to be God's children, then how come Give loves us best? The Torah says, "Thou shalt be blest above all peoples." What kind of a parent would do that to their children, put one above the rest? Basically *all* religions believe God says to them, "You are my favorites." So what is really happening is that children think God is saying to each one of them, "I love you best." If that happened in real life, the child would grow up needing a therapist. They'd think they're Mommy's favorites and therefore entitled to whatever they want.
BOB. I hope the Maker looks as kindly on free thought as on free speech.
CHIEF. Have no qualms. — Do you wish to hear still more children?
BOB. You sure I'm not holding you up?
CHIEF. I'd let you know if you were.
BOB. Well, all the prayers so far have been fairly straightforward. — Are *compound* prayers, so to speak, well received?
CHIEF. What do you mean by compound prayers?
BOB. Those addressed to multiple gods, or covering a number of conditions.
CHIEF. To answer that requires another transit — again, if you wish, accompanied by music. — A fugue, perhaps?

Music: Short segment of a Bach fugue. It fades under:

CHIEF. Let's start with ancient Asia, a continent well provided with ancient religions, and call up a venerable Mongolian:

Computer keys.

MONGOLIAN. You, O Lords of the echo in mountain passes, O Lords of the winds blowing over the sea, O Lords who dwell in the forests: During the lean years, be generous; in the months of hardship, grants us abundance; when we are in our huts, do not bring danger down upon us; and when we are outside, do not put our strength to trial. In the dark night, give us light. In the heat of day give us shade. Keep evil far from us, and goodness close to us. Play the part of the Creator and save us from all peril. Do not let our hearts tremble, for you are guardians of our lives. Bring food to our mouths and cause the sun to shine through the doors of our huts.

BOB. I had no idea that unschooled people — hut-dwellers, farmers, shepherds, hunters, primitives, prayed with such simple grace. Some of their images are very beautiful.

CHIEF. Perhaps because their lives, while they might have been hard, were uncluttered, for good or ill, they were close to the elements, to nature, close to the forces of creation.

BOB. No freeways, taxes, late late shows...

CHIEF. They had time to look long at the heavens, to welcome the sun every morning, and take leave of it every night, to watch the moon through its cycles, to speak to the Maker of the sky, earth, water, the plains, the mountains...

BOB. The eternal fitness of things.

CHIEF. I'm now going to call up a prayer of a Peruvian shepherd; and then of an African grandmother, both communing in their world:

Computer keys.

PERUVIAN. O Creator, thou who said, "Let there be light," grant to the Sun that when he rises, he may see peace everywhere. Preserve him so that he may give light to those whom he has created. O Sun, give light to this nation and keep it ever sane and happy.

Computer keys.

MENSAN WOMAN. Rising moon, may you be for us a moon of happiness. May the young become strong and the grown keep their strength; may the pregnant woman be delivered, and suckle her young. Let the stranger come to the end of his journey, and those who stay, dwell safely in their homes. Let the flocks that go to feed in the pastures return safely. May you be a moon of harvest, a moon of soundness and good health.

BOB. May I ask — (*Interrupts himself.*) — Am I taking up too much of your time?

CHIEF. We have great funds of time in Heaven. Go on.

BOB. I know there are wide ranges of prayer, and many differences among them. But are there preferred modes, postures, etiquette, protocols? I mean forms of address that are more effective, more likely to get through, than others?

CHIEF. Odd you should ask. Just recently, no more than two or three hundred years ago, we had a visitor from a world in the galaxy you call M51, who asked the same question. The answer is that there are no set rules. What counts most is the thought, even the *impulse* to the thought, of *prayer* — and of course the sincerity, scope, substance, and urgency of its message.

BOB. Where I come from there are very strong protocols. Some call for standing at prayer, others for swaying, or shouting, or dancing, or feasting, or fasting, or immersion. Some even consign their prayers to prayer wheels. Ah, the good old prayer wheel! Bloodless revolution! What a handy, timesaving device! "Forgive-forgive-forgive-forgive-forgive — pardon-pardon, pardon, pardon, pardon."

CHIEF. We don't joke about any form of prayer in Heaven.

BOB. I'm sorry.

CHIEF. Apology accepted.

BOB. But aren't there instructions, or suggestions, for proper prayer, just as there are for the right way to brush teeth?

CHIEF. Your own civilization abounds in suggestions. Come with me to the Protocol Section, and I'll call up some random samples for you. This way.

BOB. How wonderful, not to need carpeting…to walk on air, in a manner of speaking.

Music: Walking on air, in a manner of speaking.

CHIEF. This is the Protocol villa. Are you familiar with a certain Apostle once on your planet, named Mark?

BOB. Of course. From the Gospels.

CHIEF. Here, in his own voice, is a suggestion about prayer:

Computer keys.

MARK. When you pray, if you have anything against anyone, forgive, that your Father may forgive your trespasses.

CHIEF. And another from a fellow Apostle, Matthew:

Computer keys.

MATTHEW. When praying, do not use vain repetitions, for you Father knows your needs before you ask Him.
CHIEF. You'll find a good number of suggestions in Judaism, like these two from the Talmud:

Computer keys.

TALMUD. Even as you pray for the good among you, you are duty bound to pray for the bad. (*Pause.*) Pray in any language you understand.
CHIEF. And these two from the Koran:[5]

Computer keys.

KORAN. Pray to God morning and evening, and employ the rest of the day in useful avocation. (*Pause.*) Do not pray when you are drunk, or until you know what you are saying.
CHIEF. And this from a Japanese source:

Computer keys.

KUROZOMI. When prayer does not help you accomplish your purpose, know that something is lacking in your sincerity.
BOB. To me that's hedging a bit, somehow. The merchant who prayed for enormous profits, and the warrior who prayed for success in killing a Pawnee, and the thief who prayed for divine help in stealing horses — all of them were sincere, I'm sure.
CHIEF. Heavenly discourse does not encourage this kind of colloquy. You make a good point, but perhaps it's something you might want to take up with the Japanese when you return to your planet. For now, I will demonstrate through one last example, that the Secretariat is not averse to being amused by suggestions on the posture of prayer. It's an amiable trifle called *The Prayer of Cyrus Brown*, written by one Mr. Sam Foss just about a century ago on your time scale:

Computer keys.

KEYES. The proper way for a man to pray,
Say I, Deacon Lemuel Keyes,
And the *only* proper attitude,
Is down upon his knees.

---

5. Now often spelled as Quran or Qur'an.

WISE. No. — The only approvable way to pray,
    Say I, the Reverend Wise,
    Is standing straight with outstretched arms
    And rapt and upturned eyes.
SNOW. Oh, no no no, say I, John Snow,
    Such posture is too proud —
    A man should pray with eyes fast closed
    And head contritely bowed.
BLUNT. It seems to me one's hands should be
    Austerely clasped in front
    With both thumbs pointing toward the ground,
    Say I, the Reverend Blunt.
BROWN. Last year I fell in Hodgkin's well,
    (My name is Cyrus Brown)
    And both my heels was sticking up
    My head a-pointing down,

    An' I made a prayer right then an' there —
    Best prayer I ever said,
    The prayingest prayer I *ever* prayed
    A-standing on my head!
BOB (*chuckling*). Then humor is acceptable in Heaven? I hadn't thought that likely.
CHIEF. Why not? Isn't it believed by most, if not all your religions, that man was made in the image of God?
BOB. I think so, yes.
CHIEF. Then it follows that if humans bear the likeness of their Maker, the capacity for smiling and laughter also derives. It takes very little, sometimes, for a prayer to go from serious to amusing. Here is just such a passage, made by a woman named May Webb, asking for the staff of life:

Computer keys.

WEBB. Give me good digestion, Lord
    But also something to digest —
    But where and how that something comes
    I leave to you who knoweth best.
BOB. Grace before nutrition. — Another question, if I'm not abusing your patience.
CHIEF. Go ahead.

BOB. It seems to me that the most eloquent, or at least best-expressed prayers, should come from clerics or theologians who are dedicated to religion — or from writers, who are dedicated to words.
CHIEF. Let's find out. — Theologians first? John Donne was a clergyman.
BOB. No-man-is-an-island John Donne?
CHIEF. The same.

Computer keys.

DONNE. Let me, in spite of me, be of so much use *to* God's glory, that by His mercy to my sins, other sinners may see how much sin He can pardon.
CHIEF. And St. Teresa of Ávila, Carmelite nun, founder of many convents:

Computer keys.

ST. TERESA. From silly devotions and from sour-faced saints, good Lord deliver us.
BOB. I never thought that devotions could be silly, but who am I to argue with a saint?
CHIEF. It's easier to argue with writers. Some of your greatest have pondered prayer, or composed their own. Choose at random.
BOB. What about — um — (*Thinks.*) — say — Lord Byron. But then he wasn't a religious type, was he?
CHIEF. Let's ask him.

Computer keys.

BYRON. There are those who say I have no devotion:
But set those persons down with me to pray,
And you shall see who has the properest notion
Of getting into heaven the shortest way —
My altars are the mountains and the oceans
Earth, air, stars — all the springs from the great Whole
Who has produced, and will receive, my soul.[6]
BOB. Aha. — I don't want to be greedy, but were there any prayers from Samuel Pepys, the diarist?
CHIEF. Some.

Computer keys.

6. *Don Juan*, Canto III, CIV, by George Gordon Byron (circa 1821)

PEPYS. — March 22, 1660: I pray God to keep me from being proud (*Pause.*) — July 1, 1660: This morning arrived my fine camlet cloak, with gold buttons, and a silk suit, which cost me much money, and I pray God to make me able to pay for it.
BOB. Practical. — It seems to me the French should be pretty good at praying, what with Notre Dame and the Sacré Coeur on their home ground. Can we try Victor Hugo?
CHIEF. Why not?

Computer keys.

HUGO. Certain *thoughts* are prayers. There are moments when, whatever the attitude of the *body*, the soul is on its knees.
BOB. I'm glad I asked.
CHIEF. I seem to recall there are even nursery rhymes about prayers. Do your remember any?
BOB. It's been a long time.
CHIEF. Try goosey goosey gander.
BOB. Let me see now — "Goosey goosey gander
Whither shall I wander?
Upstairs and downstairs
And in my lady's chamber — (*Hesitates; then:*)
There I met an old man
That would not say his prayers;
I took him by the left leg
And threw him down the stairs."
(*Laughs.*) Harsh treatment for a non-conformist, especially an old one. — A last question, if I am still persona grata.
CHIEF. Gratissima.
BOB. Prayer often takes musical form — hymns, chants, cantatas, oratorios. How are those received?
CHIEF. With pleasure. There has been current, for a few millennia, the temptation to adopt, as the classic language to be spoken in the court of Heaven, no less a tongue than music, and there are even some in the Secretariat who believe that prayers and petitions rising Heavenward from all the worlds, should first be intercepted and translated into music for delivery to the Highest Ear. That is of course a question of policy, and has yet to be resolved; but you may take my word for it that music has high rank here, and that your species especially should be thankful for music, for the instruments of music, and for the makers of the instruments of music — also for the greatest and

most wondrous instrument of them all, the one which can form words and set them like gems in a fabric, and endow them with meaning, playing on the mind a spirit bowstring; the various, tender, pungent, pulsing human voice.

BOB. That's kind of poetic, what you just said.

CHIEF. Poetic? In your and all other worlds, the best of prayer is poetic. Do you have an interest in poetry as well as prayer?

BOB. To some extent. Have you heard of Emily Dickinson?

CHIEF. Heard of her? She works here in the Secretariat.

BOB. Really? Holy smoke! I mean — uh — just smoke. I'd die to meet her!

CHIEF. That would not be convenient at this time. But eventually it could be arranged.

BOB. There's a verse she wrote about Heaven, which has always stayed with me.

CHIEF. I'm listening.

BOB. "And so upon this wise I prayed —
Great Spirit, give to me
A heaven not so large as yours
But large enough for me."[7]

CHIEF. She'll be pleased to know she's well remembered. — Have you ever written poetry yourself?

BOB. From time to time. I'm not too good at it.

CHIEF. Why don't you try writing a prayer poem?

BOB. When I get back, it's something I might just venture to do.

CHIEF. No. Here and now.

BOB. Well, I'm not sure I —

CHIEF. It will serve as your exit visa.

BOB. No, no. I'm a lawyer. I deal with briefs and torts and contracts, which are to poetry as a street map is to Camelot.

CHIEF. Are you saying there are no lawyer poets? No sensitive writing coming out of what you call the legal profession?

BOB. Only one or two that I know about. A Midwesterner named Edgar Lee Masters, who wrote —

CHIEF. He's been here for more than fifty of your earth years. Very highly respected. — Hasn't there been, over time, a good deal of sensitive writing by barristers in your own country?

BOB. Well, yes, I suppose. Some.

CHIEF. Suppose? Must I remind you of your Jefferson and Lincoln? Both lawyers? (And they are here, too, both in creative capacities, and enjoying it very much. They'd be disappointed to learn that you, a

---

7. From Emily Dickinson's poem, *Part One: Life*, XXXIX, published posthumously in 1924.

countryman of the same calling as themselves, minified the grandeur and felicity of their writing.)

BOB (*defensively*). Well, I didn't quite mean to —

CHIEF. Never mind. You are obviously *not* a prisoner of depositions and affidavits. You are interested enough in such a grand abstraction as prayer, to come all this way to inquire about it. So don't tell us you cannot write a prayer out of all you've seen and heard and read and experienced.

BOB. I just wouldn't know where to begin.

CHIEF. Begin with yourself and those around you on your planet. Don't write it to please me or the Secretariat. Make it an Earthly prayer, not a heavenly one. We both know there are many differences in the concepts of the Maker — sects and creeds and schisms and bitter and bloody antagonisms. And still, prayer is common to them all.

We know there were thinkers among you, a few years back, who decided that God was dead. Word of that reached us. You might question whether in your own heart God has come back, or has ever been away. Your prayer should not reflect anything of what you have learned here — indeed this occasion will be soon forgotten when you awaken. But above all, be honest.

BOB (*almost a groan*). That's no easy assignment. I'm not at *all* sure I can do it.

CHIEF. Oh, come now. You're not going to be graded. This is not a school, but the Sovereign Domain of Heaven, full of amplitudes.

BOB. Still, I'm not sure I can write an *acceptable* prayer. Not in the cosmic *capital* of prayer.

CHIEF. Oh, don't speak of cosmic. One world at a time. Are you afraid of searching for what you most *want* to say? Are you too *timid* for that?

BOB. Well, when you put it that way —

CHIEF. Very well. I'll take you now to an Elysian setting, one of several little parks throughout the Secretariat. There you may write for as long as you wish, with your choice of implement — feathery pen, or laundry marker, or a keyless computer that takes down your thoughts as they come to you. And you may write on parchment, or rag paper, or velvet, or silk. And if you wish music while you are writing, you have only to *think* of what you want to hear.

BOB. And I thought *we* were technically advanced!

CHIEF. I'll drop in after a while to see if there is anything you need. — This way, please.

Music: Passage to Elysium Park Twenty-Six.

BOB (*to himself*). Where to begin? (*Pause.*) Writing a prayer *here*? In Heaven? In the Big League? I'm really not equipped...What have I gotten myself into?...Well, the Chief said to put down what I think... Maybe some music *would* help. And I'm thinking Beethoven...

Music: Beethoven for ten or fifteen seconds, then under:

CHIEF. How's it coming?
BOB. I can't tell. It seems I've been writing here for hours. How long has it been, in Earth time?
CHIEF. About ten days.
BOB. At that rate I think maybe I have another week to go.

Music: Up again, and down for:

BOB. Good, bad or indifferent, it's finished.
CHIEF. That in itself is good. Please read it to me.
BOB. *Read* it?
CHIEF. We make allowances.
BOB. In a way, it's as much a prayer to Man as it is to God.
CHIEF. Make no disclaimers. Just read it.
BOB. Very well. (*Clears throat.*)

Music: Sustained simple line, quietly behind:

BOB. We print your name on dollars
And are sure you stand over everything we say is under God
And all nations assume you are on their side and always have been, war in and war out,
And every religion understands you better than every other religion, and you in turn lean towards each with special inclinations.

You are called on to bless babies and aircraft carriers
And you are ceremoniously and endlessly praised on the basis that flattery will get us somewhere.

But there are those who pray as though tendering a bribe payable on installments
So as to accumulate years in this life and credits in the next.
Some of us make you out a broker who supplieth needs and wants
Attorney who defendeth against hard claims

Expunger of guilts who cleareth the conscience so we may be free
    to muck it up again
Housekeeper of the soul who cometh in to clean once a week;
King of accountants auditing our secret selves,
Liquidating our trespasses as we liquidate those who trespass
    against us,
Keeping batteries of books filled with fateful identifications,
Entering as much the fall of a sparrow as the crash of a plane.

But there have been complaints against you — charges of malfeasance,
Implications of sleeping on the job, trigger temper, proneness to
    vengeance,
Tantrums that have consumed too many of the innocent with
too few of the heinous.

CHIEF. Go on.

BOB. Some of your public begrudge you the benefit of doubt and doubt
your beneficence
    Protesting that it was antic of you to begin with, if we are to swarm
        like maggots on a rind too meager to support our duplicating
        billions.

Some say the noblest ideas were set down by man
And that you have been served by holy ghost writers beyond your
    deserts.
They say that the whole conspicuous distance between the worm
    and Einstein, the drone of the bee and Beethoven,
The entire interval has been filled with struggles trailing blood:
Ages of frightened proto-men, heavy with ignorance, recoiling
    in profligate floods, perishing in earthquakes, staggering
    into the unknown,
Their wails and brute chants and broken grunts fructifying at last
    into songs and sonnets and hallelujahs to your glory.
    — Well, dissidents suggest that during this grand span you sat it
        out; that in the vasty meanwhile you went off to fish in
        deeper currents.

Lately it was announced that you are dead
Which means several things besides the receiver being off the
    hook when we dial you.
It means that time must carry on by itself,

And stars pinwheel through incandescent deserts and bottomless
    voids, all on an orderly hunch;
It means the arching upward from the mud has been a drunken
    course, and purposeless, and hardly worth the trip;
It means the very mansion of existence has no windows, and is
    just a big white elephant boarded up and haunted by your
    mistakes;
It means that springtime is a come-on and a put-on, and not at all
    a show of dogged life, a riot of chlorophyll, a surge of sap
    and elixirs from wells so deep no radar pulse can ever
    return to tell what and where it touched;
It means that the love of man and woman is a table of percentages,
    and their desire a disease of the id;
It means that birth is a happening between pills,
and old age a phase held together by plastic parts;
It means that the heart of man is replaceable as soon as the donor is
    legally dead
And death is a package deal with the best advertised mortuary.

So, God: if you are alive and in that heaven we have come to know
    is spotty with systems of gravity, each pulling for itself,
Then perhaps you must flex the muscle of divine authority to get
    back in office
Because your antique miracles have been trumped by solemn
    science:
Daily the patent office registers intenser magic than the burning
    bush:
The serpent from the rod becomes a ruby laser;
The leper is healed by mycins;
The blind draw vision from an eye bank.

That being the case, dear busy God, please manifest thyself
    through one superlative, new-minted covenant:
Create for the lot of us — all nations indivisible — an Act of God
    more stupendous than mere parting waters or a
    standing sun
A miracle harder to come by, that would, if consummated,
    cause dry bones from all the hundred holocausts to meet
    and dance,
And charter stars to sing together in the brightest chancels of
    imponderable space.

And this is what that miracle would be:

That man should love his kind in all his skins and pigments,
And kill no more.

Repeat:
That we should love our kind
And kill no more.

Yes, granted, such a miracle is asking very much of you
But it is long past time to ask.

Silence.

BOB. That's it.

Silence.

BOB. Aren't you going to say anything?

Again, silence.

BOB. Is it that bad? — Unspeakable bad? (*Now with a sense of alarm.*) What's happening? Why are you fading away? What's going on? And the walls, too — dissolving!

A loud fire-alarm-like bell.

BOB (*stunned*). That must be a cosmic alarm! The heavens are collapsing!

The fire alarm modulates to the ringing of an ordinary bedside alarm clock. We are back where we started, in Bob and Joan's bedroom.

JOAN. For heaven's sake, Bob, turn off the alarm clock!

Alarm clock off.

JOAN. What's going on with you? First you toss and turn all night, and then you sleep through the alarm. You'd better get a new clock, that one's loud enough to wake up the dead.

BOB (*sleepily*). Yuh, I will.

JOAN. You talked in your sleep.

BOB (*waking up*). I did? What did I say?

JOAN. You kept repeating, "forgive…forgive…pardon…pardon." — Are you keeping something from me? Something you want to be forgiven for?

BOB. No, no, no — but I did have a strange —

JOAN. And you also said, later, "I'd love to meet her…dying to meet her." Who might *that* be?

BOB. I don't remember everything I dream. — What else did I say?

JOAN. Some of it I couldn't make out, but the last thing you mumbled was, "What have I gotten myself into?"

BOB. Hmm.

JOAN. I ask the same question. What *have* you gotten yourself into?

BOB. It's coming back a little…yes…I had a great dream. A *great* dream.

JOAN. I'll bet. Just how great?

BOB. It was — I'm beginning to remember now — yes — it was heavenly.

JOAN (*with suspicion*). *Heavenly?*

BOB. Come on, let's get up. I'll tell you about it over breakfast.

Music: Curtain.

CORWIN ON
THE SECRETARIAT

Before a live audience at the Museum of Television & Radio in New York, this program was enacted by Hume Cronyn and his daughter, Tandy. It was performed before both a live and radio audience, and used as a device something I had written earlier on a separate occasion — the long declamation beginning with the phrase:

> "We print your name on dollars and are sure you stand over everything we say is under God and all nations assume you are on their side and always have been, war in and war out, and every religion understands you better than every other religion, and you in turn lean toward each with special inclinations.
>
> "You are called on to bless babies and aircraft carriers…"

There was no way of measuring the audience's reaction to the show, and since the audience was not detained for an opinion fest, there was no way of measuring its effect. However, there is no rule against No Decision and the author insists on that.

FROM THE EDITOR

Corwin is referring above to *Prayer for the 70s* performed by Eddie Albert on the *Ed Sullivan Show* on April 6, 1969 and again on November 23, 1969. Albert asked Corwin to create a piece for him to perform on television. Nothing came to mind. Corwin told him that he was unable to think of something suitable. But Albert was persistent. Corwin later recalled, "One night, as I was about to turn in, I emptied the contents of my pockets, and a dollar bill caught my eye. I read the words 'In God We Trust.' That was how it began. 'We print your name on dollars.'"

Eddie Albert's reading of *Prayer for the 70s* struck such a chord with viewers that Doubleday & Co. subsequently published it as a book in 1969. The Plantin Press printed a special limited edition of 100 copies in 1972. The poem is also included in Corwin's 1978 book, *Holes in a Stained Glass Window*.

MEMOS TO A NEW MILLENNIUM

The sixth and final in the series *More By Corwin* was broadcast over NPR on December 31, 1999 beginning at 11:30 p.m. It was written especially for Walter Cronkite, who served as the Narrator. Also is the cast were Richard Dysart, Mala Powers, Elliott Reid, Louis Nye, Steve Franken, Phil Proctor, Alice Backes and Orson Ossman.

The music was by Elmer Bernstein.

Mary Beth Kirchner produced. The author directed.

Music: Introduction, dipping under:

WOMAN. The new millennium.
NARRATOR. Say it slowly. There is no hurry. It will be with us for the next thousand years.

Music: Up to completion.

NARRATOR. Our calendars are based on the birth of an infant in a manger twenty centuries ago. It was one of very few global covenants ever made without having to fight over it — an agreement to number our years from the impress of that nativity.

Not everybody was satisfied with the arrangement, especially cultures that had much older calendars. But right now, this being the last day of the last month of the last century of the second millennium, you have only to put a simple question to every knowing civilization in the atlas. Ask them what date they will print in their newspapers tomorrow.
VOICE. January 1, 2000.
NARRATOR. Even though the new millennium will have arrived on schedule and to nobody's surprise, it will be the biggest of all late-breaking news — a tick of the clock precisely at midnight — a special midnight, but one out of three hundred and sixty-five thousand midnights. And its effect will be to deliver us from a set of seven bloody centuries, 1300 through 1999. Toward that deliverance, a good many of us have been busy raking the leaves of history, anticipating the future, hoping that in the new era, the family of man will get along better than it has up to now.

Sound: A busy but not intrusive pattern, sustaining for a while under:

NARRATOR. Plethora is the word for the down-drags of looking back, the *ifs, maybes and could-bes* of looking ahead — all this and more, going on as we speak. And on this last day, fireworks, blaring horns, banging drums, singing, dancing, clamors like the raucous caucusing of crows, jubilations unlike anything since Noah grounded the ark, unprecedented in scale if only because there are billions *more of us present* than ever before, to *see a New Year* in.

Throngs in Times Square, Piccadilly Circus, Hong Kong, Sydney, Rio, Capetown — toasts, hugs, kisses, torrents of excitement, all of it to honor a pivotal moment out of the foreverness we call eternity — a mere fragment of time, good old mysterious Time, the igniter of the Big Bang from whose lingering fallout we are incidents.

Music: Ungrieving end-of-the-world passage.

NARRATOR. We the people — most of us, anyway — give credit to God for the special effects of creation, starting with time. But the measurement of time is our invention. It was we who came up with the calendar, the sundial, the hourglass, the clock, the pendulum, the metronome, the stopwatch — and also that chronic nag, the parking meter.

They all deal with numbers — another human invention, and a big one. Not only big, but they can be intensely personal, since all Americans, at least, are known by numerals as well as names:

WOMAN CLERK. And may I have the last four digits of your Social Security number, please?

NARRATOR. Numbers. Street number. Telephone number. Registration number. License number. And then the day-to-day numbers we live by...

MAN. Two equinoxes, four seasons, 365 days delivered in twelve uneven months...

NARRATOR. And the register of numbers raised to greatness by association:

WOMAN. The Four Horsemen...

SECOND MAN. The Seven Plagues...

BOY. The Ten Commandments...

MAN. The Twelve Disciples...

WOMAN. The Twenty-Third Psalm...

MAN. The Four Hundred...

NARRATOR. No question about it, numbers have character, have pedigrees and powers; they stand for events so momentous they *need no Author* identification. You know the range:

GIRL. ...the seventh day.

MAN. 1492.

WOMAN. 1620.

BOY. 1776.

MAN. 1861 to 1865.

WOMAN. 1914 to 1918.

GIRL. 1939 to 1945.

MAN. 2000.

NARRATOR. So according to our formulary, we now become creatures of Millennium Three. And the first thing on the agenda, after a good night's sleep, will be to go about living in that millennium, equipping it, shaping it, deciding what to do with it. Given this commission, we have incentive to ask questions and seek answers on all wavelengths, write legible prescriptions, set goals, draft memos for new morrows.

A fair start might be to ask a few people old enough to know what a millennium is, and who care about such matters, what they would wish for between now and Millennium Three.

MAN. First of all — peace. We've had enough wars. More than enough.

WOMAN. Environment. Clean the sky. Purify the waters. Save the earth to save ourselves.

BOY. I hate to think of people without homes — living inside cartons, you know? — in all kinds of weather — freezing cold, wind, rain? Couldn't we, you know — uh — (*Pauses.*)

NARRATOR. For starters, then, three sparse items: Keep the peace, clean up our act by tidying the stage, and give shelter. Questions worth pausing for a reply.

Music: Interlude.

MAN. As I said, enough fighting. War is hell. Sheer hell. Maybe in the new millennium we might, at last, honor a proposition recommended long ago by Aristophanes — *Make Love, Not War.*

NARRATOR. It slanders hell to compare it to war, because the hell of mythology and religion, although superheated and stocked with torments, are in their way, discreet and proper. Only the wicked are punished. The guiltless receive better accommodations. But in war, innocence is never spared: babies, nursing mothers, old men, cub scouts, nannies, washerwomen, scholars and gentlemen, the lame, the halt, the blind, all are expendable. When countries come to blows, the protocols of legitimized murder don't bother with distinction. A missile does not stop to ask a bistro which way to the barracks. Blasted homes, fused glass from broken bottles, scalded milk, cremated populations.

MAN. Many think it's just human nature to fight wars — therefore, when war is inevitable, why go to the trouble of trying to prevent it?

NARRATOR. To believe peace impossible is the surest way to make it so. Those who scorn the peace-keepers, who call them "do-gooders" and "bleeding hearts," need to be told that the bleeding heart seeks to prevent the bleeding head.

As for making love, not war, no society in the world would reject that prospect if it were put to a vote, because love belongs everywhere. As device alone, what equals love? Each of us was *ordained* by an act of love, and the count is high. And not we alone. Is it merely instinct when birds forage far for their young, when a bear rears in fury if its cub is threatened, when your cat brings you the gift of a done-in gopher, when your dog quivers with joy on your return from an errand?

The census-takers tell us that so-and-so many billions live here and there, and give us percentages of this and that — but no count is made of moist lips and caressing hands, of games played in the playground of the senses, of rooms lighting up in the mansions of the body. Love looms like the Himalayas; the equator cannot girdle it; it's fair in the darks of Africa; it teems in oases and archipelagos; — *and yet* — time and again the yields of love are corralled, marshaled, armed, set against each other, and, in progressively hideous ways, destroyed. Usually by despots — just a few, that's all it takes — a Caesar; a Napoleon; a Hitler; a Stalin; they and all their jackals — old men, mostly, their kidneys in decline, their speech a diplomatic parsley dipped in the blood of the young.

DIPLOMAT. His Excellency wishes to acknowledge receipt of your communication of the fourth, and to assure you that his Government has no intention of interfering with the integrity of your sovereign people.

CHAMBERLIN. I return bringing PEACE WITH HONOR!

DIPLOMAT. Accept, Sirs, renewed assurances of high consideration...

NARRATOR. The lingo is polite as varnish, sincere as the cables from casualty counters to next of kin:

CABLE. We regret to inform you...

NARRATOR. And after communiqués are exchanged, and respects transmitted like greetings on Mother's Day, War comes.

Millennium Three, please learn, and learn fast, that the regimented years whisk us off fast enough, as do antagonisms of chance, want, hunger, crime, fire, flood, earthquake, and killing winds. Nature's own bedevilments — the virus, the malevolent gene, the stumbling heart, take enough prisoners without gratuitous war.

The due rank of peace is proudest of all earthly dignities. Perhaps in the new millennium our sons and daughters can learn to enjoy that pride, and to live by it.

Music: Seal off with a passage reminiscent, though not literally, of "We Ain't Gonna Study War No More."

GIRL. The environment...the ways we're offending Mother Earth.

NARRATOR. We've punched holes as big as a continent in the ozone layer, we've gorged ourselves on resources that can't be replaced, we've dumped toxins in landfills that are likely to leak, we've percolated greenhouse climates from the bad breath of our engines and furnaces, and, by doing all those things, we've cadged from our children's future the sufficiencies and protections that are rightfully theirs.

It's not as though nobody had warned us. Half a century before the Wright Brothers, Henry Thoreau wrote:

THOREAU. Thank God man cannot as yet fly, and lay waste the sky as well as the earth! We are safe on that score for the present.

NARRATOR. But the present sped away, and before long thousands of flying machines laid waste not only the sky but cities beneath. And then much of what war did not do by way of insulting the earth, we ourselves accomplished by slow and steady measures — proof positive that whatever wisdom we may have come by, has not increased nearly as much as the need for it.

We claim to have drawn wisdom from the oldest archives — from Ecclesiastes, Proverbs, sages, prophets, philosophers. But none of the ancients could have foreseen the unreliability of their descendants — the actuality that we, who have divined some of the profoundest mysteries of creation, would also annihilate millions like ourselves in world-engulfing wars. How could we possibly expect Plato, Confucius, and other legendary wise men, to have guessed we'd be such clumsy wardens of the trusts mandated to us? After all, we were granted special status:

GENESIS ...dominion over the fish of the sea, and over the fowl of the air, and over every living thing that moveth on the earth...

NARRATOR. But had we been assigned to *destroy* certain living things in our charge, we could not have been more proficient. Of the fish of the sea:

CONSERVATIONIST. The cod is gone from the Grand Banks. Overfished. The salmon is in full retreat. The sardine has all but disappeared from the eastern Pacific. The dolphin is trapped is fishing nets set for tuna, and destroyed. The whale is in constant peril...

NARRATOR. As to our dominion over the fowl of the air: early last century the naturalist Audubon[1] reported having watched a flock of passenger pigeons pass in a stream that lasted three whole days:

AUDUBON. *Billions* of this beautiful pink-tinted bird with dark grey feathers and a long tail...at times they were so thick they darkened the sun. It was magnificent.

NARRATOR. Said in 1813, when their number was estimated at nine billions. In 1914, the *exact* count, was ONE. A single passenger pigeon remained. The rest had been killed for feathers, or for food, or for sports, or because they damaged crops. The sole survivor, given the name Martha, died in the Zoological Gardens of Cincinnati.

---

1. John James Audubon (1785-1851)

As of last month, more than forty percent of the world's arable soil, once held together by trees, grass and underbrush, had in the name of progress and development been stripped, whereupon it dried out, crumbled and was eventually washed out to sea.

So all in all we have been careless caretakers of our ward. We have slashed forests, dirtied skies, drained wetlands, overgrazed pastures, stunted mountains, acidified rain, degraded rivers, turned cities into smudge-pots, and driven once abundant species to the brink of extinction or over it...

It's a hell of a record.

A few post-scriptive memos, then, to Millennium Three:

Music: First of a montage of amenable chords, linking under:

NARRATOR. Item: Be kind to trees. They give fruit, shade and ornament, and — bounty of all bounties — oxygen, the breath of life.

Music: Punctuation.

NARRATOR. Item: Insist that every oil tanker and freighter plying waters anywhere be toilet-trained.

Music: Punctuation.

NARRATOR. Item: Assign to the vaunted ingenuity of science the distillation of zero polluting fuels, so that our skies may be clear of pestilences.

Music: Up to conclusion.

BOY. Uh — if you remember — about the homeless? — living on the streets — in cartons?

NARRATOR. Ah, well, there are no rents or levies in cardboard housing; the only taxes are on health and dignity. Certain amenities are absent, such as walls and a roof, yet the floor is always firm — authentic sidewalk pavement. But no frills — no chairs, no bedding because no bed, no clothesline because no clothes, no toilet, no sink, no mailbox, no address...

BOY. Without an address you can't take a book out of a library, did you know that?

NARRATOR. ...no books, no periodicals. Maybe a few newspapers — old ones, to roll up and stuff in chinks against hard weather. And pasteboard doesn't wear well: whatever its color to begin with, it goes iron-grey, it warps; when wet it turns to mush. And décor is lacking. To be sure, there are inscriptions on cartons just as on temples and public buildings, only they're not carved in stone, they're just printed:

MARKING. This Side Up.

SECOND MARKING. Handle Carefully.

THIRD MARKING. Made in Taiwan.

FOURTH MARKING. Refrigerate After Opening.

NARRATOR. The poor are always with us, and have long been, so we mustn't scold the departing millennium harshly on that score. The dispossessed may go unsheltered, but they're not unnoticed:

FDR. I see one-third of a nation ill-housed, ill-clad, ill-nourished...[2]

POLICEMAN. If there's an ordinance against sleeping on a park bench or under an overpass, then it's my duty as a policeman to clear the area. It's the law.

LANDLORD. They're an eyesore — they upset tenants in the condo — idlers, vagabonds staking out wherever they choose. This is a high-rent district, and their loitering has a bad effect on property values.

WOMAN. They say we don't want to work. Well, there was an ad in the paper offering fifteen jobs. Over eight hundred of us stood in line, hoping to be hired.

SOCIOLOGIST. The assumption that the homeless are mostly no-gooders who avoid work, is unfair to a class that can't reply through lawyers, lobbyists, or public relations counselors. By official count, the incidence of fraud among welfare recipients has never exceeded four tenths of one percent, whereas the IRS estimates that thirty-four percent of private income nationally goes unreported.

NARRATOR. Poverty is an old as hunger, but in a world where massive government buildings, super-supermarkets, sprawling theme parks, city-sized airports and colossal stadiums rise overnight, where a star pitcher averages five thousand dollars for every ball he throws, where an executive fired after a few months on the job can take home ninety million dollars in severance pay; where the cost of waging wars compares to the expense of health and housing as Mount Everest compares to a sand dune, it ill becomes the well-housed, well-warmed and well-fed, to carp about sidewalk space for the poor. Hence to the doers and mentors of Millennium Three, a modest suggestion: dismiss the crotchet that destitution is God's punishment for indolence or sin, and that the hungry are hungry by choice. Again, Scripture tells us:

---

2. Franklin D. Roosevelt, *Second Inaugural Address* on January 20, 1937.

SCRIPTURE. The poor shall never cease out...
NARRATOR. But adds a caution:
SCRIPTURE. Never mock them.

Music: End of segment, and into interlude sustaining briefly under:

NARRATOR. No jury is grand enough to indict or exonerate the late millennium. But since lessons of history cost high enough, and the cost keeps rising, the least we can do is study them. Certain things we know already: There will be a long wait for a brave new world. The besotted old one will not just pack up and check out on the morning of January 1, 2000. Everything will carry over — business as usual, good and bad times, quirks of policy, frettings of government, effusions of art, neuroses of the stock markets, mergers, marriages, divorces, yo-yo whimsies of fame. There will be heroes and abominations, paucities, generosities, atrocities, events so momentous they'll be identifiable by a word, or a bar of music, a place name, the mere sound of which brings instant recognition.

Music: Four-note motif of the Beethoven Fifth.

WOMAN. Eden.
MOSES. Let my people —
MAN. Gethsemane.
JESUS. — for they know not what they —
HAMLET. — be or not to be —
JEFFERSON. When in the course of —
HALE. I only regret that I have but one —

Music: Opening bars of the Marseillaise.

LINCOLN. — will little note nor long remember —

S-O-S in code, and repeat.

FDR. — live in infamy —
MAN. Buchenwald.
ARMSTRONG. One small step —

Music: Beginning of Bach or Bernstein fugue, which fades slowly under:

NARRATOR. The good news, though sparse, is that there are among us dedicated volunteers, people of conscience. And we need them, because the rest of our lives will be spent within the compass of their concerns. They've resolved to do what most of us can't take time to even attempt: to heal old wounds and prevent new ones; to guide us through channels of change that one day may be our only escape from menaces inherited by the new millennium.

For certain, our sons and daughters will be as unpredictable as *we*. The treasures, trash, obligations and dilemmas left by us, will belong to them. Nor does it take a seer to warn us that the future, like Nature, makes no pledges. It's well and good to love Nature when she's friendly, but don't count on her.

And let's be cautious, too, about prognosticators. Take certain pronouncements by figures well known to us, starting with a President of the United States. Here is Rutherford B. Hayes in 1876, concerning the newly invented telephone:

HAYES. An amazing invention, but who would ever want to use one of them?

NARRATOR. Andrew Carnegie, in 1900:

CARNEGIE. To kill a man in the near future will be considered as disgusting as we in this day consider it disgusting to eat one.

NARRATOR. Thomas Edison, in 1922, on the development of commercial radio:

EDISON. The radio craze will die out.

NARRATOR. Lee De Forest, inventor, in 1926:

DE FOREST. While technically television may be feasible, commercially I consider it an impossibility, a development of which we need waste little time dreaming.

NARRATOR. Henry Ford, in 1928:

FORD. People are becoming too intelligent ever to have another big war.

NARRATOR. John Foster Dulles, not long before the attack on Pearl Harbor:

DULLES. Only hysteria entertains the idea that Japan contemplates war on us.

NARRATOR. Darryl Zanuck, head of the Twentieth Century Fox Films, in 1946:

ZANUCK. Video won't be able to hold onto any market after six months. People will soon get tired of staring at a plywood box every night.

NARRATOR. And reaching back, there was Nostradamus, famous for the accuracy of his prophecies. He made a prediction in the sixteenth century which expired only a few days ago:

NOSTRADAMUS. Between November 23 and December 21 in the year 1999, the final battle between the forces of good and evil, the battle of Armageddon, will take place.

NARRATOR. Perhaps the only fully guaranteed prediction is that the sun will rise tomorrow and shine on all calendars in the world that are exposed to its light.

Music: A chuckle.

NARRATOR. In the vast store of speculations on the new millennium, this program will amount to little more than a pebble on the face of a glacier; but having gone this far, it might be sluggardly not to put forward this last notion: that anything mankind has made or committed, can be changed. Especially our mistakes. No doubt it would be heavy sledding to implement our wistful memos — but isn't war heavy sledding? And responding to natural disasters? And building a space station? And finding cures for AIDS and cancer?

Music: Sneak in subdued peroration, and hold behind:

NARRATOR. Need it take a breed of giants to refine priorities, sanitize values, cleanse the house we live in, humanize the body politic? Are such ends beyond the reach of the same species that writes poems and symphonies, gives us Shakespeare, Leonardo, Beethoven, Lincoln, Einstein, dictates to the atom, tames tigers and rivers, bores tunnels under the sea? From the very beginning, when our ancestors breathed through gills, hasn't every waggle, every thrust, every inch plodded, every proliferating cell in our pedigrees, been in response to Challenge?

What are the odds that we're not through growing?

What are the odds that maybe we're just getting started?

Music: Rises, but then subsides for a fermata under:

Music: Up to conclusion.

CORWIN ON
MEMOS TO A NEW MILLENNIUM

The idea of cashing a piece of journalism on the Millennium originated in the mind of Mary Beth Kirchner who had gone to the trouble of approaching the Corporation for Public Broadcasting for a grant of monies wherewith to pay for the services of no less than Walter Cronkite as narrator of a piece of journalism I had in mind to greet the Millennium of 2000. I met this grand old man when he was a definite senior citizen, after he had been voted the most trusted man in America by one of those polls that occur spontaneously in American life.

Now Walter had piloted a sailing boat ex Nantucket Island, where he kept it. In the summer of 1999, when observing the Millennium was front and center in the calculations for its celebration, I conceived of a project to be narrated by Cronkite and prepared a manuscript for him. Cronkite's fee was formidable: it began at $5,000. I prepared a copy for him, and sent it off to his home on Nantucket Island, not knowing he was already at sea. Mails take forever to be delivered under sail and then the Atlantic in summer is no season for delivery. I assumed that Walter was at sea and I would have to wait until my script caught up to him. It finally did, and his response was immediate and enthusiastic. It was joyously received, and I went to work immediately on the production phases, which included hiring Elmer Bernstein to prepare a score for this now important production. Bernstein complied with one of his last works for orchestra, based on a script that Cronkite had approved. It was possibly the last score he wrote before he died untimely.

This reminiscence constitutes the entire story of my relationship with both Cronkite and Bernstein, whom I sorely miss. I saw Cronkite subsequent to the loss of Bernstein, and met Mrs. Cronkite shortly before her death. It was not long before Walter joined her in death.

FROM THE EDITOR

This was not the first time that Cronkite read Corwin's words on the air. In 1978 CBS aired a weeklong series of specials titled CBS *On the Air: A Celebration of Fifty Years.* The nine-and-a-half hours of programming concluded with the ode *Network at Fifty*, read by Walter Cronkite and written by Norman Corwin. *Network at Fifty* was also published as a book in 1979.

Memos to a New Millennium was Norman Corwin's final play for radio. It was a fitting way to wind up a radio career that had started seventy years earlier. Corwin knew the Twentieth Century intimately. They had both made history together. To the very last, he remained an unapologetic optimist. And he made me one, too.

GLOSSARY OF TERMS USED IN THIS BOOK

Written by Norman Corwin:

AD LIB: To extemporize, improvise, invent, doodle—whether in speech, sound, or music. Actually, good ad libbing should be carefully rehearsed so as to *sound* impromptu, for in radio as in nowhere else, the literal meaning of the phrase (from the Latin *ad libitum*—"at one's pleasure," or "as one wishes") cannot be honored. The slightest background phrase, wriggling through the dialogue of principals on-mike, can do wonders in the way of heightening realism. Example of a bad ad lib for a city-room: "So I said to her, 'Listen, Toots, are you wall burp miff pipkin or snaffagaffle with me tomorrow night?'" Example of a good ad lib: "Give this a #10 head and send this copy back to Morgan and tell him to cut it down. It's top-heavy." In cases where it is important to create authentic atmosphere (as in the background of a crowd at a ball game, or workers in the above city-room), ad libs should be written and rehearsed just as carefully as set speeches.

BACK: To support, as with music, sound, or cast ad libs, any speech or effect which holds the center of the microphone stage.

BACKGROUND: Sound, speech or music, used either separately or in combination, to back other elements.

B.G.: Background.

BLEND: To mix the various components of an effect simultaneously. Thus, if the sound of a dive-bomber is coming from Microphone A, a movement of the Mahler Third from B, a stream of consciousness from C, and an echo effect of a beating heart from D, all at the same time, the engineer would obviously have to do some tall blending to form these into an intelligent combination. So would the author.

BOARD: The engineer's control panel, through which all elements of the show must pass. Each microphone on the studio floor is controlled by a volume-dial on the board and can be faded individually. On the average big network studio board there are channels for eight microphones.

BUILD: To increase the power of an effect.

CROSS-FADE: To fade in one effect while the other is faded out. It corresponds to the "dissolve" in motion pictures.

DOWN: When applied to speech, a direction to distinguish between a personal narrative, aside, inward, or contemplative quality, and direct address to another person; see Up.

ECHO: The effect produced either electronically or mechanically to give hollowness or the impression of space, as in a large auditorium.

ESTABLISH: To register solidly an effect before reducing it in favor or another component of the program. Once a background sound has been convincingly established, it can be subordinated and yet maintain presence by a sort of carry-over suggestion. For instance, if the scene is a boiler factory, it is not necessary to make a loud din for more than a few seconds. After that, the listener will take your word for it, and there is no point in continuing to beat him over the head. You "bring down" the sound after having established it, so that when Burton the boilermaker speaks, he can be heard above the boilers.

FADE: To diminish or increase (fade in) volume, whether by changing positions relative to the microphone or by electrical means on the control board.

FILTER: An electrical device used to alter tone characteristics by eliminating or augmenting various frequencies. Thus low frequencies may be eliminated or "filtered" to leave only high frequencies.

MONTAGE: A kaleidoscopic succession of brief scenes, speeches, sounds, music, or any of these in combination.

MOTIF: A thematic phrase or passage of music which is reproduced or varied through the course of a script; often, a short musical figure serving both as means of transition and as an aid to the identification of a character or setting.

OFF: Abbreviation for off-microphone; see Perspective.

PEAK: As used in this volume, the height of an effect.

PERSPECTIVE: The relationship of an element to any other, or to the microphone. As with a movie camera visually, one must establish perspective aurally through the microphone. The listener must know where he is in relation to characters or scenes, and unless there are varying perspectives in a performance, the total impression will be one of flatness and unreality.

REACTION: The response of an individual or of a group to a speech or happening.

SEGUE: The musical tradition, without a break, from one tempo or mood or key to another.

SNEAK: To introduce music or sound softly behind dialogue or narration.

SOCK CUE: An immediate, sudden, and vigorous entrance. Musically, it is most often used to indicate a smash opening or climax.

TRANSITION: The change, or passage, from one scene or time to another.

UNDER: Behind another effect.

UP: When applied to speech, a direction to distinguish between a personal narrative, aside, inward, or contemplative quality, and direct address to another person.

VIGNETTE: A short scene; especially when it is a component of a montage.

WIPE OUT: To obliterate, overwhelm, drown out, as when music takes a scene away from speech or sound.

ABOUT THE AUTHOR

Norman Corwin was born May 3, 1910, in Boston, MA. He began his career as a newspaperman for the *Springfield Republican* before moving into radio. Corwin joined CBS in 1938 at the request of CBS vice president of programming William B. Lewis. Hired initially to produce and direct a poetry series with his name in the title, *Norman Corwin's Words Without Music*, Corwin penned his first original scripts for this series, resulting in critical recognition from *Time* magazine.

He reigned supreme at CBS during the war years, acting as writer-producer-director of series such as *Twenty-Six by Corwin*, *An American in England*, *Passport for Adams*, and *Columbia Presents Corwin*. Additionally, Corwin was responsible for two of the greatest radio programs of the era: the very first four-network broadcast, *We Hold These Truths*, celebrating the 150th anniversary of Bill of Rights on December 15, 1941, (winning him the George F. Peabody Medal) and his masterpiece, *On a Note of Triumph*, marking the end of the war in Europe on May 8, 1945.

In 1946, Corwin was given the inaugural Wendell Willkie One World Award. His prize was an around-the-world trip honoring the 1942 excursion taken by Willkie on behalf of President Roosevelt. Returning to his reporter roots, Corwin made this a working trip, traveling with a wire recorder to chronicle his findings in the immediate aftermath of World War II. This resulted in his final series for CBS, the thirteen-part radio documentary *One World Flight*. In 2009, Corwin's personal journal from that trip was finally published as *One World Flight: The Lost Journal of Radio's Greatest Writer*.

Corwin joined nascent United Nations Radio as Chief of Special Projects after leaving CBS, writing, producing, and directing powerful radio drama such the Peabody Award winning *Document A/777*. Segueing into motion pictures, he penned the screenplay for the Kirk Douglas film *Lust for Life*, earning Corwin an Academy Award® nomination. Corwin later won an Emmy®, the duPont–Columbia Silver Baton, and was inducted into the Radio Hall of Fame.

A prolific writer all his life, Corwin wrote numerous books, including *Thirteen by Corwin, More by Corwin, Untitled and Other Radio Plays, Dog in the Sky, Megalove and Overkill, Holes in a Stained Glass Window,* and *Trivializing America.* Corwin wrote two Broadway plays: *The World of Carl Sandburg* and *The Rivalry.* He scripted thirteen of the twenty-six episodes of his 1971–72 television series, *Norman Corwin Presents.* After dipping his toe back into radio with an original script for *The Sears Radio Theater* in 1979, Corwin found his unique voice and talents once again in demand during the 1990s as National Public Radio provided him a national platform one last time with the series *More by Corwin.*

A Note of Triumph: The Golden Age of Norman Corwin, a documentary film about his legendary radio broadcast, won the Academy Award® in 2006.

Norman Corwin died in Los Angeles, CA, on October 18, 2011, at the age of 101. Among his last writings are the comments penned for this book.

ABOUT THE EDITOR

Michael James Kacey is a Los Angeles based filmmaker whose recent work includes *The Poet Laureate of Radio: An Interview with Norman Corwin*. He authored the book *Long Night's Journey Into Daybreak: 10 Things You Need to Know Before You Make Your First Feature Film*, based on his own "reel-life" experiences making the dark indie-drama *Daybreak*. Mike has also directed several radio recreations of Norman Corwin's work and delivered the presentation *Norman Corwin: The Most Influential Voice You've Never Heard* to students at Kings College in Wilkes-Barre, PA. His current project is the feature film documentary *Radio Changed America*.

INDEX

14 August, 112, 122

Adams, Ashby, 72
Albert, Eddie, 265
Alfred I. du Pont – Columbia University Award, 112, 285
All Things Considered, 94
American Radio Archives, 9, 93
Andrews, Dana, 148
Asner, Ed, 150
Astin, John, 72

Backes, Alice, 210, 266
Baer, Parley, 72
Basehart, Richard, 42
Beaver, Walt, 150, 240
Bergen, Edgar, 93
Bernstein, Elmer, 266, 277
Boardman, True, 72
Bouchon, Paul, 12
Boyer, Charles, 42
Bridges, Lloyd, 124
Brogden, Steve, 93
Bunche, Dr. Ralph, 36, 37

California Artists Radio Theater (CART), 72, 148
Carroll, Pat, 112
CBS, 6, 7, 9, 41, 72, 87, 110, 112, 122, 277, 285
CBS Documentary Unit, 12
Cervantes, 179
Charoff, Melanie, 240
Citizen of the World, 12, 41
Cobb, Lee J., 12, 41, 42
Coleman, Ronald, 42
Corey, Jeff, 210
Corporation for Public Broadcasting, 124, 277
Crawford, Joan, 42

Croft, Mary Jane, 72
Cronkite, Walter, 266, 277, 278
Cronyn, Hume, 240, 265
Cronyn, Tandy, 240, 265
Curse of 589, The, 180, 209
de Santos, Joseph, 12
de Havilland, Olivia, 122
Dewey, Warren, 124, 150, 180, 210, 240
Discovery, The, 209
Document A/777, 42, 71, 233
Dryden, Robert, 12
Duff, Howard, 148
Duffin, Shay, 72, 93
Durning, Charles, 150, 179
Dysart, Richard, 266

Ed Sullivan Show, The, 265
Eggar, Samantha, 72, 93, 148, 150, 180
Erdman, Richard, 72
Erlenborn, Ray, 72
Evans, Maurice, 42
Evatt, Herbert, 45, 67

Fabray, Nanette, 72, 93
Ferrer, José, 42
Fifty Years After 14 August, 112, 122
Franken, Steve, 72, 210, 240, 266
Freeman, Kathleen, 72

Gardner, Reginald, 42
Gediman, Dan, 112
Gilmore, Art, 72, 93
God and Uranium, 122
Gough, Michael, 150
Grice, Bonnie, 124, 210
Griffith, Andy, 72

289

Halperin, Marty, 72, 124, 150, 180, 210
Harlan, John, 72, 148
Heflin, Van, 42
Henning, Linda, 72, 93
Herd, Richard, 148
Hermann, Bernard, 6, 7
Hersholt, Jean, 42
Hill, Steven, 12
Holes in a Stained Glass Window, 265
Holland, Sidney G., 55
Horne, Lena, 42
Hunt, Marsha, 42
Hyphen, The, 209

Irving, Charles, 12

Kane, Byron, 72
Kaplan, Marvin, 72, 150
Kean, Gerald, 12
Kernis, Jay, 94, 110
Kiley, Richard, 179
Kirchner, Mary Beth, 9, 112, 124, 150, 180, 210, 240, 266, 277
Knox, Alexander, 42
Kurali, Charles, 112, 122, 210

Labor Day, 102
Landau, Martin, 124
Laughton, Charles, 42
Lear, Norman, 5
Lee, John R., 148
Lemmon, Jack, 124
Lewis, Elliott, 72
Lloyd, Norman, 72, 93, 150

MacLeish, Archibald, 34
Maltin, Leonard, 93
Markel, Fletcher, 72
Markham, Monte, 148, 210
Mary and the Fairy, 209
Mann, Paul, 12
Manson, Alan, 148
Memorial Day, 95
Memos to a New Millennium, 266, 277, 278
Michel, Werner, 12, 41
Mitchell, Shirley, 150
More by Corwin, 124, 150, 180, 210, 240, 266, 286
Morning Edition 110

Murray, Lyn, 42
Mutual Broadcasting System, 42, 71
National Holiday Series, 94, 110
National Public Radio (NPR), 72, 94, 109, 110, 112, 122, 124, 150, 180, 210, 240, 266, 286
Network at Fifty, 277
Nimitz, Fleet Admiral Chester W., 38
No Love Lost, 124, 148
Nolan, Jeanette, 72
Norman Corwin Presents, 209
NPR Playhouse, 72
Nye, Louis, 210, 266
Olivier, Sir Laurence, 42
O'Reilly, Elizabeth, 240
Ossman, Orson, 266
Our Lady of the Freedoms and Some of Her Friends, 210, 237, 238
Owens, Gary, 7

Peabody Medal, 71, 285
People, Yes, The, 15, 108
Peterson, Melinda, 240
Powers, Mala, 150, 210, 266
Prayer for the 70s, 265
Price, Vincent, 42
Proctor, Phil, 148, 210, 240, 266
Pursuit of Peace, The, 42, 71

Rasovsky, Yuri, 150, 240
Rayburn, Bryna, 12
Reid, Elliott, 72, 150, 210, 240, 266
Reiner, Carl, 93, 180
Riddle, Nelson, 72
Robinson, Edward G., 42
Roosevelt, Eleanor, 64, 71
Roosevelt, Franklin D. (FDR), 113, 114, 118, 233, 273, 274
Ryan, Robert, 42

Sandburg, Carl, 15, 23, 24, 108, 286
Sears Radio Theater, 72, 93, 286
Secretariat, The, 240, 265
Semmler, Alexander, 12
Shatner, William, 124, 150, 180, 209, 240
Shaughnessey, Charles, 150
Shepherd, Ann, 12

INDEX 291

Stange, Ken, 150, 180, 210,
Strange Affliction, The, 72, 93
Swenson, Karl, 12
Times Gettin' Hard, Boys, 23, 24
Thousand Oaks Library, 9, 93
Together Tonight! Jefferson, Hamilton, and Burr, 148
Trout, Robert, 119

United Nations Radio, 71, 285

van Stuwe, Hans, 12
Vaughn, Hilda, 42

Waldo, Janet, 72, 93, 150
Walker, Zack, 240
Warner, David, 72
We Hold These Truths, 71, 285
Webber, Peggy, 9, 72, 93, 148
Welles, Mel, 72
Welles, Orson, 6, 112, 122, 123
Wendell Willkie One World Award, 41, 285
Williams, Emilyn, 42
Windom, William, 72
Writer With The Lame Left Hand, The, 150, 179

Young, Robert, 42

Zuckerman, Steve, 240

Bear Manor Media

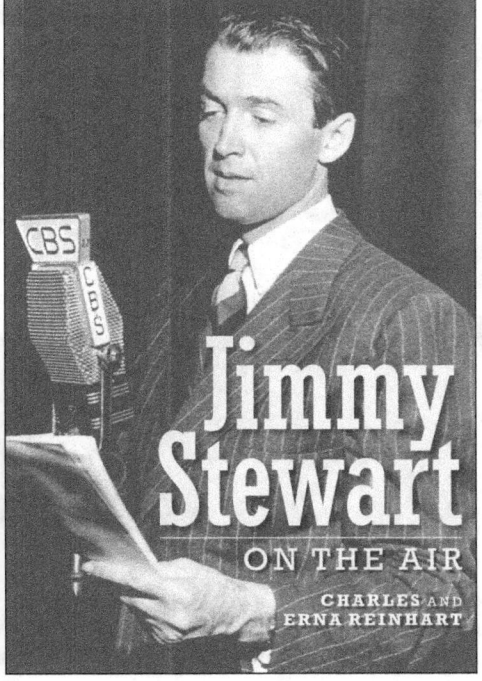

Classic Cinema.
Timeless TV.
Retro Radio.

WWW.BEARMANORMEDIA.COM

www.ingramcontent.com/pod-product-compliance
Lightning Source LLC
Chambersburg PA
CBHW060555230426
43670CB00011B/1837